D0853819

THE
PAUL HAMLYN
LIBRARY

DONATED BY
THE PAUL HAMLYN
FOUNDATION
TO THE
BRITISH MUSEUM

opened December 2000

WITHDRAWN

Colour Plate I. Page from the catalogue of Mintons China Works showing 'Arrangement for Butchers Shop' and 'Arrangement for Fish Shop'. Courtesy Royal Doulton Tableware Ltd.

COLLECTING VICTORIAN TILES

COLLECTING VICTORIAN TILES

Terence A. Lockett

Illustrations by Geoff Taylor
and Stephen Yates

Antique Collectors' Club

© Copyright 1979
Terence A. Lockett
World copyright reserved

Reprinted 1982, 1984, 1988, 1994

ISBN 0 902028 82 0

All rights reserved. No part of this publication may be reproduced, stored in a retrieval system or transmitted in any form or by any means electronic, mechanical, photocopying, recording or otherwise, without the prior permission of the publishers

While every care has been exercised in the compilation of the information contained in this book, neither the author nor the Antique Collectors' Club Ltd. accept any liability for loss, damage or expense incurred by reliance placed on the information contained in this book

British Cataloguing in Publication Data:
A catalogue record for this book is available from the British Library

Other books by Terence Lockett:
The Rockingham Pottery (with Arthur A. Eaglestone)
Davenport Pottery and Porcelain 1794-1887

THE PAUL HAMLYN LIBRARY
WITHDRAWN
THE BRITISH MUSEUM

738. 60941
LOC

Printed in England on Consort Royal Satin from Donside Mills, Aberdeen, by the Antique Collectors' Club, Woodbridge, Suffolk IP12 1DS

Contents

PRICE REVISION LISTS

The usefulness of a book containing prices rapidly diminishes as market values change.

In order to keep the prices in this book updated, a price revision list will be issued annually each year. This will record the major price changes in the values of the items covered under the various headings in the book.

To ensure you receive the price revision list, complete the pro forma invoice inserted in this book and send it to the address below:

ANTIQUE COLLECTORS' CLUB
5 CHURCH STREET, WOODBRIDGE, SUFFOLK IP12 1DS

Antique Collectors' Club

The Antique Collectors' Club was formed in 1966 and now has a five figure membership spread throughout the world. It publishes the only independently run monthly antiques magazine, *Antique Collecting*, which caters for those collectors who are interested in widening their knowledge of antiques, both by greater awareness of quality and by discussion of the factors which influence the price that is likely to be asked. The Antique Collectors' Club pioneered the provision of information on prices for collectors and the magazine still leads in the provision of detailed articles on a variety of subjects.

It was in response to the enormous demand for information on 'what to pay' that the price guide series was introduced in 1968 with the first edition of *The Price Guide to Antique Furniture* (completely revised 1978 and 1989), a book which broke new ground by illustrating the more common types of antique furniture, the sort that collectors could buy in shops and at auctions rather than the rare museum pieces which had previously been used (and still to a large extent are used) to make up the limited amount of illustrations in books published by commercial publishers. Many other price guides have followed, all copiously illustrated, and greatly appreciated by collectors for the valuable information they contain, quite apart from prices. The Antique Collectors' Club also publishes other books on antiques (including horology and art), garden history and architecture, and a full book list is available.

Club membership, open to all collectors, costs little. Members receive free of charge *Antique Collecting*, the Club's magazine (published ten times a year), which contains well-illustrated articles dealing with the practical aspects of collecting not normally dealt with by magazines. Prices, features of value, investment potential, fakes and forgeries are all given prominence in the magazine.

Among other facilities available to members are private buying and selling facilities, the longest list of 'For Sales' of any antiques magazine, an annual ceramics conference and the opportunity to meet other collectors at their local antique collectors' clubs. There are over eighty in Britain and more than a dozen overseas. Members may also buy the Club's publications at special pre-publication prices.

As its motto implies, the Club is an organisation designed to help collectors get the most out of their hobby: it is informal and friendly and gives enormous enjoyment to all concerned.

For Collectors — By Collectors — About Collecting

The Antique Collectors' Club
5 Church Street, Woodbridge, Suffolk IP12 1DS, England

List of Colour Plates

Introduction

In recent years there has been a very considerable growth in interest in Victorian tiles. Many people have begun to concentrate upon tiles as their foremost collecting activity, and many more have added a few tiles to their general collections. An even greater number drawn by the sheer attractiveness of the designs have been moved to purchase examples to enhance the décor of their houses or flats. This widespread interest is not really to be wondered at, as the range of Victorian tiles is so wide and covers the whole stylistic spectrum from neo-Gothic, through Persian and Renaissance revivals to the Aesthetic Movement and art nouveau. The decorative subjects of the tile designers are equally eclectic and cover interests as divergent as nursery rhymes, landscape, sport, literature and abstract and geometric patterns. It is this very diversity of design which today's students find so fascinating, and it is with these in mind, as well as for collectors, that a detailed guide to sources for further study has been provided in Chapter Three.

It is hoped that besides providing information for collectors of tiles and students interested in design, this book will make some contribution to the study of Victorian design in general, although it should be stressed that this is not a study of architectural ceramics. Throughout, the chief focus has been upon tiles as pictures, either representational or as patterned design, geometric and abstract. Thus there has been a deliberate concentration upon the actual designers of the tiles. Much hitherto unpublished material has been included on designers such as Moyr Smith, William Wise, Thomas Allen, Stacey Marks, Walter Crane and Lewis F. Day, to name some of the more prominent figures. Details of the series they designed for the great tile factories has been collated, and it should be possible for the dedicated collector deliberately to set out to collect the entire output of an individual designer, in the manner in which collectors with a predeliction for completeness so frequently exhibit.

Thus this book has basically a two-fold aim, to assist the collector in identifying and classifying the tiles of the period 1840-1910, and hopefully, to make some contribution to our knowledge of decorative and industrial design in Victorian England.

Finally a word on the illustrations; those throughout the text are prefixed 'Figure', while the collections of tiles in Chapter Six illustrating the design subjects are prefixed 'Plate'.

T.A. Lockett
July 1979

Acknowledgements

Many people have played an important part in the writing and production of this book, but none more so than my wife, Isabel. It was she who first began to collect tiles some twelve years ago, largely, I suspect, as a counter-balance to my own ever-enlarging collection of English pottery and porcelain. Before very long I too was bringing home floral patterns and Moyr Smiths, to swell what still remains basically Isabel's collection. From time to time in the text that follows you will read phrases such as "we have noted" or "we were fortunate in discovering"; this is not the author indulging himself in the royal plural, but an indication that the research and discovery of the past decade has been a shared experience which we have both enjoyed enormously.

The illustrations for the book have been prepared with great skill and meticulous care by Geoff Taylor and more recently by Stephen Yates. I am most grateful to them both for identifying themselves so closely with what I was seeking to achieve. I am also indebted to Judy Robinson for so capably and cheerfully typing my revised manuscript.

A host of people in official positions have given generously of their time and provided me with every facility to study the collections of wares, or documents for which they were responsible. I am particularly grateful to Paul Atterbury, Historical Adviser to Royal Doulton Tableware Ltd., for constant help, advice and encouragement over many years, and to Hugh Gibson, and Bill Fisher also of Royal Doulton. Alyn Giles Jones who catalogued the Minton archives at Bangor University gave me total co-operation and made my visits to North Wales stimulating social occasions, as well as fruitful research expeditions.

Arnold Mountford and his staff, especially Pat Halfpenny, at the City Museum and Art Gallery, Stoke-on-Trent, have always responded most readily to my many calls for assistance. The kindness of Bruce Tattersall, formerly Curator of the Wedgwood Museum at Barlaston, Ron James, formerly Curator, Clive House, Shrewsbury and David Sekers, formerly Director, the Gladstone Pottery Museum, is much appreciated. At Spode I received assistance from Leonard Whiter, Harold Holdway and particularly from Paul Wood of the Design Department. John Ribbets kindly allowed me to photograph the de Morgan tiles from the Manchester Polytechnic Collection.

Norman Emery at the City Library, Stoke-on-Trent, was unfailingly generous both with his time and in pointing out sources of evidence. We were made most welcome by Tony Herbert and Tim Evitt of the Ironbridge Gorge Museum Trust, and Rosamond Allwood of the Wolverhampton Museum refreshed our enthusiasm with the splendid exhibition she mounted there. Roger Pinkham at the Victoria and Albert Museum generously shared some of his research information with me, as indeed have many people who have written to me over the years. These are too numerous to list here and I hope each of them will accept personally this collective 'thank you'.

Nearly all those listed above have generously given permission for tiles or documentary material in their keeping to be photographed for reproduction here. Additionally, I must thank the following individuals who have either lent tiles or informed me of the whereabouts of interesting items or supplied me with information: Andrew Borthwick, Richard Dennis and Jocelyn Lukins, Anthony Cross, Margaret Henderson Floyd, Nick Hedges for photographs, Harold Jones, Elizabeth Adams, Julian Treuhertz, Arthur and Muriel Eaglestone, Gillian Eastwood, Anthony Thomas, Sadia Walsh, Hilary Evans, Hartley Asquith and Alan Smith. In particular, I have received most generous help with information, with unusual tiles, and through constant encouragement, from Reginald Haggar and Audrey Atterbury.

Chapter One

Historical

It is a truism to state that tiles are amongst the earliest examples of man's use of ceramic material for decorative purposes. In the historical time-scale Victorian tiles were very late comers. However, it is not the purpose of this book to trace the origin and development of tiles through the various epochs both pre- and post-Christian. The tiles of Egypt, Mesopotamia (including the Tower of Babel!), Rome, China, India and 'the unsurpassed tile-architecture of Persia', the medieval European masterpieces and the Renaissance products from Italy, all these provide a rich back-cloth and often a source of inspiration to the Victorian tile maker. The history of these wonderful and colourful wares has been admirably told and illustrated in the works of Arthur Lane, W.J. Furnival and especially in the beautifully illustrated volume by Anne Berendsen (see bibliography for details).

Closer to our own time and culture are the Dutch delft and the tiles produced in England in the eighteenth century. Excellent books by C.H. de Jonge and Anthony Ray have been written on these topics. It is appropriate that Plate 1(1-6) is devoted to wares of this type for they occasionally come the way of the collector of Victorian tiles and serve as valuable aesthetic touchstones. Indeed, the Sadler and Green printed wares are in certain respects the forerunners of the mass-produced wares of the Victorian age for in the words of that well-known affidavit of 27th July, 1756, the two men "without the aid or assistance of any other person or persons, did, within the space of six hours, to whit, betwixt the hours of nine in the morning and three in the afternoon of the same day, print upwards of 1200 Earthenware tiles of different patterns at Liverpool ... more in number and better and neater than one hundred skilful pot painters could have painted in the same space of time."[1]

As the fashion for delftwares declined in the 1780s so did the printing of tin-glazed tiles for fireplaces and similar wall surfaces. Nor to any extent did printed or painted creamware tiles take their place, though some fine examples are occasionally encountered (Figure 1). Thus the making of tiles dwindled away at the end of the eighteenth century.

When tile making reappeared in the third decade of the nineteenth century it took an entirely different form. The new wares were the thick and heavy encaustic floor tiles, the production of which was to continue uninterruptedly from the early 1830s. They represent one of the three main streams of tile making in the Victorian period. A second category of manufacture was of tiles to be used in major architectural schemes, either as a decorative element in the structure, or as adornment for the walls, examples of which span the years from the smoking-room at the House of Commons (1851) to Harrods' Meat Hall (1902).

The third type of tile is that with which this book is chiefly concerned,

Figure 1. Solid clay, creamware tile transfer printed on-glaze in black with a design symbolic of Peace. 7ins. by 7ins. Signed in the print 'T. Baddeley, Hanley'. Maker unknown — Baddeley was an engraver. c.1810. Courtesy City Museum and Art Gallery, Stoke-on-Trent.

Figure 2. Detail of portrait of Herbert Minton by H.W. Pickersgill, R.A. Courtesy Royal Doulton Tableware Ltd.

and takes us back in a sense to Sadler and Green and the simple pictorial tile for "hearths, fireplaces, wall linings, baths, friezes, skirtings, flower boxes and cabinet work."[2] This type of tile, the decorative or art tile, was not produced in any great quantity before 1860, but from 1870 to c.1910 hardly a house, school, chapel, pub, palace, or cathedral was erected that was not embellished somewhere or other with decorative tiling.

To understand and appreciate the wares we collect, it is helpful to know something of their history and of how they were made. The story has been told before of the growth of the tile industry — most notably by Jewitt, but parts of it are worth repeating, and certain elements may usefully be expanded upon.

Jewitt records[3] that Herbert Minton (Figure 2), son of the founder of the great Minton firm, became interested in the production of encaustic floor tiles in 1828, but his experiments had not proceeded far when, in 1830, Samuel Wright of Shelton took out a patent for "a manufacture of ornamental tiles". Not being a commercial success he sold his moulds and patent rights to Herbert Minton who agreed to pay Wright a 10% royalty on all tiles sold. Minton set aside one small room and three men for experimental production. He used brass moulds instead of Wright's plaster ones, but failure was repeated. Nevertheless in 1835 he issued his first printed catalogue of pseudo-medieval encaustic tile designs, and the following year executed a hall floor for Mr. Booker of Liverpool. In this same year, 1836, John Boyle joined Minton in partnership in what was a very thriving earthenware business and seemingly was resentful of the time and energy Minton was devoting to tile experiments. However, encouragement was forthcoming from Harriette, Duchess of Sutherland, and a tiling contract was completed at Trentham Hall. By this date other firms were venturing into the encaustic tile business, most notably Copeland and Garrett, arch rivals in porcelain manufacture and near neighbours of Minton in Stoke, and the Worcester Works of Chamberlain & Co.

In June 1840 another important technical advance was signalled when Richard Prosser of Birmingham took out a patent for making a variety of articles from clay in a powdered state — buttons, tesserae, floor tiles, glazed tiles, etc., by the use of a screw press, hence the name 'dust-pressed' tile. Herbert Minton quickly bought up half the English patent rights (again Boyle was unenthusiastic), and under the supervision of his engineer, John Turley, the manufacture of white glazed tiles began in August 1840. These were not the thick floor tiles but thinner wall tiles. Nevertheless, it was the encaustic floor tiles which commanded most of Minton's attention especially after he had formed a friendship with the fashionable architect and leading inspiration of the Gothic revival, A.W.N. Pugin, who was in the Staffordshire area in the early 1840s working on Alton Towers and Cheadle Parish church. The co-operation of the manufacturer and the architect was an important example of that unity of industry and art for which so many theorists, especially Sir Henry Cole, struggled so long to achieve in the new machine age (Figures 3 and 4).

Commissions increased, most notably in 1841 with the flooring of the Chapter House at Westminster. A second catalogue, 'Old English Tile Designs', appeared in 1842. Then followed a most successful demonstration of Prosser's tile press to the Royal Society of Arts on 8th March, 1843, and three years later a further exhibition at a soirée given by the Marquis of Northampton attended by Prince Albert, the Duke of Wellington, Sir Robert Peel and several bishops. Following the example of Josiah Wedgwood, Herbert Minton had introduced his wares at the highest level. Now other well-known designers and architects such as J.M. Blashfield, Digby Wyatt and Owen Jones worked in conjunction

Left: Figure 3. Tile design by A.W.N. Pugin, pen, pencil and wash. Labelled 'Jardiniere No.6' and 'tiles for top octagon', dated 1850. Courtesy Royal Doulton Tableware Ltd.

Figure 4. Encaustic tile inlaid in white on black with design of a pigeon. 5¾ins. Designed by A.W.N. Pugin. Mark: 'MINTON & Co. PATENT. STOKE UPON TRENT'. c.1850.

Figure 5. Imitation medieval encaustic tile. A block printed design in orange upon a solid brick-red body. This is not a true encaustic tile but indicates a cheaper and surer way of achieving the desired effect. No mark. Maker unknown. c.1860-1870.

with him to develop the adoption of geometric and encaustic floor tiles "into extensive use in the rebuilding of churches, noblemen's mansions and other public buildings." The commissions included a tile floor for the Queen at Osborne House in 1844 and, of course, corridor floors for the magnificent House of Commons in 1852.

Meanwhile, in 1841, Boyle left the firm and in 1845 Michael Daintry Hollins joined it, followed in 1846 by Samuel Barlow Wright, son of the patentee. In 1849 Herbert Minton's nephew, Colin Minton Campbell, also became a partner.

The Wright patent had originally been for fourteen years, and when it came up for renewal in 1844 Minton jointly renewed it for seven years with George Barr and Fleming St. John of the Chamberlain & Co. Works in Worcester. Jewitt maintained that little if any profit had been made in the first period of the patent, so generous was Herbert Minton and so thorough and expensive were his experiments and innovations.

A further important development took place in 1848 when F.W.M. Collins and Alfred Reynolds showed Herbert Minton trials they had made of "transferring to pottery, impressions taken from the flat surface of metal or stone" whereby "broad and flat layers of colour could be produced, and several colours transferred at the same time to the ware" (see p.50 for details). On 14th March, 1848 a patent was taken out "for improvements in ornamenting china, earthenware and glass". Technically, this was a most important step forward and although many failures had to be endured before suitable colour pigments were found and success assured, the Collins and Reynolds patent for 'block printing', as it is simpler to describe it, provided an important link in the chain of development of printed decorative tiles. Its first major recorded use is in the designs of Pugin for the walls of the smoking-room at the House of Commons, the tiles of which were printed by the Collins and Reynolds process. Block printing really came into its own in the 1870s, and many of the printed series were done in this fashion, termed by Mintons themselves as 'New Press' (see p.50).

Further impetus to the production of decorative tiles was imparted by the glaze experiments conducted by Minton's Art Director, the great French ceramicist Leon Arnoux, who took up his appointment in 1848.

He worked to produce the opaque enamel, or so-called *majolica* glazes, with which to colour floral and abstract tile designs, and though these were first produced c.1850, it was again not until the 1860s and 1870s that vast quantities were made. Many examples of this decorative treatment are illustrated later. Ultimately opaque glazes too were superseded by the translucent colour glazes used in the 1890s and on the art nouveau tiles of the Edwardian era.

Other technical developments followed as the flood tide of church and chapel building and restoration increased the demand for encaustic tiling beyond even the expectations of Herbert Minton who, when he died in 1858, was the acknowledged master of encaustic tile production. Only after his death did the competition become formidable. In 1855 S.B. Wright and H.T. Greene, again of Mintons, invented a process whereby encaustic tiles could be formed mechanically from the wet, plastic clay, thus considerably speeding up production. In 1863 Boulton and Worthington patented a method of dust-pressing encaustic tiles, an important extension of Prosser's methods.[4] This new method was employed first by T. & R. Boote but did not oust the plastic clay encaustic tiles and the two types were produced contemporaneously for many years. Finally, in 1873 the Maw company introduced a steam driven press into their factory.

Whilst these technical innovations were taking place, the pattern of demand was subtly shifting. The use of tiles which had found favour with royalty in the 1840s, had by the 1860s percolated through to the middle class. Stimulated by fashion arbiters such as Charles Eastlake's *Hints on Household Taste,* and the extensive use of decorative tiles in many public buildings, the demand for decorative wall tiles had greatly increased amongst the middle classes. It was at this particular moment that the firm which had provided the inspiration and leadership in the industry for forty years broke up.

The story of the dissolution of the Minton and Hollins alliance is a complicated and tortuous one, but basically the partners Colin Minton Campbell (the Minton China Works connection) and Michael Daintry Hollins, who had joined the firm in 1845, split up in 1868. Campbell took the porcelain and earthenware business with its galaxy of foreign artists and its international fame. Hollins took the tile works; he also took the celebrated name Minton Hollins & Co., and in after years his catalogues continued to advertise the success of the Minton factory prior to the 1868 split. Legal complications about the use of the Minton name followed in 1871 and 1875 (see p.59) and some rift between the former partners must have developed in this period, for Hollins erected a huge new factory in Shelton New Road, Stoke (still standing and recently cleaned), and thus, after c.1870 Minton Hollins & Co. were to all intents and purposes a new firm. They continued primarily as encaustic tile makers until, like everyone else, they were caught up in the tile boom of the 1870s and 1880s and produced every type of tile in the repertoire. Though technically it might be correct to regard Minton Hollins & Co. as the legitimate successors of the old firm, as Jewitt, Furnival and Barnard appear to do, yet in spirit, in artistic endeavour, and in many other respects the successor to Herbert Minton was Colin Minton Campbell of the Minton China Works. It was he who retained a set of the old pattern books, he retained Arnoux and his staff of artists and designers, and he or others in the firm retained a drive and purpose akin to that of Herbert Minton. For it was from Minton's China Works (henceforward always called Mintons in this book) that the real impetus to the manufacture of decorative art tiles came. Perhaps the key to this lies in the opening in 1871 of the Kensington Gore Art Pottery Studio (Figure 6).

Figure 6. Business card for Minton's Art Pottery Studio, designed by H. Stacey Marks. c.1870.

The importance of Minton's Kensington Studio has perhaps never been fully recognised, though there is a very lively account of an enterprise which was sadly terminated by a fire in 1875.[5] In that brief four years was determined one of the major directions into which the decorative tile business was to go — the printed and painted pictorial series.

Into the Studio came Hannah Barlow and a host of others such as William Wise, H.W. Foster and Edward Hammond, who were to serve Mintons as decorators and designers for many years. Almost certainly it was to the Studio that Moyr Smith came with his designs for the first of the really popular and trend-setting series of designs for the Biblical series (see p.124). Christopher Dresser also produced certain designs which are still preserved in the Mintons archives when working at the Studio, see Plate 21(116). The Rheads' account of the Studio is a fascinating starting point but not the last word and further research upon its importance and seminal influence would surely be fruitful.

Certainly, it was from the Studio that design ideas flowed to Mintons, and — presumably in the premises vacated by Hollins — the large scale manufacture of printed, pictorial tiles began in the early 1870s. The fashion was soon established and though Mintons gained a headstart on their rivals, others such as Copelands, Minton Hollins & Co., Maws and Wedgwood soon followed them into the field. The break up of the old Minton and Hollins connection as it turned out did no real harm to either side. Hollins with £30,000 valuation compensation built a new and modern factory, Colin Minton Campbell fashioned a new product and created a new market.

Two final points perhaps need stressing. One of the constant themes of the art mandarins of Victorian England was the divorce which they claimed existed between art and industry. The tile makers as much as anyone tried to reconcile the two. The employment of outside designers, starting with Pugin and Wyatt and progressing through Moyr Smith and Christopher Dresser to Walter Crane, Lewis F. Day and Alphonse Mucha, was a serious, and not unsucessful, attempt to bring the best in art and design to the general public through the medium of the mass produced tile. The élitists might scoff at this and turn to the handmade and consciously artistic products of William Morris, the Martin brothers or their less sincere imitators, but the union of art and industry preached so ardently by Sir Henry Cole in the late 1840s and 1850s was achieved in some measure in the work of the Victorian tile makers.

What is perhaps even less frequently recognised or acknowledged is that the leaders of the tile industry, Mintons and Copelands, were the most successful manufacturers of pottery and porcelain of the age. Wedgwood too, when their fortunes revived in the 1860s and 1870s, established a high standard. It was only as the century progressed into its last two decades that pre-eminence passed into the hands of the mass producers, such as Maw & Co., Minton Hollins & Co., Craven Dunnill and a host of lesser names. Even then it is significant that all these, and Pilkingtons, at one time or another manufactured 'art pottery'.

Chapter One Footnotes

1   E.S. Price, *John Sadler, A Liverpool Pottery Printer.*
2   Maws Catalogue, n.d.
3   Jewitt, Vol.1, pp.196-206.
4   Furnival, pp.459-463 for technical details.
5   The Rheads, in an excellent chapter, pp.347-362.

Chapter Two

The Collection

The tiles which the collector is seeking will have come from a variety of sources — "Walls, Hearths, Fire Places, Furniture, Flower boxes etc."[1] We shall not consider the encaustic or inlaid floor tile, since their bulk and weight make them rather unsuitable for the ordinary collector. Nor will much be said of the very attractive and beautifully coloured architectural schemes which T. & R. Boote amongst others advertised for the dairy, the fish shop and the butcher. Colour Plate I shows a fine example from the Minton catalogue. The quintessence of such architectural decoration is Harrods' Meat Hall, but however spectacular it might be, this and similar designs exist as exemplifications of what could be achieved, rather than as quarry for the collector. Many such architectural schemes are described and admirably illustrated in Julian Barnard's work. It is the single — or short run — decorative and pictorial tile which the collector seeks and with which this book is concerned.

The tile collector, unlike the collector of pottery and porcelain, cannot add variety to his collection by the choice of objects of differing shapes. Tiles are flat, decorated on one side and, with only occasional variations, are of a standard square shape. Variety is achieved by decoration. Most collectors after a period of general collecting tend to move into a specialised field and here the range and variety of decoration adequately compensates for the uniformity of shape.

The most obvious form of specialisation, particularly for anyone who has come to tiles from pots, is to collect the range of products from one factory. An interesting and rewarding collection could be accumulated in this way. Certainly with the large firms such as Mintons, Minton Hollins or Craven Dunnill there is plenty of scope, though if the chosen factory were Wedgwood, de Morgan or Pilkington the cost could be relatively high. The drawback to this approach is the comparative scarcity of marked examples from many of the less well-known producers. Even some of the larger firms such as Craven Dunnill were rather limited in the scope of their output (in their case because they produced few pictorial tiles). This is not to say that factory of origin is not a worthwhile approach, indeed one would hope to see before too long, complete monographs devoted to the products of a single maker based upon collections formed in this manner.

A similar approach might be to collect a few specimen tiles from the largest possible number of makers. This too would provide an interesting collection, though the dominance of the large firms would surely cause the collector undue disappointment as specimen after specimen proved upon examination to be Mintons or Minton Hollins. Thus many lovely tiles of high quality with admired decoration would have to be left because one already had enough examples of the work of that particular firm. We have found this to be the case in our own collection, and the arrangement of this book reflects the rejection of that particular approach.

Decoration is the primary feature of a tile, thus a collection based upon types of decoration is a third possible approach. The most obvious candidate is the printed/pictorial decoration with the allied literary and historical interest which this type of tile engenders. Our own collection has tended to veer in this direction as many of the accompanying illustrations testify. If, however, the collector finds the printed decoration rather mechanical and repetitive, then an equally strong case can be mounted for a collection of moulded tiles, of coloured glaze effects or of on-glaze enamel painting. Any of these would provide excellent and decorative displays. More specialised still would be a collection based upon the work of an individual artist or designer. William de Morgan is an outstanding example and one whose work is already much admired, collected and correspondingly expensive. Moyr Smith too is an established name, but an interesting collection could be made of the works of some of the designers depicted here, especially William Wise (see p.192), George Cartlidge (see p.180), Lewis F. Day (see p.88), or of other decorators and designers whose work we have been able to identify.

In order to assist the collector as much as possible, the approach that has been adopted in the present work is the 'theme' or 'subject' approach. Having rejected the 'factory of origin' classification, and concentrated upon decoration, it was decided that classification by subject — landscapes, nursery rhymes, animals or whatever, would enable comparisons to be made of the merits of the work of separate factories and of individual artists, both in the treatment of similar themes and in the application of different technical processes to designs of a comparable nature. The tiles of the Victorian era are a microcosm of the art history of the period. This is part of their attraction. The thematic approach allows us to trace, through the development of significant designs, the artistic moods of the Victorian age. The influence of Pugin and the Gothic revival can clearly be seen in the geometric and abstract designs of the 1850s and 1860s. The flowering of the aesthetic movement, with the almost universal adoption of the lily, peacock and sunflower as ornamental motifs, is likewise revealed. So too is the cult of the medieval. The inspiration of the work of the Pre-Raphaelites, of William Morris and of other key figures is reflected in the pictures on the tiles for the hearth and the flower box. Furthermore, some of the characteristics of the Victorians, their sentimentality, their love for the romantic and the picturesque may be seen in the work of the decorative tile manufacturer. On these and other themes and influences we shall expand in the appropriate sections. The thematic approach is the one which allows the greatest scope for discerning and charting the prevalent styles, influences and motifs in the design and decoration of the Victorian tile.

Additionally, a thematic approach allows a much greater freedom for the collector to choose examples from the very expensive to the comparatively cheaply-priced tile within his selected theme. Thus the collector of flower motifs can range — as the illustrations show — from the expensive rarities of Walter Crane's work for Pilkingtons, Plate 12 (70 and 71), to the inexpensive but attractive specimen depicted in Plate 6(32), which research has revealed is a design registered on 2nd February, 1887 by the Decorative Art Tile Company, Hanley. A happy coincidence for the collector combining rarity with cheapness.

This thematic treatment is strongly recommended to the would-be collector. It provides variety and flexibility and, if the choice of subject or subjects is not too restricted, ensures a reasonable framework so that the collection does not get out of hand numerically. But whatever advice may be offered here, it will be the individual collector who determines the scope of his or her own collection. This is as it should be.

One of the subsidiary attractions of tile collecting is that the pleasure of junk shop hunting is retained. As most collectors of ceramics have found in recent years, there are so few pieces of Bow, Rockingham, delftware or Derby to be found unrecognised in the junk shops that visiting them, as one did fifteen or twenty years ago, is now largely a waste of time. With Victorian tiles, for the present at least, it is different. The market stalls, the back street junk emporia or the small provincial 'antique' shops are still worth a visit and the enquiry "any Victorian picture tiles?" If you are fortunate and the answer is "yes", you may be offered tiles still *in situ* in small items of furniture. The 'Aesop's Fables' tiles, Plate 32 (181-186), were set in a long wooden plant pot stand. Other examples have come from square plant pot holders, bamboo tables, chairs, and most frequently, from the backs of washstands (Figure 7). Recently the practice of removing the back panel from the stand and taking out the tiles seems to have declined. As tiles have gained in popularity they have been retained as decorative features in the stripped and refurbished washstand.

Many tiles bear evidence of having come from fireplace surrounds (Figures 8 and 9). The accumulation of plaster on the back and black lead or paint on the face of the tile should not deter the collector. The

Figure 7. Washstand with marble top. The back inset with ten tiles each moulded with an art nouveau floral motif. Maker unknown. c.1900. Courtesy Sarah Richardson.

Figure 8. Part of a page from the Maw & Co. pattern book showing a majolica fireplace and four bosses representing the seasons (see also Plate 45(256). Courtesy Royal Doulton Tableware Ltd.

quality of the glaze is usually so high that accretions can be carefully removed and the original shining surface restored. Quantities of plaster can be eased off, after soaking in water, but some cements do not come away easily and are best left. A lump of cement on the back is preferable to a freshly-chipped or shattered tile. Slight chips from the edges of the tile may have to be accepted when one is buying an unusual or attractive piece. Its removal from a wall or fireplace by a demolition contractor has not always been accomplished with loving care and delicacy.

As consolation, a slightly damaged tile should be cheaper than a perfect one. Large-scale demolition of late Victorian and even Edwardian property, in many of our Northern and Midland towns especially, has considerably increased the supply of decorative tiles, but as clearance programmes of sub-standard housing built in the 1870-1910 period are completed and property is modernised, with the old coal-burning grates and fireplaces removed, so the supply of tiles will diminish. What may now seem plentiful and inexpensive may in a very short time become both scarce and dear. It is certainly not beyond the bounds of possibility that sets of pictorial tiles by William Wise or Moyr Smith could attain a similar status to the printed 'pot-lid', and correspondingly be as expensive and as sought after. The variety of design was much wider in tile design than in pot-lids, as the lists of series published here will testify, but rarities in this field, as indeed in the field of under-glaze blue transfer printed earthenware, will increasingly command what may now seem to be 'ridiculous' prices.

It is never very easy to write helpfully about prices. With an annual inflation rate of 12-15% at the time of writing (1979) and with a class of ware which is attracting serious attention from collectors, dealers, writers and researchers, any 'price guide' has to have wide margins and needs to be up-dated frequently, which annual supplements to this book will do. What follows, therefore, is perforce a general outline, and a fuller, detailed guide is given at the end of the book. At the top of the scale, the £200 paid in 1973 for a set of six (all different) of Walter Crane's 'Flora's Train', Plate 12(70 and 71), designed for Pilkingtons seemed excessive at the time, since which date the value of the pound has halved! The ordinary, but attractive printed and coloured geometric or floral pattern at between £2 (rock bottom) and £6 — dependent upon mark, condition etc. — is not unreasonable. Art nouveau coloured glazes examples tend to be in the £4-£10 range, whilst Wedgwood tiles are always more expensive than those of comparable makers — £20-£25 for an 'Old English' or month tile Plate 44(252) and Plate 45(253 and 254), is not uncommon. Mintons printed sets of Moyr Smith designs (6ins. size) have been selling in the past year or so for sums ranging from £6-£15 per piece dependent upon quality, colour and rarity. Eight inch tiles are more expensive than six inch, other factors being equal. Blue printed picture tiles are more expensive than brown or black for a comparable pattern, though this may be only a reflection of the current high interest in blue printed wares. A multi-coloured print will be more costly still. William de Morgan tiles are really a specialised field. Certainly as regards prices they are in a class of their own. Attractiveness — as with de Morgan's work is one criterion, so is condition, and rarity too plays a part. A floral or patterned design which can be attributed to a specific artist or designer — for example Lewis F. Day at Pilkingtons has an enhanced value. Sets of tiles tend to be more expensive *pro rata* than single examples.

These are only guidelines to current trends. The only sensible advice one can give is to remind the collector to keep a sense of proportion, and never to pay more than he can reasonably afford. It is a very delicate

Figure 9. Four fireplace designs, coloured. One for Lord Thynne. From the Minton archives (Jones, Minton MSS, No. 1841). Courtesy Royal Doulton Tableware Ltd.

balance. Tomorrow he may see the identical tile at half the price of the piece he covets today. Alternatively, he may have to wait many years for another chance to add the rarity to his collection. By that time today's 'too dear' may well seem to have been 'a giveaway'.

A collection of tiles may be displayed in a variety of ways. The tiles can be accommodated on plate racks or shelves — indeed narrow shelves or tile racks could be specially constructed for them so that they could be displayed vertically. Two other methods of display are illustrated. Plate 1(3) shows a tile in a commercially produced, opaque plastic wire spring plate holder hung from an angle pin. This is the easiest, simplest method of display and the wire is relatively unobtrusive. The holders cost about 25p each and their use facilitates the reorganisation of the display. Plate 1(2) shows a more elaborate method of display. Here the tiles are framed, which means that the side edges which are sometimes unsightly, are hidden, and a colourful frame can be provided to match and supplement the attractiveness of the individual tile. Frames may be made from strips of picture-framing wood backed by plywood, hardboard, or secured at the back by strong, fabric adhesive tape. Our own frames were constructed with a hardboard back and a chipboard surround. The chipboard is bought in ready-cut squares and the centre is marked to size and cut out with a coping saw. This leaves a residue of tile-sized pieces of chipboard, but guarantees that there is no jointing of corners which might require a level of practical competence quite beyond the ability of the present writer. The chipboard frame is smoothed, checked for size, and then nailed to the hardboard. It can then be covered with a suitable material, cut to size and stuck down. Hessian, felt, PVC and other plastic materials in a variety of colours can all be used as coverings. A loop of string through the back and two or three triangular brass fasteners on the front to secure the tile, completes the job.

In this type of frame the tile is presented very attractively and can readily be taken out to examine the mark on the back or any other features of interest. However, the work can be time-consuming and if the collection is growing fast, new acquisitions quickly outstrip the time available for framing them. The cost of such self-made frames is only a little above that of the plate hangers, averaging say 30p each, depending on the quality of the covering material. As an alternative, these frames may be painted, given a wood stain or sprayed with paint.

The foregoing applies to single tiles, or at the most pairs. Tile panels or runs of five or more tiles tend to be very heavy and unless one is a particularly competent handyman, professional advice on framing is advisable. Finally, certain impact adhesives may be used, sometimes in conjunction with a hook fixed to the back of the tile, thus providing one further method of hanging tiles for display.

If the collector does not wish to display all his pieces, those in store can easily be housed in the bottom of a cupboard or somewhere similar. To avoid damage a piece of foam rubber or bubble plastic of the right size between each tile in a stack affords good protection.

Whatever method one adopts in displaying a collection, or indeed whatever motives prompted the initial acquisition of a tile or two — whether for interior decoration or to satisfy the urge to 'collect something' — it is to be hoped that displaying the possession will be only the beginning and not an end in itself. Any collection however small and

Figure 10. Butcher's shop window containing set of twelve tiles designed and etched by William Wise from two series 'Animals of the Farm' and 'Village Life'. c.1880-1890.

apparently unimportant can give redoubled pleasure to its owner if it is a live collection. A dead collection sits immovable on a shelf or in frames, like a lump of baked clay. But a living collection is one which is capable of giving something to its owner over and above the pleasure of beholding it and counting its investment value. For some collectors it is the literary or historical associations which their pieces evoke which gives this added pleasure and brings the collection to life. For others it is the thrill of discovery and research, the pursuit of knowledge.

It is not necessary to engage in scholarly research to enjoy one's collection to the full; but many collectors do gain satisfaction from reading around their subject and cataloguing the collection. Indeed, making a catalogue is a useful beginning to more detailed research. A simple card index entry for each tile is all that is required. The size, colour and design, the mark, the artist, the pattern number and factory of origin should be noted. A record of when and where the tile was purchased and how much was paid for it is all that is needed for a simple catalogue. Those who have never attempted to keep such a record would be surprised at what pleasure can be gained from doing so, and from adding to it from time to time notes on similar tiles seen in museums, exhibitions, catalogues of sales, magazines or books.

The keen student may wish to go further and begin to investigate the source of a particular set of designs; to piece together the life of the artist whose work he admires; to trace the history of the factory whose tiles he collects. All these possibilities, and many more, are open to the amateur and the non-specialist. The initial steps are sometimes very difficult. But, as progress is made, perhaps with the help of a trained historian, a helpful librarian, or through an extra-mural class, a familiarity develops with old newspaper files, the catalogues of the local history library, the resources of the record office and the contents of the parish chest. In the next chapter we shall discuss some of the specific sources we have used in writing this book, and throughout full references have been given to other primary and secondary source material.

This chapter ends with a tantalising picture (Figure 10), of a dozen William Wise tiles *in situ* in a butcher's shop in Whaley Bridge. This display and a splendidly preserved butcher's shop in Warwick Street, Carlisle, are powerful reminders of the attractiveness of Victorian tiles in their original situations. Long may they remain there to thwart the trendy, modernising shop fitter and the envy of the tile collector!

Chapter Two Footnote
1   Minton Tile Catalogue, c.1880.

Chapter Three
Pattern Books, Catalogues and Documentary Material

Much of the detailed information presented in this book has been gleaned from surviving documentary material. It is perhaps fortunate that serious interest in Victorian tiles has developed before too much historical source material has been forgotten or thrown away. There is a wealth of information still in existence, and we are most grateful to all those noted in the acknowledgements for their generosity and kindness in making readily available material in their care. What is described in this chapter and elsewhere is only what we have been able to discover and utilise, it is by no means all that remains. There are whole categories of documents such as the records of the Tile Manufacturers' Association which have not been touched, and undoubtedly much more information will come to light relevant to specific factories, their patterns, series and architectural schemes. There is an abundance of material for future researchers to work upon.

Apart from historical documentary material, which will be discussed later, three main sources of information have been used: artists' designs, the factory pattern books and published printed catalogues. It is important to distinguish between these as they will be constantly referred to in the detailed survey of the tiles.

A number of collections of original artists' sketches, drawings, water-colours and general designs exist. These originals have been preserved by Mintons, Wedgwood, Copeland and Maw and will be described later. Usually these drawings represent the first stage in the tile making process; they are the original designs of the artist, submitted in the hope of acceptance or commissioned for production. These originals or copies of them by the artist would also be used by the engraver or etcher for producing the copper plates from which transfer prints would be taken. It is a real privilege to see and handle this original work especially when the design is for a tile which one cherishes in one's own collection.

Once a design had been accepted and engraved or etched, it would be assigned a number and entered in the factory pattern book. For Mintons, Copeland, Wedgwood and Maw, such pattern books have been preserved in whole or in part. They usually take the form of a printed 'pull' from the copper plate stuck down in a book, numbered, placed in sequence and decorated in the appropriate colours, or with written instructions as to the type of decorative finish. The same pattern might appear several times in a pattern book, each time with differences of colour or decorative detail (the addition, say, of gilding), and each separate entry bears a different pattern number. In the later chapters where pattern numbers are quoted for designs, it is always the first entry, the lowest number noted, which is recorded. Most of the factories discussed would certainly have more than one set of pattern books.

There would probably be a master copy such as Copeland keep in their 'pattern safe,' and probably a separate copy for the printers, with either offprints or relevant sets of coloured examples for the paintresses to work from. The Mintons archives also contain several sets of printed designs which, though left loose, have been carefully coloured, possibly even by the original designer himself. These pattern books are very important for establishing a chronology for the introduction of the patterns. As is recorded later (p.204), the Copeland pattern books contain a most helpful series of dated entries indicating when patterns were 'sent to London' in the period 1840-1880, thus enabling us to date with reasonable accuracy the introduction, not only of the dated patterns, but those in between. Such reference points are found less frequently in the pattern books of other manufacturers but with the help of other relevant information a comparative chronology can be established for the introduction of most of the Mintons and Wedgwood patterns and less certainly those of Maw. It is for this reason that in the text and captions we have quoted the pattern numbers, even though in most cases these **do not** appear on the tiles themselves. Their relative position is important. The dates which are given are the approximate **first** introduction of the pattern. The tile in your collection may bear a design introduced in 1878, but it could have been produced fifteen or even twenty years later. There is no way in which the actual date of manufacture can be determined other than when firms altered their marks, ceased production, or provided similar specific reference points.

Further help in accurate dating can be provided by the printed catalogues issued by the various firms. Once a design was in production it would in due course appear in a printed trade catalogue which gave details of all the designs currently on offer, with their pattern numbers for convenience of purchase. When a design ceased to be popular it would disappear from the printed catalogue as did the Moyr Smith sets from the post-1900 Mintons catalogue, and it would be reasonable to assume that once the design had been withdrawn from the catalogue, it would rarely if ever, be produced again. These published catalogues were beautifully produced in full colour lithographic printing. They were intended for the trade to use for the purpose of ordering and matching. The cover of an edition of the Mintons catalogue of c.1883-1885 reads:

"Mintons Tiles. Selected patterns of Enamelled Tiles, for Walls, Hearths, Fire Places, Furniture, Flower Boxes, &c., reduced to a scale of 1½ inch to a foot. Full-sized Prints of any particular Patterns that may be required will be sent on application to MINTONS (Limited) CHINA WORKS, Stoke-upon-Trent, or their London Warehouse, 28, Walbrook, (opposite Cannon Street Station.) This book of patterns is entered at Stationers' Hall. Price Seven Shillings and Sixpence."

The Stationers' Hall records have all been transferred to the Public Record Office where, no doubt, a copy of this catalogue will be located. One feels sure that examples of the catalogues from the various manufacturers may still be found in the offices of some of the older builders' merchants and similar firms. We have been fortunate in securing a copy of the Minton Hollins and Co. catalogue from which some of the illustrations have been taken (Colour Plate II).

Using the three primary sources of information noted above, it is

Colour Plate II. Page from the catalogue of Minton Hollins & Co., showing painted art tiles "for Grate Cheeks and Hearths". Author's Collection.

Colour Plate III. Page from the catalogue of Mintons China Works showing a range of tiles "chiefly of Persian design". Courtesy Royal Doulton Tableware Ltd.

Left: Figure 11. Coloured design for tile panel depicting a peacock by Leon Victor Solon for Mintons. The design was in a folder marked "not executed". (Jones, Minton MSS, No. 1841). c.1895-1900. Courtesy Royal Doulton Tableware Ltd.

Figure 12. Coloured design in red and white of tile panels depicting a tropical bird and fish and water rushes in the Japanese style. Designer unknown, executed by Minton for Thomas Goode, London. (Jones, Minton MSS, No. 1841). c.1875. Courtesy Royal Doulton Tableware Ltd.

possible to add to our knowledge of the output of several of the major tile makers.

By far the largest collection of material is that contained in the Minton archives which have recently been professionally and expertly catalogued by Alyn Giles Jones, Archivist, University College of North Wales, Bangor. This catalogue will be referred to frequently throughout this book as a reference for specific items in the Mintons collection. The material is now in Stoke in the keeping of Royal Doulton Tableware (who now own the old Mintons factory) where, under suitable safeguards, items are available for study.

There is a very considerable collection of art material[1] relating to tiles, amounting to over fifty catalogued items, and in several cases a single item may contain upwards of a hundred drawings, coloured prints or similar work. There is a certain amount of repetition and some of the large folios are labelled "not executed". Nevertheless original work by Stacey Marks (see p.135), Moyr Smith (see p.121), L.V. Solon (Figure 11), William Wise (see p.192), H.W. Foster (see p.183) and several other artists such as Mussill and Henk, is contained in the fascinating if somewhat heterogeneous collection which ranges from doodles and preliminary sketches to beautifully finished designs which had been submitted to clients and bore the request "Return to Mintons, Stoke-on-Trent." In the captions and elsewhere frequent reference is made to this art material where it exists for relevant patterns. In contrast to Figure 11, which depicted a "not executed" design, Figure 12 shows a coloured design from the archive collection for two panels in the Japanese taste. These panels were incorporated in a building and can be seen to this day on the side of Thomas Goode the china retailers, 17-19 South Audley Street, London, W.1.

The Minton archives also contain an almost complete set of tile pattern books. To date we have traced thirteen in all. There is some duplication and certain gaps remain which might well be filled when additional material, which has come to light since the catalogue was compiled, is fully recorded. As they stand these thirteen patterns books,[2] dating from the 1830s through to the early years of the present century, contain the following pattern ranges 21-254, 441-501, 884-1860, 2168-3111. The gap between patterns 1860 and 2168 is rather unfortunate as in this range fall several of the series which are discussed here such as 'Animal Groups' Plate 19(105-107), 'Old English Sports and Games' Plate 42(235), 'Views' Plate 14(78 and 80). This gap is partly filled by a miscellaneous pattern book[3] which includes examples of most of the important printed series in the missing range as well as other patterns which start in the 800s and, with many gaps, continues to over 2,000.

From these most valuable books we can learn something of the enormous range of pattern production undertaken at the Mintons China Works over an eighty year period, and make an attempt at a chronology of patterns. The early patterns are mainly encaustic designs, though some plaques and panels are included and floral designs also appear in the 1850s and 1860s. The first printed series on record is pattern 1335, 'Old Testament', designed by Moyr Smith. This series is quickly followed by the same designer's 'Industrial,' 'Early English History' and 'New Testament' series. These are noted in detail and illustrated later (Plates 27, 47 and 52). From other evidence (see p.122) it seems very unlikely that these designs were in production as early as 1870, a date often given for this type of work. A more likely date is 1872-3. Pattern 1607, 'Waverley', also by Moyr Smith, was exhibited at Paris in 1878, and tiles in the series 'Animals of the Farm', pattern 1699, by William Wise are dated 1879 on the copper plate. Patterns 1753 and 1756 in the pattern book have one of the very few dates found in any of the books, for there is a note saying "trial for 12 March 1880".

This is only a skeleton chronology, the extension beyond 1880 is tentative, and is based upon a design registration for 1896 appearing beside a pattern in the 2770 range. Thus we find that just over 1,000 new patterns had been introduced in this sixteen year period, or a rough average of sixty patterns a year. This compares with an average seventy-five new patterns a year in the heyday of 1878-1880, and probably about sixty-five in the period 1872-1880. If we accept this tentative scheme we can assign approximate dates to some of those tiles whose numbers are traceable in the catalogue or the pattern books and this has been done and noted in the captions. It is worth stressing that even these apparently late dates give Mintons several years' start in the printed pictorial patterns on their rivals at Copeland, Wedgwood and Maw.

Several editions of the colour printed catalogue (including one of early encaustic designs) are in the Minton archives[4] and three different editions are in the City of Stoke-on-Trent Library at Hanley.[5] One of the most important features of these coloured catalogues is that each of the earlier ones begins with a "List of the Various Series of Picture Tiles". It is from these printed lists that we have quoted extensively in the captions to the illustrations and elsewhere in the text. The three volumes in Hanley cover virtually the whole range of tiles. The earliest of the three, c.1884, contains 24 sheets of coloured illustrations and includes all the important pictorial series as far as pattern 2015 — the 'Albert Dürer' series — as well as many hundreds of miscellaneous, geometric, abstract and floral patterns. The second volume would seem to date from c.1896. Some of the earlier sheets are omitted or combined and new patterns take us to sheet 52. The third volume is c.1905, and by this time all the earlier pictorial series have been omitted, including all the Moyr Smith designs, though some of the William Wise views and cattle prints remain. The bulk of the designs from sheets 50-70 are in the art nouveau style. Price lists are also included in these catalogues and one learns that most simple printed designs on 6-inch tiles sold at 3s. 6d. a dozen (e.g. 'Industrial' in blue and white). The 'Tennyson Idylls' series in white blue and brown 6-inch were 4s. 6d. a dozen, the 'Classical Figures with Musical Instruments' in white, blue, brown and yellow, 8-inch size, 11s. a dozen and 'Waverley' in four colours 8-inch size 12s. a dozen, the same price as the 'Medieval musicians' 8-inch size, in coloured glazes. A price list of 1891 with an 1894 addendum[6] gives more detail:

"The 3/6d per dozen quoted in this list for Tiles 6in x 6in decorated in one colour, is the *price when done on a white body either White or Yellow glaze,* on BUFF, IVORY, DRAB or RED body the price is 3d a dozen extra; and for *all* 6in x 6in patterns done on SAGE, OLIVE or TURQUOISE body, 1/- a dozen more than for other coloured bodies.

"8in x 8in when done on SAGE, OLIVE or TURQUOISE body are 1/6d a dozen more than the price here quoted for other bodies."

The Minton archives also include several Photograph Books which contain photographs of ware produced and several are devoted to tiles.[7] The record in each is rather fragmentary and as a different numerical sequence is used to that employed for the pattern book and catalogue, there is a risk of confusion. What is particularly helpful about the photograph books is that they illustrate a number of designs which may never have gone into quantity production, but which undoubtedly were actually made. For example, there are photographs of a set of 6-inch tiles of the 'Seven Ages of Man' (see p.136), by Stacey Marks, in which the figures are of quaint bird-like creatures not unlike the grotesque birds fashioned by the Martin brothers. Another study "after H.S. Marks" depicts the months of the year represented by small boys standing in a line. It it painted on a panel 16ins. by 8ins. "in Indian blue by Mrs. Keats and Miss Turner". There are many photographs of completed panels and quasi-architectural sketches, and it could well be that many of these were special and unique commissions. One of the books opens with a splendid photograph of the tile panel executed at St. Pancras Station. In short, these are most useful source books and furnish ample material for anyone who wishes to pursue the work of a particular designer in more detail. One of the more fascinating sidelights was to note how frequently the name of Antonin Boullemeir, one of the great Minton ceramic artists, appeared in the books either as a painter or designer of panels depicting *putti*. Due to lack of space, it has not been possible here to describe all the individual subjects in their relevant sections later in the book, and only the major series will be dealt with. Lastly, mention should be made of some of the historical documents relating to Minton tile production which have been consulted.

The Artists' Wages Book[8] provided interesting information on William Wise the designer (p.192), though somewhat disappointingly no reference so far has been traced to payments to the freelance artists such as Stacey Marks and Moyr Smith. The relevant patents and the various agreements with Prosser, Wright and Barr already noted on p.18-20 are also to be found. An interesting set of accounts — one amongst very many — is contained in a Summary Book[9] which gives comparative figures in pounds sterling for the various classes of wares sold in the years 1883-1898:

Abstract of nett sales 1884-98. Abbreviations used are: CG — China Gilt; CU — China Ungilt; EE — Enamelled Earthenware; T — Tiles; F — Figures.

	CG	CU	EE	T	F
1884	39001	10823	30569	25166	463
1887	29027	6759	22581	21215	181
1890	28262	7342	23222	18710	189
1893	28383	6132	18548	18129	85
1894	19999	6311	15915	16832	49
1896	30031	7209	17177	17898	29
1898	28316	7767	15738	17138	61

The strength of the tile section throughout this period is apparent from these figures, though the relative position clearly was weakening at the close of the century *vis-à-vis* fine china.

The Minton records are undoubtedly the most considerable we have encountered and the excellent catalogue (now completed by an Index) is a great help in finding one's way through a very extensive range of material. Because of its wide scope and general usefulness detailed treatment has been given to the Minton archives. However, artistic and documentary material is also quite plentiful from other tile makers.

The Copeland records are most instructive. The present firm of Spode retains a full set of six pattern books for all the tile designs covering the period c.1840-1900, and in addition about two hundred original watercolour and pen and ink sketches for tile designs. Details of these sources are given on pp.204-208. We have not so far come across a printed catalogue for Copeland and the impression conveyed by the pattern books is that the scope and extent of their business was very much less than that of Mintons. This is really implicit in the fact that most of their tiles were made from the plastic clay and not the more efficient mass-produced dust-pressed tile. Furthermore, in the pattern books there are a considerable number of 'private patterns' such as that for pattern 733 of c.1868 against which is entered "Private. This pattern done only for N. Owen & Co. Rotherham". Numerous similar private patterns were executed for Steel & Garland of Sheffield, Carr Bros. & Wilson, Sheffield (see p.144), W. Corbitt & Co. of Rotherham and Nisbet & Son, Glasgow. All of whom would seem to be stove grate manufacturers.

Wedgwood also produced tiles on a much less substantial scale than Mintons for about thirty years c.1870-1900. A good deal of light can be thrown on the types of tiles produced by the surviving records in the

Wedgwood Museum, Barlaston. The most important single item is a blue bound volume of tile patterns. This does not comprise the complete range but starts at pattern T 242 and proceeds more or less in sequence to pattern T 547. Each pattern is printed in the book, which clearly was made up well after most of the designs had been produced. The patterns from T 242 to T 268 are the conventional floral and abstract designs. From T 269 onwards (see p.191) pictorial series occur with frequency and the introduction of this style can be dated with reasonable accuracy as the set of months entitled 'Early (or Old) English', pattern T 275, was registered in March 1878 (see p.171 for further details). The various designs are fully described in the appropriate sections in Chapter Six. The dating of subsequent series is not at all easy as, unlike the Minton pattern books, the entries are not in strict sequence, though it would be reasonable to assume that the ship patterns, Plate 59(334), T 493-T 497, were comparatively late. Two patterned designs T 469 and T 544 both carry design registration numbers, the former indicating a date of 1886, the latter 1892. Thus the intermediate ship patterns would appear to date from c.1889. On this pattern number evidence all the pictorial series except the ships and a few of the American scenes fall between the dates of 1878 and 1885. The Wedgwood pattern numbers prefixed by the capital T do frequently appear on the tiles, and as the T seems unique to Wedgwood they provide a helpful method of attributing unmarked examples.

Also preserved at Barlaston is a folder of drawings and tile designs by the artist Thomas Allen (see p.140 for details) and a printed colour catalogue of c.1902 for encaustic and mosaic pavements and general architectural schemes, which does not include any of the printed pictorial designs. Such designs did appear in the usual printed catalogue, for a few very tattered fragments are in the Wedgwood Museum. As research into nineteenth century ceramic production intensifies it is highly likely that more interesting materials, both artistic and in printed form, will be discovered amongst the vast treasury of the Wedgwood Museum. Regrettably there are only a very few tiles in the superb factory collection of Wedgwood pottery and porcelain.

If the production of tiles by Josiah Wedgwood & Sons Limited was comparatively small, that of the Maw Company of Jackfield, Shropshire was immense (Figure 13). By the end of the century their volume of production would seem to have overtaken that of both the Minton China Works and the Minton Hollins concern. Much of the Maw Company tile work consisted of encaustic and architectural tiling, but they were responsible for some interesting patterned and pictorial tiles and again we are fortunate in having substantial documentary evidence to assist both understanding and identification. The material is located in the Shrewsbury District Library, as well as in the Clive House Museum and at the Ironbridge Gorge Museum Trust library in Ironbridge. In quantity and quality it would certainly furnish the basis for an interesting study of the development of the factory. Abstract books at Shrewsbury give details of orders supplied between 1913-1926, bank books for part of the same period, early twentieth century minutes of meetings of the directors, and several volumes of catalogues for dado schemes, Anglo-Roman, geometric and encaustic tile pavements and publicity material — complete with excellent photographs of tiling commissions carried out by

Figure 13. Photograph of Maw & Co., Benthall Works, taken in 1973 after the works had closed in 1969.

the firm in pubs and hotels mainly in the Birmingham area. The printed catalogues advertise pavements, etc. "designed and arranged by M. Digby Wyatt, G. Edmund Street, George Goldie, H.B. Garling, J.P. Seddon and Others," and there are eleven volumes[10] of design books, each volume approximately 20ins. by 14ins. packed with a fascinating collection of drawings, watercolours and prints, virtually all of which are for "encaustic tiles, arms, crests, monograms, embossed patterns etc." Equally fascinating, but not particularly relevant to this present book, is an account book for the years 1895-1899 with details of work done in "opal lustre", "ruby lustre", "tiles for panels" and so forth.[11]

An earlier account book[12] for the years 1891-1894 gives the price of tiles on 6th March, 1891 as "6 x 6 white, 3/9 a yard, strips for lustre, 6/6 a yard, various intaglios, 4/3 a yard and printed, 4/9 a yard." This volume also contains interesting details of payments to work people: "To Andrew Childe Painter 10d per hour w.e. May 13 (1891) 43½ hrs £1/16/3" which included painting "2 lustre vases, Crane's design". On another occasion Childe paints: "Lustre vases, Virgin & Lamps, tiles for Japanese room". Other names recorded in this book are:

Walter Evans, "painter, sketching in pattern books 1½ hrs"

William Moore, "painter"

W. Browne, "painter", "persian work"

J. Rutter, "painter" — a pair of lustre panels 16ins. by 4½ins., "six hours"

S. (T. or G.) Edge, "barbotine painter and gilder", he spent 57½ hours on an "underglaze panel of London Bridge" 3ft. 9ins. by 2ft. 9ins., then another 61 hours in three separate sessions "touching up London Bridge"

J. Meredith, "painter"

Thomas Evans (no description, but a painter)

Charles H. Temple, one of the major designers at the factory who was largely responsible for the firm's exhibits at the 1893 Chicago World's Fair

Jones, "painter".

The paintresses were named on 22nd April, 1891 as Miss Felton, Miss Harper, Miss Bright, Miss Ray and Miss Connor. It should be borne in mind that these artists were decorating pots as well as tiles. But there is no doubt that tile work was an important feature, and this is exemplified by a Wages Book for 1894-98[13] where in addition to the names already cited entries occur for:

Frank Allcock, painting lustre and majolica

A. Oakes, persian brushwork, gilding "in lustre room"

Alfred Potter, "painting and enamelling 6 x 6 landscapes in colour"

J. Wilde, painting lustre at "prices per yard", "seconds" at 2s. per yard. Wilde regularly earned £3 a week by such piece work, and on occasions £4 or £5. On 24th March, 1896 he took home £7 5s. 11½d.

These three account books give fascinating glimpses of the workings of this vast pottery and tile business in the 1890s. They help us to understand the human dimension which lies behind the wares, and supply a valuable corrective should we be tempted to a too close adherence in our research to the mundane and acquisitive business of pattern numbers, dating and attribution.

However, to return to such mundane business, two more items in the Shrewsbury-Maw collection deserve note. The first is a large printed catalogue (Figure 14), similar to the Minton ones discussed earlier. The second is a form of pattern book which has been compiled by cutting up the printed catalogue and sticking the appropriate coloured pictures in pattern sequence with a note describing the finish to be applied. Where no coloured print was available, the title of the tile was entered against the appropriate number. The patterns start at 2001 on page one and proceed to 2746 on page thirty. Additionally, between pages sixty-four and seventy-eight some mosaic patterns in the numerical range of pattern numbers 1051-1348 are depicted, and in other parts of the book fragments of other pattern sequences are given. For the collector's purpose it is the patterns in the first range, 2001-2746, which are of interest. Unlike the Minton patterns, each tile in a series was assigned a separate pattern number, thus a full series occupied twelve places in the book. This is very helpful as it enables all the subjects in a series to be identified, and all have been listed in the appropriate following sections. The predominance of the work of Walter Crane (see pp.90 and 168) in the period c.1878 is important. Very little can be deduced as to the date of these patterns, except to note that 'Nox' (see Colour Plate VI) and similar Crane designs were exhibited in Paris in 1875. As these are in the pattern range 2176-9, and the earliest pictorial pattern is 2134, we can deduce that these patterns were not in production much before 1875 — if at all (see also p.150). The last series of pictorial patterns is numbered 2664, but there is no indication of the date, though on stylistic grounds one would put it well into the 1880s.

The Ironbridge Gorge Museum Trust material relating to Maw is currently in two locations. The Library is housed at the central premises in Ironbridge. Here are to be found further examples of catalogues including a splendid bound volume of *Tiling* by Maw & Co. with C.H. Temple's name on the cover and a further note that this is the "colonial edition". Illustrated in full colour are decorative wall and panel schemes designed by Lewis F. Day (£20 for a hand painted panel 8ft. by 4ft.) and a simple floral wall design with a lion frieze designed by Walter Crane. Another bound catalogue with prices for 1900 contains several pages tipped in, culled from the catalogues of other manufacturers such as

Figure 14. Page from Maw & Co.'s printed catalogue. Showing designs from series such as 'The Seven Ages of Man', 'Signs of the Zodiac', 'Biblical Scenes' and 'Aesop's Fables'. All are referred to in the appropriate sections in Chapter Six. c.1885. Courtesy Royal Doulton Tableware Ltd.

Carter & Co. Indeed the collection contains complete catalogues from Robert Minton Taylor (encaustic designs), Carter & Co. of Poole, a most helpful Craven Dunnill catalogue dated 1879, the Ruabon Terra-Cotta catalogue, Gibbons, Hinton & Co. of Brierley Hill and the Wedgwood encaustic and pavement tile catalogue. This is only an indication of the material available; there are various other Maw printed catalogues depicting "Tile Pavements" etc., several large volumes contain "Examples of Ancient Pavements, Tiles and Mosaic" with drawings of such, and the Library also houses an interesting collection of source books from which tile designs — mainly encaustic — were copied, and a good collection of loose drawing and design material. Taken together with the two Shrewsbury deposits, this is a most valuable group of documentary and source material for the Maw and Craven Dunnill concerns.

At the Maw factory site under two miles away (Figure 13) some fascinating developments are in the offing. The Trust is renovating the factory building, part of which, it is hoped, to open to the public in the summer of 1980. Here will be displayed a fine collection of Maw and Craven Dunnill tiles, panels and encaustic, mosaic and architectural ceramics. A great deal of work is currently in progress on the cataloguing of literally thousands of moulds and other material found on the site, and a most fascinating development is the scheme to make this a working Museum, where tiles and art pottery will be made to the original moulds, designs and glaze colours for sale to the public, and where restoration and conservation work on existing tiled buildings or decorative schemes can be carried out. The well publicised removal and current restoration of the large tile panels from the Charing Cross Hospital is one example of the type of work which Tony Herbert and Tim Evitt and their staff are hoping to undertake in the future. One can readily forsee the importance the Ironbridge Gorge Museum Trust's tile project will have for the future study of the subject, both in the documentary sense and in the development of the tile gallery which should constitute a unique reference collection of the products of this huge concern.

The four sets of documentary material that have just been described are of major importance, and the scope of the records associated with these four firms goes well beyond the narrow confines of their tile production, indeed three of the quartet are far better known for their pottery and porcelain products than for their tiles.

Another enterprise which produced both art pottery and tiles was Pilkingtons Tile and Pottery Co. Ltd. of Clifton Junction near Manchester, perhaps best known as the makers of 'Royal Lancastrian' pottery. Tiles were first made by Pilkingtons in 1893 from local clay, but as production expanded the dust-pressed method was used. The firm was guided in its early years by one of the truly great potters of the period, William Burton, formerly of Wedgwood. He assembled around him a team of fine artists and craftsmen and was able to commission work from some of the leading designers of the day such as Walter Crane, Frederick Shields, Lewis F. Day and C.F.A. Voysey. Tiles from their designs were shown at the Paris Exhibitions of 1900 and 1908, and in 1901 at the Glasgow Exhibition. A catalogue of the latter is in the City of Stoke-on-Trent Library, Hanley,[14] and from it one can glean much information on Pilkingtons' products.

Figure 15. Front view and interior of Pilkingtons' stand at the Franco-British Exhibition 1908. Taken from the Illustrated Review *of the exhibition, p.211.*

Important panels 30ins. by 12ins., designed by Walter Crane, depicting 'Sight' and 'Taste' from a set of 'Senses' are illustrated. So too are some remarkable panels 3ft. 6ins. by 18ins. painted on 6-inch tiles of 'The Carnation', 'The Lily', 'The Iris' and 'The Rose' designed in his characteristically free and attractive style by Alphonse Mucha. A number of rather unusual 6-inch and 12-inch by 6-inch tiles in low relief, designed and modelled by J.R. Cooper, show the 'Queen of the Tourney' and 'Knights and Heralds' (four designs). The catalogue also illustrates fourteen different designs mainly of art nouveau floral motifs by Lewis F. Day (see p.88) all finished in attractive coloured glazes. 'Celtic Scroll' and 'Peacock Feather' are two of John Chambers works illustrated, and C.F.A. Voysey's 'Tulip Tree', 'Fish and Leaf', 'Bird and Lemon Tree' and 'Vine and Bird' are also shown.[15] The six designs from 'Flora's Train' by Walter Crane (see p.90) are also included.

This then is an important catalogue enabling a start to be made on the correct attribution of these most attractive tiles to their designers. One can safely predict that these pieces will be much more sought after in the future than they have been.

The City of Stoke-on-Trent Reference Library is also the location of a fine colour printed catalogue issued by T. & R. Boote Ltd. The catalogue is printed in French and Italian as well as English and, though many good single tiles are shown, the eye is really caught by the large architectural designs for the dairy, the fish shop and the butcher. The Boote firm was a very large concern and carried out many important contracts which are listed in the catalogue, amongst which are the Blackwall Tunnel, St. Stephen's House, Westminster, and the Government Offices, Rangoon. A similar Boote catalogue dated 1903 contains a preponderance of examples of floor tiling as does an 1893 Boote catalogue of *Encaustic, Mosaic and Ornamental Tile Pavements* and these are less helpful to the collector.

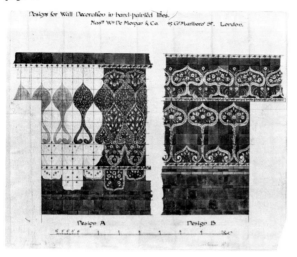

Figure 16. Two 'Persian' coloured designs for "Wall Decoration in hand-painted tiles by Messrs. Wm. de Morgan & Co. 45 Gt. Marlboro' St." c.1890. Courtesy Victoria and Albert Museum.

The last firm we wish to single out is Minton Hollins & Co. This was created in 1868 after the break-up of the original firm of that title (see p.21). The curious fact is that, although the Minton Hollins Company became probably the largest tile producing firm in the country, their output of decorative and pictorial tiles was overshadowed by that of Colin Minton Campbell's Minton China Works. A copy of the Minton Hollins catalogue in the City of Stoke-on-Trent Library bears this out. The catalogue shows a firm producing several hundred designs of 'art tiles' with printed, painted and glaze effects, but they lack the individuality of the work of Mintons and Wedgwood. The pictorial series which have come to light or appear in the catalogue are noted in the appropriate sections, but they are relatively few in number and unfortunately no printed check list of the titles in each series appears in any of the catalogues we have seen. The firm does not seem to have attempted to compete by the large-scale employment of outside designers other than of Moyr Smith. Probably the sales of floor tiling and of patterned and floral pieces made it unnecessary for them to enter seriously into the pictorial series market. Because of this apparent paucity of pictorial and figure designs we have tried to illustrate a correspondingly larger number of Minton Hollins tiles in other categories, some of which are taken from the tile catalogue in our own collection. Of all the firms studied this, it is felt, would most repay further study, for there is surely a good deal of documentary material as yet untapped.

Both at Stoke and in the Victoria and Albert Museum, catalogues and other material exists which the serious student would want to consult. The full list would be too tedious to print here. The material in the Victoria and Albert Museum is fully catalogued in a multi-volume work which is an invaluable source of reference[16], and a careful search before visiting the library for material relevant to a particular line of enquiry would save many hours of frustration. Printed catalogues from Maw, Mintons, Minton Hollins & Co, and material relevant to William de Morgan (Figure 16), the Campbell Brick and Tile Company, Burmantofts and many other aspects of the subject are contained in the National Art Library collection.

At Stoke, in addition to the sources already mentioned in this chapter there are catalogues and other material relating to: Minton Hollins & Co. for encaustic tiles; parquetrie by the Tamworth Encaustic Tile Co.; Peakes, terracotta and paving tiles; Wengers Ltd., for colour materials; the Ruabon Terra-cotta Brick and Tile Works; terracotta "designs for Tile Pavements Plain and Encaustic" manufactured by William Whetstone, Coalville; mosaic floors and hearths of the Crystal Porcelain Tile Works, Cobridge; and J.G. & J.F. Low of Boston, U.S.A. All these items and many others are fully catalogued in the excellent Reference Library at Hanley. At the nearby City Museum two catalogues from Sherwin & Cotton are located as well as a single sheet of coloured designs from Stubbs & Hodgart of Longton (see Figures 64 and 65).

In this lengthy review of the type of material available to anyone who is interested in pursuing research, only the surface has been touched. There is plenty of scope both for finding out more from the sources already noted, and for the discovery of new evidence. The starting points have been indicated, these together with the fine tile collections at the Gladstone Pottery Museum at Longton and the important material at the Ironbridge Gorge Trust's Museum, should enable collectors and students to enhance their understanding and appreciation of the tiles in their own collections.

Chapter Three Footnotes

1   Minton MSS, Nos. 1609-1661.
2   Minton MSS, Nos. 2337-2345A and 1836, 1824 and 1842.
3   Minton MSS, No. 1842.
4   Minton MSS, Nos. 1366-1375.
5   Ref. No. LM 155. 4246 MIN.
6   Minton MSS, No 1312.
7   Minton MSS, Nos. 1642/3/4/5.
8   Minton MSS, No. 662.
9   Minton MSS, No. 1328.
10 Catalogue reference 5229-5239.
11 Catalogue reference 4119.
12 Catalogue reference 4118.
13 Catalogue reference 4120.
14 Reference LM, 155. 4272.
15 G.A. Godden illustrates the 'Peacock Feather', 'Bird and Vine' and 'Bird and Cherry Tree' in *British Pottery, An Illustrated Guide*, p.363.
16 *The Victoria and Albert Museum: National Art Library Catalogue*, G.K. Hall, 1972.

Chapter Four

Technical Definitions

Throughout this book a number of terms are used which may require some preliminary definition. In this section simple definitions are given for processes and decorative techniques. References are given for those who would wish to pursue a particular matter further.

Manufacture:

Dust clay. The clay used to make tiles by pressing in the method first patented by Richard Prosser in 1840 had to be ground, sieved and dried. Before pressing it was slightly dampened to ensure adequate cohesion.[1]

Encaustic tile. A term used to describe floor tiles, usually ¾-1in. thick, on which the pattern is formed by inlaid blocks or strips of clay of different colours. The encaustic pattern is made in slip clay with plastic bodied tiles, and of dust clay after the 1863 Boulton and Worthington patent for dust pressing encaustic tiles.[2]

Faience. A term used rather loosely both in the nineteenth century and subsequently. Used here to mean architectural decorative ceramics.[3]

Geometric tiles. Basically floor tiles of many shapes and sizes which when fitted together formed an attractive pattern. Each geometric tile was of one colour only.

Mosaic tiles. A mosaic pattern was formed of small pieces of differently coloured tile pasted face downwards on a drawn pattern paper. The whole was cemented and when placed in position the covering paper was removed. This was a laborious business and Maws developed a dust-pressed tile which simulated mosaic late in the nineteenth century.[4]

Plaque. Used here to describe single tiles of large size, that is more than 8ins. square. Many plaques were made in sizes 12ins. by 6ins. or 12ins. by 8ins.

Plastic clay. This was the normal type of clay used in the manufacture of pottery and porcelain. It is malleable and ductile and can be 'thrown' on a wheel. All tiles were formed from plastic clay before the dust pressing process was invented, and subsequently many encaustic tiles and plaques were formed of plastic clay. Most of Copeland's 6-inch decorative tiles were of plastic clay.

Slip. Clay in a liquid state is termed slip. Frequently used to give a white or cream coating to the surface of a tile prior to printing or painting. A stiff slip was used for the inlay of encaustic tiles and for tube lining.

Terracotta. Architectural ornament sometimes of sculptural form, it is unglazed and is of a red or reddish brown colour. Low fired.

Tesselated pavement or tesserae. Terms much used by tile makers in their advertisements. They mean little more than a patterned floor scheme usually geometric or more accurately mosaic in nature.[5]

Tile press. A machine first patented by Richard Prosser for forming tiles by the compression of dust. Furnival describes the working of a Boulton press as follows:

"The operation of these presses may be described as follows:- The stop of the bottom die or plate having been set to the proper depth for yielding a tile of the desired thickness ... and the top die or plunger having been raised to full height ... the presser wipes the die clean with a greasy rag. Then from a heap of prepared damp clay-dust placed on the press bench, the presser pushes or scoops laterally into the mould sufficient clay-dust to fill it, and strikes the surface level with a straight-edge. The top die is then lowered, by a hand-movement of the screw forcing it down into the mould, compressing the dust-clay slowly, so as to allow time for the contained air to escape from the dust during this first pressing. The top plunger die is then rapidly raised again a short distance, and immediately very rapidly and powerfully lowered, so as to impart greater pressure on the contents of the mould, and so form a firm, compact tile.

"The top plunger is then quickly raised to full height, or at least several inches clear of the mould orifice, and the tile forced up and out by foot-gear acting under the bottom plate or die. The tile is now sufficiently hard to bear removing by hand, ready for fettling and placing previous to burning ...

"The expedition with which these powerful screw-presses are operated can be imagined from the fact that in some instances 6-inch by 6-inch tiles are pressed at the rate of eighteen hundred a day from one machine."[6] (Figure 17.)

Decoration:
Barbotine. The term used when the design or picture is painted on the tile in coloured slip. Such tiles are not encountered very often, but are easily recognisable. See Colour Plate X for an example.

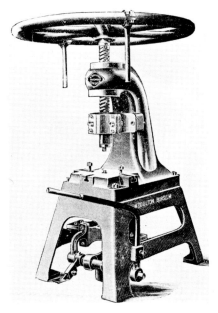

Figure 17. Dust-tile press of the horse-head type. Made by W. Boulton Ltd., Burslem. Taken from Furnival, p.454 (see bibliography.)

Biscuit painting. Some tiles were painted in colours under the glaze. This is particularly the case with tiles and panels which were to go outdoors or were likely to have to endure heavy wear which would have spoiled on-glaze enamel decoration. Underglaze prints were quite frequently supported by additional biscuit painting in colours. See Plate 9(50) and Plate 62(350) for examples.

Embossed pattern. A pattern moulded in relief on the surface of the tile. See Plate 48(273 and 274) for examples.

Enamel painting. The term is used to indicate hand painting in colours done over the glaze and then fired at a relatively low temperature c.800°C. See Plate 18(99 and 100) for examples.[8] Such painting was often done in addition to transfer printed outlines which might be either under or over the glaze.

Glaze. The impervious glass-like coating which covers the biscuit surface of the tile. Much use was made of coloured glaze effects which might be either opaque or, towards the end of the century, translucent. It is the latter which is intended when the phrase "decorated in coloured glazes" is used hereafter. (Figure 18.)

Incised decoration. Tiles are occasionally decorated by incisions being made in the plastic clay. When such incisions remove a clay slip of one colour to reveal a body of another colour beneath this is termed *sgraffito*. Hannah Barlow, however, in her work — see Plate 23(128 and 129) — rubbed coloured stain into the incisions which formed the design. The body of her tiles was of uniform colour.

Majolica. Another somewhat indeterminate historical term originally applied to tin-glaze wares thought to come from Majorca. Used in the nineteenth century to indicate a coloured glaze ware.[9] Many of the opaque coloured glazes were developed by Leon Arnoux at Mintons after 1850. These and the later translucent glazes were applied to moulded and embossed tiles or tile panels and decorative embellishments.[10]

Figure 18. Tile (glaze) dippers at work. Taken from Furnival, p.716 (see bibliography).

Pâte-sur-Pâte. A rare form of tile decoration primarily developed by Marc Louis Solon at Mintons for decorating porcelain wares.[11] A picture was built up in relief on a dark ground by repeated applications of a white slip. In appearance it is not unlike Wedgwood's jasper ware.[12]

Sgraffito, see also incised decoration. Fine examples of this technique are two large tiles signed by M.L. Solon depicting *putti* practising the potter's art, as seen in Barnard, Plate 10. Sgraffito tiles are very rare but some are said to have been made at Maws.[13]

Slip painting. See barbotine. But note that an 'engobe' of slip is the coating, usually white or cream, often given to the surface of the biscuit tile before receiving a decoration under or over the glaze.

Transfer printing processes. The basis of all transfer printing on tiles is the transfer of a design from a prepared metal plate by means of an inked tissue paper to the face of the biscuit ware. Once transferred it is fixed by firing in the 'hardening on' kiln and subsequently glazed and fired again. There are three basic ways in which the metal plate — usually copper — could be prepared.

a. Engraving. This process whereby the pattern is scored out of the surface of the copper plate by the use of a sharp tool in a series of lines or dots (stipples) which together form the required picture. An engraved, heated, copper plate is inked, the ink fills the shallow depressions which form the pattern, the surplus is cleaned off and special transfer paper is placed on the inked plate which is then passed through rollers and thus the pattern is 'transferred' to the paper. This is well known and was the method by which the Staffordshire potters printed millions of wares in underglaze blue in the first half of the nineteenth century.[14] Many tiles were decorated with single colour underglaze prints derived in this fashion from an engraved copper plate. See Plate 16(90) for an example.

b. Etching. This method gave a much finer, softer and more detailed result than could be obtained from an engraved copper plate. In etching the copper plate was covered with a thin film of an acid-resistant wax. The etcher then drew the picture in fine lines on the wax taking care that the copper was exposed by the etching tool. When completed the etched plate was immersed in a bath of acid. The acid attacked the exposed part of the copper plate ('biting in') and thus were formed the shallow depressions suitable to receive the printing ink as described above. See Plate 19(105), Plate 44(249) and Plate 55(311) for examples of etched designs.

From time to time etched copper plates might be touched up by an engraver. Conversely some engraved copper plates were given a final touch of depth or delicacy by the etching process.

Copper plates for tiles produced by both etching and engraving processes are still retained in the room of the head engraver at Mintons (Royal Doulton Tableware Ltd.).

Both engraving and etching were satisfactory for only single colour printing — though some tablewares had been produced at Davenports by a multi-colour process in the 1830s — and both under and overglaze painting had been used on tiles to support the printed outline and this could be multi-coloured.

c. Block printing. Printing in more than one colour was practised at Mintons especially as a result of the Collins & Reynolds patent of 1848 (see p.20). Although Furnival gives a brief description[15] of a multi-colour printing process very similar to block printing, this development has never been fully described previously. Jewitt was aware of the importance of this development of the Collins & Reynolds patent for the printing of decorative tiles for he notes:

"The process was applied to the decoration of earthenware and china generally, both useful and ornamental; but has proved to be more successful with flat surfaces. It was at an early period applied to ornamenting glazed tiles, and quickly supplanted the old and more expensive method of ground laying ... there is now a very extensive trade done in these tiles, which are very beautiful and every variety of design ... the combinations of colours and the arrangement of the patterns give them a brilliancy all their own" [16]

It is because of the extensive use of the block printing process on Minton tiles including many of the series, for example Plates 27 and 28 (155-158), that the following description of the process is quoted in full just as it occurs on a document in the Minton archives.[17] It is contained in a memorandum prepared at the works by J. Steel in 1953 in connection with the Burslem College of Art centenary Exhibition.

"Block printing New Press in Minton records can rightly be called the forerunner of lithography on pottery, in that a finished print would show from two to four colours when laid down on a piece of ware.

"In the production of patterns the outline of a design was marked out very lightly on a piece of zinc and a print taken off the zinc. This print was then laid down on a thicker piece of zinc and all the metal outside the limits of the design routed away to the required depth leaving the design in relief. In the case of three colour designs the process would have to be repeated three times, care being taken that each part of the design would fit in with the whole pattern.

"One of the zinc plates with part of the pattern — say the leaves — would be fastened down to a flat surface by means of pegs, and the printer would go over it with a rubber roller covered with colour picked up from a stone at the side of the press. At the head of the press was a movable frame at right angles to the engraved zinc plate and on this were very sharp pins sticking out horizontally to which a sheet of printers' tissue paper was attached. After fixing the paper the frame was dropped to lie flat on the colour-covered zinc plate and the printer then turned a handle bringing down onto the tissue paper a heavy metal slab which caused the paper to pick up the colour, after which the frame was raised, the paper removed and replaced by other sheets according to the number of prints that were required, each print being hung over a line.

"When enough prints had been taken, the zinc plate with the pattern in relief was replaced by another showing a different section of the pattern — say the ground-work — and the operations described above repeated.

"After the removal of the second zinc sheet the third one came into operation, and it must not be forgotten that these three zinc sheets were so pinned down on the bed of the press that each part would register correctly to make the full pattern, and to ensure that, the paper had to be pinned in exactly the same position each time the zinc plates were changed.

"After a complete print in all the colours had been obtained the paper would be laid down on a piece of biscuit earthenware and rubbed either with a hard brush or 'stumper', a piece of flannel tightly rolled and bound with a cord. The paper would then be peeled off or washed away with a damp sponge and the article was ready for firing.

"According to our records, Block, or New Press, printing first came into operation in 1849 as far as pottery is concerned, but the decoration was done on tiles even earlier."

Finally, it should be noted that block printing in monochrome was also extensively practised, for example the 'Aesop's Fable' series was so printed, Plate 32(181-186).

d. Lithography. A multi-colour printing process akin to block printing. Its possible use on tiles is rather obscure, but the following quotation from a letter in the Minton archives is helpful:

"We understand that M. Rataud came to Mintons in the early 1890s and developed a lithographic process. Meeting with success, he left Mintons and established himself as a producer of lithographic transfers about 1893. Mintons first used lithographs in 1894. This would have been on earthenware."[18]

The term has often been used incorrectly in the past to describe tiles which were block printed.

Tube lining. Some tiles have raised lines which have been 'piped' on, in the fashion of cake icing. The technique is not dissimilar to slip-trailing as practised by the country potter. The lines effectively separate the glazes of different colours which are subsequently applied and serve to outline the design. See Plate 70(398 and 401) for examples. Many *moulded* tiles which employ coloured glaze effects are incorrectly described as 'tube lined'.

Chapter Four Footnotes

1   Furnival, pp.451-453.
2   Op. cit., pp.444-465.
3   Op. cit., pp.749-779.
4   Op. cit., pp.804-805.
5   Op. cit., pp.456-457.
6   Op. cit., pp.453-463 and 559-563 contain full details, diagrams and photographs of various types of tile press.
7   Op. cit., pp.562-563.
8   Op. cit., pp.737-738.
9   Wakefield, pp.83-95.
10   Furnival, pp.188-190.
11   Godden, *Victorian Porcelain,* pp.170-188.
12   Furnival, pp.582-587.
13   Op. cit., pp.591-593.
14   Coysh, pp.7-8, for further technical details.
15   Furnival, p.600.
16   Jewitt, Vol.2, p.206.
17   Minton MSS, No. 1405.
18   Minton MSS, No.199.

Colour Plate IV. A selection of colour finishes on popular printed tile series from Mintons China Works all designed by Moyr Smith. Left-hand column: 'Shakespeare'. Centre column: Tennyson — 'Idylls of the King'. Right-hand column, first and second: Thomson's 'Seasons'; third: 'Anacreon'; fourth from 'Classical Figures with Musical Instruments'. Author's Collection.

Chapter Five
List of Principal Tile Makers and Their Marks

The following list has been compiled from information contained in G.A. Godden, *Encyclopaedia of British Pottery and Porcelain Marks,* 1964; Llewellynn Jewitt, *The Ceramic Art of Great Britian,* 2nd edn. 1883; Julian Barnard, *Victorian Ceramic Tiles,* 1972; W.J. Furnival, *Leadless Decorative Tiles, Faience and Mosaic,* 1904 and Rosamond Allwood, *Victorian Tiles,* 1978.

Additional information not found in these works has been included and, where relevant, a reference to the source is made.

Most of those tiles which are marked carry a clear imprint of the maker's name or initials and it has not been felt necessary to reproduce exact to-scale marks. If required such information is available in the books cited above.

Adams & Bromley, c.1895, tile decorators. No known wares or marks.

Adams & Cartlidge Ltd., Vine Street, Hanley, c.1900-1910. Successors to Sherwin & Cotton in the production of George Cartlidge's moulded portrait tiles, see Plate 48(275). Marks: 'Made by Adams & Cartlidge Ltd., Vine Street, Hanley.'

A.M. Ltd., England, c.1908 + . Not identified.

Architectural Pottery Co., Poole, Dorset, 1854-1895. Founded by T.S. Ball, John Ridgway (of the famous family of china manufacturers of Cauldon Place, Hanley), T.R. Sanders and F.G. Sanders. From 1861 the latter two ran the firm. The company produced a wide range of encaustic and wall tiles. William de Morgan decorated on their biscuit ware. In *Kelly's London Directory 1876,* they had a London agency at 11 Adam St., The Adelphi. For details of tile production see Jennifer Hawkins, *The Poole Potteries,* Victoria and Albert Museum, 1978. Bought out by Carter & Co. in 1895. Marks: 'A P Co' or the firm's name in full.

Art Tile Co., Dudley, c.1900. In *Kelly's Post Office Directory 1900.* No known wares or marks.

Art Tileries, Stourbridge, Worcestershire, c.1895. Tile decorators. No known wares or marks.

J.H. Barrett & Co., Boothen Works, Stoke-on-Trent, c.1896-1924 + . Successors to Adams & Cartlidge and Sherwin & Cotton in the production of Cartlidge's portrait tiles (see Chapter Six, Section 9). A marked example shows Conrad Dressler, inventor of the tunnel oven, which the firm was the first to install for tile firing c.1913. A good collection of portrait tiles and later wares is in the City of Stoke-on-Trent Museum. Marks: the firm's name. Also probably 'J H B' in monogram on printed tiles, see Plate 6(34) and Colour Plate X.

Barry & Co., Woodville Tile Works, Burton on Trent, Staffs., c.1880. "Encaustic, mosaic, geometrical and white glazed tiles for baths &c." only. Mark: none recorded.

Bates, Dewbury & Co., Mayer St., Hanley, c.1900. Recorded in *Kelly's Post Office Directory 1900*. No known wares or marks.

Birch Tile Co. Ltd., Clarence St., Hanley, c.1900. Recorded in *Kelly's Post Office Directory 1900*. No known wares or marks.

J.M. Blashfield, 1840-1875. Early maker of encaustic tiles in London. Was at Stamford in Lincs., 1858-1875, producing "terracotta as applied to every purpose, glazed or enamelled tiles ... enamelled architectural enrichments for internal use". An interesting figure (see Jewitt, Vol. I, pp.432-438) whose firm was responsible for the remarkable series of terracotta panels depicting pottery processes which are to be found on the Wedgwood Memorial Institute in Burslem. They look particularly fine after their recent cleaning. No known marks.

Thomas & Richard Boote Ltd., Burslem, established 1842, producing parian and ironstone china. Tile production, 1850-1963. They made many coloured glaze tiles of a good standard and colourful architectural schemes. Several catalogues survive (see p.43). Patented a process for dust-pressing encaustic tiles in 1863. Had a London showroom at Waltham Buildings. See Plate 9(52) and Plate 43(245) for examples. Marks: the firm's name or initials 'T.B. & S.' Also trade mark of a couchant greyhound between two laurel leaves beneath a crown.

T.G. & F. Booth, Church Bank Pottery, Tunstall, 1883-1891. They became Booths Ltd., general earthenware manufacturers. Said to have produced transfer printed art tiles c.1887. Mark: the initials 'T.G. & F.B.'

Broseley Tileries, Broseley, Salop, c.1860-c.1920. Probably only geometrical and encaustic tiles. Responsible for the flooring tiles at the Royal Academy and Lincoln's Inn. (See M. Messenger, *Shropshire Pottery and Porcelain*, Shrewsbury Museum, 1974). No marks recorded.

Robert Brown & Co., Paisley Earthenware Works, 1876-1933. This was an extension of the firm Ferguslie Fire-Clay Works established in 1839. "Plain and coloured pavement and walltiles &c". Mark: 'BROWN, PAISLEY' with a crown between.

Brown-Westhead, Moore & Co., Cauldon Place, Hanley, 1862-1904. They were extensive earthenware and china manufacturers. Very few tiles have so far been recorded. See Plate 22(123). Mark: the firm's name and 'Hanley, Ravenscroft Patent.'

Burmantofts Faience, Messrs. Wilcox & Co. Ltd., Leeds, 1882-1887. From 1887-1904 Holroyd & Armitage. Much architectural work in coloured glazes, for example panels on the side of the Midland Hotel, Manchester. Some single decorative tiles, see Plate 23(130 and 131). Also makers of art pottery. Terracotta production was continued after 1904 by the Leeds Fire-Clay Co. Ltd. Marks: 'BURMANTOFTS FAIENCE,' and incised monogram of 'BF', sometimes with the B reversed.

T.W. Camm, 1866-1870, later **Camm Bros.**, Smethwick, Staffs., c.1870-1880. Decorators only of painted tiles "allegorical and historical" in subject, of a high standard according to Jewitt (Vol. II, p.454). Marks: the firm's name, possibly also the initials 'C * B.'

Campbell Brick & Tile Company (later Campbell Tile Co.), 1875 to the present day, though now the firm is part of H. & R. Johnson-Richards Tiles Ltd. Founded by Colin Minton Campbell of Mintons China Works and Robert Minton Taylor, to produce encaustic and geometric floor tiles in opposition to Minton Hollins & Co. (see p.21). Soon branched out into many types of tiles though architectural decoration was their speciality. They had a London showroom at 206 Gt. Portland St. West as early as 1876 described in *Kelly's Directory* as a "depot for ornamental tiles, encaustic, majolica earthenware, plain, painted and enamelled". In 1896 the address is given as 340 Gray's Inn Road. Catalogues survive, see p.44 (See also *Pottery Gazette* for 1st October, 1896.) Marks: the firm's name, sometimes encircling the initialled points of the compass.

Carter & Co. Ltd., Poole, Dorset, established 1873. From 1921 traded as Carter, Stabler & Adams Ltd., Poole Pottery. Using local clay they specialised in glazed tile murals and architectural schemes, plain floor tiles and terracotta. Exported wares to Canada and elsewhere. (See also the entry for the Architectural Pottery Co. and Furnival, pp.196-200 for interesting details, also *Pottery Gazette* for 1st October, 1896.) Had a London showroom in 1890 at 43 Essex St., Strand. Mark: the firm's name.

Carter Johnson & Co., St. George's Tile Works, Worcester, c.1871-1895. Took over St. George's Patent Brick and Pottery Works from David Barker in 1871. Encaustic tiles noted. Mark: the firm's name.

Chamberlain & Co., Worcester, 1836-1840, succeeded by G. Barr and Fleming St. John, 1840-1848, in the same works. Encaustic tiles only. In 1844 together with Mintons bought Wright's patent (see p.20). Ceased production in 1848 and sold out to J.H. Maw in 1850. Marks: Probably 'Chamberlain's' with or without 'Worcester.'

Copeland & Garrett, 1833-1847, became **W.T. Copeland**, 1847-1867, **& Sons,** 1867-1970. Tiles made 1836-c.1900. Early encaustic tiles and then plastic clay 'art tiles' and printed pictorial sets in the 1870s and 1880s. Many examples are illustrated here. Pattern books still exist, for full details see pp.204-208. Marks: the name of the firm, usually just 'COPELAND(S)'.

W. & E. Corn or Corn Bros. Top Bridge Works, Longport (formerly one of the Davenport factories), 1891-1903, and Albert St., Tunstall (*Kelly's Post Office Directory 1900).* No known wares or marks.

C.O.V. (England), c.1890-1900. Not identified, though tiles so marked are not uncommon. Miscellaneous and floral patterns, no pictorial examples recorded. See Plate 9(51).

J.M. Craig, Kilmarnock, Scotland, c.1870-1900. No known wares or marks.

Craven Dunnill & Co. Ltd., Jackfield, Shropshire, 1872-1951 (formerly Hargreaves & Craven). Great rivals to Maws. They produced much encaustic work such as the Roman Catholic Cathedral at Shrewsbury. Designs by leading architects such as Waterhouse and Goldie commissioned. No distinctive style in decorative tiles, see Plate 9(53), Plate 18(102), Plate 19(108), and Plate 38(211) for examples. Some rare items of art pottery are known. At one stage the firm introduced a profit-sharing scheme with the workers (see Jewitt, Vol.I, pp.305-307 for details). Research is currently being undertaken on this large firm's history and output by the staff of the Ironbridge Gorge Museum Trust. Marks: the factory's name and sometimes address, and an elaborate moulded mark depicting a pottery entitled 'THE JACKFIELD' with 'CDJ' in a monogram.

Crystal Porcelain (Pottery Company Ltd.) Tile Works, Elder Road,

Cobridge, Staffs., c.1882-1890. A catalogue in Hanley Reference Library is headed: "Manufacturers of Encaustic and Plain Tiles and Mosaics for pavements and all kinds of Glazed, Enamelled and Majolica Tiles for Dado's, Walls and Hearths." The company would appear to have made a wide range, though apart from two central panels in a hearth scheme all the illustrated tiles are simple patterned ones. Marks: 'C P P Co', and a printed dove, or the firm's name.

Decorative Art Tile Co., Brian St., Hanley, Staffs., c.1885-1900 +. Decorators. See Plate 6(32) for an example which is quite common. No marks known.

Della Robbia Co. Ltd., Birkenhead, Cheshire, 1894-1901. Hand-made tiles and plaques, painted or glazed in colours, early art nouveau in style see Plate 38(215 and 216) and Plate 51(287) for examples and text p.157 for details. They made very striking art pottery. Examples are in the Williamson Art Gallery at Birkenhead. Mark: the firm's name.

William de Morgan, 1872-1907, various addresses (see p.69 for details). Initially decorated other potter's blanks, subsequently made his own tiles. Very distinctive and much sought after tiles and wares. Worked wholly in the arts and crafts tradition. Quit potting to become a successful novelist. There is an excellent biography by William Gaunt and M.D.E. Clayton-Stamm. Marks: many, some give guidance as to dating, all have name or the initials 'D.M.'

Walter Pen Dennis, Ruabon, Wales, 1891-1901. No known wares. Marks: all include the potter's name.

Doulton & Co. Ltd., Lambeth, London, 1870-c.1940, for tile production. One of the leading tile decorators. Made some plastic clay tiles which were decorated by Hannah Barlow, Plate 23(128 and 129). Many superb architectural decorations in the 1890s and early 1900s including the Winter Gardens, Blackpool, and Harrods' Meat Hall based on the designs of W.J. Neatby and others. Used Craven Dunnill blanks. (For full details of the firm's activities see, Desmond Eyles, *Royal Doulton,* and Paul Atterbury and Louise Irvine, *The Doulton Story,* 1979). Marks: on their own tiles and others, the name of the firm in one form or another.

William Eardley, 63 Lichfield St., Hanley, c.1887. Recorded as "tile manufacturer" in Frank Porter, *Postal Directory for the Potteries, 1887.* No known wares or marks.

J.C. Edwards, Ruabon, Wales, c.1870-1958. Produced a wide range of products including terracotta, mosaic, encaustic and "tiles for walls, floors, fireplaces and the like." By 1896 had nearly 1,000 employees and produced two million articles a month. (See Furnival p.203 for details.) Mark: the name of the firm or a monogram of initials 'JCE'. (See Colour Plate X.)

William England & Sons, c.1868 +. Recorded by J. Moyr Smith in *Ornamental Interiors,* 1887 as one of those tile firm's "whose productions in keramic art have become notable". Also recorded in *Kelly's London Directory 1876,* at 5 Bury Place, Bloomsbury (mosaic pavements). Marks: many tiles are marked with one word 'ENGLAND' and though this was common after 1891, it is possible that this firm also used this single word both prior and subsequent to this date as its mark. See Plate 23(132) for a possible example and Plate 29(167).

Samuel Fielding & Co., Railway Pottery (later Devon Pottery), Stoke, 1879-?. Made majolica, earthenwares and tiles. Single specimens are not uncommon. Plate 60(341) and possibly Plate 24(138). Marks: initials 'S.F. & Co.' printed and often a pattern number.

Flaxman Tile Works, ? Longton, c.1890-1930 ?. No documentary record has been found, but oral information has been supplied for the tentative dates. For examples of the wares see Plate 48(273 and 274). Mark: 'FLAXMAN', moulded.

T. Forrester & Sons, c.1895. Recorded by Barnard as decorators, no known mark or wares.

Gateshead Art Pottery, Co. Durham, c.1884-1900 +. Mentioned in a local Trade Directory for 1884 and in *Pottery Gazette* in 1899. No known wares or marks.

Gibbons, Hinton & Co., Brockmoor, Brierley Hill, Staffs. (Barnard gives Stourbridge), 1883-c.1950. Recorded in *Kelly's Directory 1900* and in *Pottery Gazette* 1899. A catalogue c.1920 is in the Library of the Ironbridge Gorge Museum Trust. No art tiles were noted. Marks: probably the firm's initials.

Gibbs & Canning, Glasscote, Nr. Tamworth, 1847-1900 +. Noted by Furnival p.203 as one of the "other large manufacturers". (Full details also are given in Jewitt Vol. I, p.424.) The principal product was high grade terracotta for architectural use, e.g. Holy Name Church and the Town Hall, Manchester, The Royal Albert Hall and the Natural History Museum, South Kensington. Tiles were recorded but the type is not specified. No known marks.

William Godwin (& Son), Lugwardine, Hereford, 1861- ? . Substantial maker of encaustic tiles of medieval design. (See Jewitt Vol.II, p.452.) They had a London agency in 1890. Mark: the firm's name and sometimes address. See Plate 64(365).

Godwin & Hewitt, 1889-1910 (later Godwin & Thynne), Victoria Tile Works, Hereford. Encaustic and decorative tiles. Mark: a shield device and the initials 'G. & H.H.', or the firm's name. See Plate 22(122). See also H.G. Thynne.

G.H. Grundy, Duffield Road, Derby, c.1895 +. Recorded in *Pottery Gazette,* 1st October, 1896, as the maker of Photo-Decorated Tiles (see p.103). Over fifty topographical subjects on 6-inch tiles are said to have been made and printed in colour. No recorded mark.

J. Hamblett, West Bromwich, Staffs., c.1890. No known wares or marks.

Hawes & Co., London, c.1876-c.1880 +. Barnard on p.161 notes the *Building News* Vol.47 criticising the firm for making imitation encaustic tiles by transfer printing under a thick glaze. *Kelly's London Directory 1876* gives the address as 1 Bloomsbury Court, Holborn. No other wares or marks known.

Heaton, Butler & Baines, King Street, Covent Garden, London, established 1862. Produced stained glass, metalwork and furniture, and some tile decoration (see p.143).

Hopkins, c.1900. No known wares or marks.

Jackson Bros., Castlefield, Hanley, c.1887. Recorded in F. Porter, *Postal Directory for the Potteries 1887.* No known wares or marks.

Jeffrey & Son, c.1900. No known wares or marks.

W.P. Jervis, Stoke-on-Trent, c.1880 +. Decorators only. No known wares or marks.

H. & R. Johnson Ltd., Crystal Tile Works, Cobridge, Staffs., 1901-the present, and the **Highgate Tile Works,** Tunstall, post 1916. Following many mergers and amalgamations now trades as **H. & R. Johnson-Richards Ltd.**, the largest contemporary tile producer. The firm incorporates many famous names: the Campbell Tile Co., T. & R. Boote, Maw & Co., Minton Hollins Ltd., Malkin Tiles, Sherwin & Cotton, etc. Responsible for the fine tile exhibits at the Gladstone Pottery Museum, Longton. Produced some interesting art nouveau pieces early this century. Marks: a shield with the word 'Crystal' and the initials 'H. & R.J. ENGLAND. TRADE MARK.'

Lee & Boulton, High Street, Tunstall, c.1896 + . An article in *Pottery Gazette*, 1st October, 1896, describes them as "manufacturers of every description of art tiles, porcelain floors, geometrical and mosaic wall and dado tiles". Their specialities were patent "Indestructible Floor Tiles" and patent "Aphthartic Glazed Tiles for walls, dadoes, grates, hearths etc." *Kelly's Directory 1900* describes them as 'Art Tile manufacturers'. Printed and coloured glaze (majolica) examples have been noted. Marks: almost certainly, 'L. & B. England'; 'L. & B. T(unstall) England'. 'L.T.' occurs on tiles identical to examples marked L. & B. England, and thus could well signify Lee, Tunstall.

Leeds Art Pottery & Tile Co., 1890-c.1900. Earthenwares and art pottery and certain decorative tiles, some marked with the firm's name (see Heather Lawrence, *Yorkshire Pots and Potteries*, pp.56, 241).

Malkin, Edge & Co., Newport Works, Burslem, 1866. Part of the earthenware firm of Edge, Malkin & Co. One of the few tile firms listed in *Kelly's Directory 1872*. In 1900 appears in Kelly's as 'Malkin Tile Works'. Jewitt, Vol.I, p.260-261 gives details of their use of the Boulton and Worthington screw press for encaustic tiles. They had a large production of the general run of patterned, printed and glaze effects as well as encaustic tiles. Pictorial series have been noted. See Plate 42(239 and 240) and Colour Plate X. They had a London showroom on Charing Cross Road. Marks: the name of the firm or initials with a greyhound device. Possibly also, 'M.T. Ltd.', though this could also apply to Marsden Tiles.

Mansfield Bros. Ltd., Art Pottery Works, Woodville and Church Gresley, c.1890-1957. Barnard suggests they were "probably only decorators". Mark: initials 'M.B.' No known wares.

Marsden Tile Co., Dale St., Burslem, c.1890-1918. Wares described in *Pottery Gazette*, 1st October, 1896, included printed floral and geometrical patterns, and a patented 'rainbow' glaze effect. They had a London showroom, 23 Farringdon Avenue E.C., and a growing export trade with "the Colonies and in South Africa". Marks: possibly 'M.T. Ltd.'

Martin Brothers, Fulham and Southall, London, 1873-1914. The four brothers were delightfully earnest and somewhat eccentric studio potters whose stoneware pots and bird models are much sought after. Some simply moulded salt glaze tiles were made, see Plate 2(12). Marks: many variations which include the names of the brothers, the initials, and often Southall.

Maw & Co., Worcester, 1850-1852, Benthall Works, Broseley, 1852-1883, and then after 1883 at Jackfield, Salop, until 1969. Very large and important firm manufacturing the full range from encaustic and architectural schemes from designs by Digby Wyatt and Owen Jones, to single, hand-decorated plaques, etc. Also art pottery after 1875. A good number of pictorial series, many designed by Walter Crane. Catalogues,

design books and accounts all survive. Full details are given in the text.
Major exhibitors overseas, e.g. Chicago World's Fair 1893, and prolific
exporters. Marks: several forms, but all contain the name of the firm.
Minton Hollins & Co., Shelton New Road, Stoke-on-Trent, 1868-1962.
In 1868 Michael Daintry Hollins took the floor (encaustic, etc.) tiling
business out of the long established Mintons China Works on a division
of the business. He subsequently built an entirely separate, new factory.
This rapidly expanded into all aspects of decorative and architectural
tiling. It was never really a serious competitor however to Mintons China
Works in printed and pictorial tiles, but nevertheless had an enormous
output of all other types. Catalogues and other documentary material
exists. An interesting description of the factory in 1879 is in James
Francis McCarthy, *Great Industries of Great Britain,* Vol.3, 1875-1880,
and quoted in Barnard pp.40-42.
 Marks: on encaustic tiles, 'Minton & Co.' On all decorative tiles,
'Minton Hollins & Co., Stoke-on-Trent', often with additional numbers
and letters (not pattern numbers).
Mintons China Works, Stoke-on-Trent, Staffs., 1830-1918. Founded in
1793 by Thomas Minton producing earthenware and porcelain. Tile
production began c.1830 under Herbert Minton. The firm was a pioneer
in many developments (see Chapter One). From 1845-1868 traded as
Minton & Hollins, and Minton & Co. In 1868 the partnership dissolved,
Colin Minton Campbell took the china works and Michael Daintry
Hollins the tile business. Soon after this the large-scale production of
decorative wall tiles began at Mintons China Works. Many printed series
were produced which are recorded here for the first time. Mintons China
Works dominated this area of production in the 1870s. Extensive
records, pattern books, original documents etc., survive at the factory,
now part of Royal Doulton Tablewares Ltd. (See text for full details, and
also entries for Minton Hollins, Campbell Brick & Tile Co., and Robert
Minton Taylor.)
 Marks: some confusion, indeed litigation over the use of the name
'Minton' on tiles (see Barnard pp.168-171 for the text of the 1875 legal
judgement). The basic marks as used on post-1868 decorated tiles are:
'Mintons China Works, Stoke-on-Trent'; and the globe mark with
'MINTON(S)' (according to Godden the 'S' was added after 1873)
through the equator. Pre-1868 tiles may be marked 'Minton & Co.,' or
'Minton & Co. Prossers Patent'. Some tiles are unmarked, even
examples from the well known printed sets.
Ollivant, c.1898. No known wares or marks.
Peakes, c.1890. A catalogue of terracotta and paving tile designs is in the
City of Stoke-on-Trent Library. No known marks.
Photo Decorated Tile Company, c.1899. Noted in Barnard p.162, almost
certainly G.H. Grundy of Derby, q.v.
Pilkingtons Tile & Pottery Co. Ltd., Clifton Junction, Manchester,
1893-present day. An important tile and art pottery firm. Many fine
coloured glaze effects in art nouveau style were produced under the
direction of the manager William Burton, after designs by Walter Crane,
Lewis F. Day, C.F.A. Voysey, A. Mucha and others. Examples are
illustrated and described in the relevant chapters. Catalogues and other
documentary materials survive. Marks: a raised 'P' on the back of the
tile.

Pinder Bourne & Co., Nile Street, Burslem, 1862-1882. Noted by Barnard p.162. Jewitt Vol.I, pp.158-159 does not record tile production. No known wares. Mark: the firm's initials.

Porcelain Tile Company, Cobridge/Hanley, Staffs., c.1890 + . Noted in *Pottery Gazette,* 1st October, 1896, as "manufacturers of encaustic and plain tiles, and mosaics for pavements, glazed, enamelled, and majolica tiles for dadoes, walls, hearths and floors." Their speciality was "vitreous floor tiles". They had a London agent. No known marks.

Prestage, c.1900. Noted in Barnard. No known wares or marks.

Pryke & Palmer, 47/48 Upper Thames Street, London, E.C., 1890s. Decorators only. No known wares or marks.

Richards Tiles, Pinnox Works, Tunstall, 1903-1968. (Successors to Corn Bros.). Glaze effects on wall tiles. Eventually merged into H. & R. Johnson Richards. No known marks.

Sherwin & Cotton, Vine Street, Hanley, 1877-1911 (Godden gives 1930). Extensive manufacturers of majolica coloured glaze tiles for all purposes. Also produced Cartlidge's portrait tiles, see Plate 48(276). See also Adams & Cartlidge and J.H. Barrett. Marks: the firm's name and a triangular device enclosing a Staffordshire knot; also 'SHERWIN'S PATENT LOCK' — a moulded back for more secure fitting and fixing.

Shrigley & Hunt, 28 John Street, Bedford Row, London and John O'Gaunts Gate, Lancaster, c.1880. A firm of interior designers only, decorating blank tiles. Mark: the firm's name. Their principal painter was W. Lambert.

T.A. Simpson & Co. Ltd., Cliff Bank Works (*Kelly's Directory 1887*) and Furlong Tile Works, Burslem, c.1885-1969. Made fairly wide range of ordinary printed and colour glaze tiles, see Plate 6(33). Examples not uncommon. Mark: the firm's name or initials, 'T.A.S. Ltd.', often accompanied by a lion and shield device.

W.B. Simpson & Sons Ltd., 100 St. Martin's Lane and 456 West Strand, London, c.1873-1910 + . Decorators only. Maw's account books record purchases of blanks from them by Simpsons, and the Order Office pattern and photograph book includes a 'Melross' series of patterns marked 'SIMPSONS ONLY'. See Plate 37(207 and 208) and Plate 44(247 and 248). *Kelly's London Directory 1876,* records them as "agents for Maw & Co. tile pavements". Also said to have used Mintons blanks. Marks: those of the original tile manufacturer, often with a shield device with the initials 'W.B.S. & S.'.

George Skey & Co., Wilnecote Works, Nr. Tamworth, c.1862-1900. According to Jewitt, Vol.I, pp.424-426 the firm made many types of terracotta, rustic wares, architectural enrichments, "paving tiles and facing bricks". Apparently no decorative art tiles. A catalogue in the City of Stoke-on-Trent Library illustrates "parquetrie designs". Mark: the firm's name.

E. Smith & Co., Coalville, Leicestershire, 1859-1900 + . Terracotta products were manufactured by George Smith c.1860, subsequently the range was widened (see Jewitt Vol.I, pp.422-423). They traded as the Midland Brick and Terra-cotta Company. Pictorial and printed tiles marked 'E. Smith' are known and not uncommon, they date from 1880 + . Series include Shakespeare, see Plate 30(171 and 172), nursery rhymes, as well as patterns, see Plate 67(378). Mark: the firm's name and sometimes the address.

Smith & Ford, Lincoln Pottery, Burslem, 1895-1898 (continued as Samuel Ford & Co. to 1939). No known wares. Mark: a horseshoe and ribbon device and initials 'S & F'.

W.T.H. Smith Ltd., Cable Pottery, Longport, Staffs., 1898-1905. Recorded in Godden, p.584. No wares known. Mark: the firm's name around a globe surmounted by a crown.

Steele & Wood, London Road, Stoke-on-Trent, 1874-1900 + . Recorded in Godden, p.595. According to *Kelly's Directory 1890,* they had premises in London. See Plate 45(258). Mark: the firm's name sometimes with an address, or an elaborate shield with both name and initials of the firm incorporated.

Stone & Co., Nonsuch Pottery, Ewell and Epsom Potteries, c.1866-1900 + . According to Jewitt they produced "paving and other tiles", almost certainly these would be encaustic and architectural, though he noted a view of Nonsuch Palace. Mark: 'Stone & Co.'

Stubbs & Hodgart, Longport, Staffs., c.1890-1900 + . A coloured advertisement sheet in the City Museum and Art Gallery, Stoke-on-Trent, depicts over thirty different designs in the art nouveau style. See Figures 64 and 65.

Sugden Bros., c.1898. Recorded in Barnard, p.164. No known wares or marks.

C.P. Sutcliffe & Co. Ltd., Higher Broughton, Manchester, 1885-1901. Recorded in Barnard, p.164, as having been bought by Maw in 1893. No known wares. Mark: a flowering plant in a pot bearing a large capital 'S' (see Godden, p.604).

George Swift Ltd., Binns Road, Liverpool, c.1900 + . Recorded in Furnival, p.203, as one of the "other large manufacturers" and on p.751 as an "eminent firm". No known wares or marks.

Tamar & Coalville, c.1899. Recorded in Barnard, p.164. No known wares or marks.

Robert Minton Taylor, Fenton Tile Works, 1869-1875. Taylor was a partner of Colin Minton Campbell and Michael Daintry Hollins 1863-1868. He left the business in 1868 and set up on his own the following year as R. Minton Taylor & Co. He was sued by Hollins of the newly-established Minton Hollins & Co., for his use of the word Minton. Taylor's business was bought by Colin Campbell in 1874 and advertisements were issued for the Minton Brick & Tile Co. Again Hollins sued over the use of the Minton name to which he claimed exclusive right for floor tiles. His claim was upheld and Taylor and Campbell then formed the Campbell Brick & Tile Co. in 1875. Taylor produced some interesting neo-delft 4-inch tiles, and some of the blanks for the murals in the Grill Room at the Victoria and Albert Museum. Marks: his name or initials and sometimes address. See Plate 64(360 and 362).

H.G. Thynne of Hereford, c.1900. A group of Thynne's tiles are in the City Museum, Stoke-on-Trent. Mainly moulded and lustre glazed pieces. See Plate 63(355). See also Godwin and Hewitt.

Charles Timmis & Co., Sheaf Works, Longton, Staffs. (in 1890 trading as **Timmis & Watkin** c.1890-1900 +). Recorded in Barnard, p.164, as decorators only, for a brief period. See Plate 9(50) for an example. No known marks.

J. & W. Wade Co., Burslem, c.1890-1900 + . Recorded in *Kelly's Post*

Office Directory 1900, as "art tile manufacturers" though Barnard lists them as decorators only. Later traded as **A.J. Wade.** No known marks.
Webb & Co., Leeds, c.1880. A tile with this mark is recorded by R.Allwood, *Victorian Tiles,* item 208.
Webb's Worcester Tileries, Rainbow Hill, Worcester, 1870-1905. According to Jewitt, Vol.I, p.258, the products were chiefly geometrical tiles, but decorative wall tiles are known, see Plate 9(48). They had a London address in 1890. Mark: the name of the firm.
Josiah Wedgwood & Sons Ltd., Etruria, Staffs. Tile production c.1870-1900+. Manufactured tiles of all descriptions, though mostly transfer printed and decorative wares. Many examples illustrated here. Catalogues, pattern books and other documents survive, full details are given in the text. Marks: the Portland vase and the firm's name. Not all wares are marked.
Ambrose Wood, Regent House, Hanley, c.1885. The tile Plate 4(20) was registered by Ambrose Wood in 1885. No other wares or marks known. Could be the same concern as Wood & Co.
Wood & Co., Boothen Road Works, Stoke-on-Trent, c.1887-? Recorded in F. Porter, *Postal Directory for the Potteries 1887,* as tile manufacturers. Barnard notes them as "decorators only". No known wares or marks.
George Wooliscroft & Sons Ltd., Patent Tile Works, Hanley, c.1880-present day. (The address is given as Etruscan St., Etruria, in F. Porter, *Postal Directory for the Potteries 1887,* and at Melville Street, Hanley, in *Kelly's Directory 1900.*) Also at 52 Finsbury Pavement, London E.C. Recorded in *Pottery Gazette,* 1st October, 1896, as making a speciality of "fresco" tiles, which "in plain colours of varied shade, are particularly suitable for the the walls of stables, as the face is not a glaze, but a body fired on with a semi-glazed appearance, which, however, reflects no glare to injure the eyes of horses"! They also produced lustre effects; 'Ironstone Adamant' tiles for floors; 'Anglo-Dutch' handmade and coloured in blue with "authentic scenes of places of interest"; and printed and art tiles. Mark: an elaborate impressed mark showing a waterwheel and the words, 'Etruria Hydraulic Tiles'.

NOTES

1. Many other firms are recorded in Directories and elsewhere who may have been decorative tile producers. For example, in the 1900 edition of *Kelly's Staffordshire Trades Directory* over 180 firms are listed as 'Brick and Tile Makers'. Some of these only manufactured common bricks or roofing tiles, but others such as the Porcelain Tile Company did make decorative and glazed wares. The same *Directory* lists separately 'Art Tile Manufacturers' (only two of these), 'Enamelled Tile Manufacturers' (three only) and 'Encaustic Tile Manufacturers' (fifteen of them). Clearly this is an incomplete list and it would be unwise to place too much reliance upon the accuracy of this source.

    Much more research is needed before the list of known tile makers can be regarded as complete. In the foregoing list every entry has been checked, and no firm has been included which seemed to have been concerned solely with terracotta manufacture and the making of common bricks and roofing tiles. A similar policy has been adopted concerning retailers. For example, *Kelly's 1876 London Directory* includes John Mortlock of Oxford Street, the well-known retailer in the list of 'Encaustic Tile Makers'. The same *Directory* lists the following who may have been tile makers, but were more likely to have been retailers. They have been omitted from the main list, and no wares or marks are known for any of them:

Ashton & Green, 14 and 15, Bury St.

Edward Barter, 19 Mear St., Long Acre.

Samuel Gibbs (possibly of Gibbs & Canning), 30 Keppel St., Russell Square.

Alfred H. Lavers.

John G. MacColla.

Albert John Tatham, 14 South Wharf, Paddington.

2. Tiles have been noted with the following initials: 'H.B. & Co.', 'K Y'; 'J.H.L'; 'L & D'; 'M.T.W & Co'; No known firm fits any of these though the last one could stand for Marsden Tile Works Co. or Malkin Tile Works, but this is only guesswork.

3. Many tiles are unmarked except for single letters either raised or impressed. Bearing in mind that the raised 'P' for Pilkingtons has often been regarded as having no significance in attribution, the following list of single letter marks is given, though we suspect that many of them have significance only for the internal organisation of the factory of origin. No attribution is attempted: C, D, H, Is, L, O, R, T, W, X.

4. Pattern numbers often occur on otherwise unmarked tiles and it might well be possible to assemble a range of patterns for a hitherto unknown factory, or one to which marked examples or a traceable registered design would provide the factory of origin.

5. It is worth reminding collectors that there were several firms which were decorators only, and thus one should not assume that every tile was decorated in the factory which bears its name. Examples of Mintons' printed series are known on unmarked blanks, on tiles marked 'Campbell Tile Company' (which is understandable) and rather strangely with a design definitely post-dating 1868 on the blanks of Minton Hollins & Co. Furthermore non-Minton designs have been recorded on their blanks, and enamel paintings by amateurs, often of a high level of accomplishment, are also encountered.

6. The use of the word 'ENGLAND' generally indicates a tile made after 1891 — to comply with the McKinley Tariff Act — and 'MADE IN ENGLAND' is a twentieth century mark.

7. The registration of designs, patterns or shapes at the Patent Office in London, took place throughout the Victorian period. The system was introduced in 1842 with the well-known diamond-shaped registration device. The placing of the year letter was altered after 1867 moving from the top space to the right corner. In 1883 the system was altered again and from 1st January, 1884 wares were accorded a simple numerical registration.

The registration number is sometimes printed on the back of the tile and thus gives considerable assistance in dating the introduction of the pattern in question, though of course the tile itself may have been made several years later. Furthermore, the name of the manufacturer or designer taking out the registration can be ascertained, an important matter on otherwise unmarked tiles. The design registration records may be consulted at the Public Record Office in Chancery Lane, London (given three days warning), or without prior notice at the Ashbridge

Repository. Alternatively the PRO will conduct a search for the requisite design number and supply a photocopy at the charge of £5.50 for each entry.

The full table of registration marks is shown below:

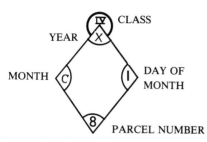

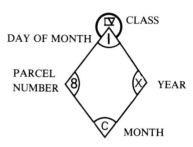

Pattern Registered January 1st, 1842   Pattern Registered January 1st, 1868

YEARS

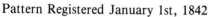

	1842-1867 *Year Letter at Top*				1868—1883 *Year Letter at Right*		
A	=	1845	N = 1864	A	=	1871	L = 1882
B	=	1858	O = 1862	C	=	1870	P = 1877
C	=	1844	P = 1851	D	=	1878	S = 1875
D	=	1852	Q = 1866	E	=	1881	U = 1874
E	=	1855	R = 1861	F	=	1873	V = 1878
F	=	1847	S = 1849	H	=	1869	W = (Mar. 1-6)
G	=	1863	T = 1867	I	=	1872	1878
H	=	1843	U = 1848	J	=	1880	X = 1868
I	=	1846	V = 1850	K	=	1883	Y = 1879
J	=	1854	W = 1865				
K	=	1857	X = 1842				
L	=	1856	Y = 1853				
M	=	1859	Z = 1860				

MONTHS (BOTH PERIODS)

A	=	December	G	=	February	M	=	June
B	=	October	H	=	April	R	=	August (&
C			I	=	July			September 1st-
or O	=	January	K	=	November (&			19th 1857)
D	=	September			December 1860)	W	=	March
E	=	May						

DESIGN REGISTRATION NUMBERS 1884 to 1909

	Rd.No.		Rd.No.		Rd.No.
1884	1	1894	224720	1904	420000
1885	19754	1895	246975	1905	447000
1886	40480	1896	268392	1906	471000
1887	64520	1897	291241	1907	494000
1888	90483	1898	311658	1908	519000
1889	116648	1899	331707	1909	550000
1890	141273	1900	351202		
1891	163767	1901	368154		
1892	185713	1902	385500*	*From 1st January, 1902,
1893	205240	1903	402500	approximate numbers only

Chapter Six

The Wares

Notes

Where no acknowledgement is made in the captions, the tiles illustrated in the following Plates are from the author's collection.

In order to avoid pointless repetition, the marks of the major firms, Mintons China Works, etc., are not given in full each time they occur in the captions and text. The full standard marks are given with brief details of each manufacturer in Chapter Five. However, any unusual variation is recorded.

The sequence for the Plate captions is always, top left, top right, middle left, middle right, bottom left, bottom right.

1. DUTCH AND ENGLISH DELFT

The Dutch and English delft tiles shown in Plate 1(1-6) were only indirectly the forerunners of the Victorian decorative tile. Dutch tiles were made from solid clay and not dust-pressed, and they were given an opaque tin glaze rather than a clear, liquid lead glaze. Despite these and other considerable technical differences, it is not entirely inappropriate to include a small selection of them in a book on Victorian tiles, for the collector may well be offered the Dutch pieces, and because of their attractiveness, find it difficult to resist adding them to their Victorian counterparts. They make a stimulating contrast.

The four Dutch examples range in date over two centuries. The cow Plate 1(1) is typical of an early type, other subjects noted are fish, and quite frequently, soldiers. These early tiles tend to be strong in the blue colour and noticeably thicker than their eighteenth century counterparts.[1] The hawk in Plate 1(2) is a most attractive piece of decoration, with a softer blue than in Plate 1(1). Examples may be seen in the Victoria and Albert Museum, and others are illustrated in colour, together with very attractive flower and butterfly studies.[2] The Renaissance vase, Plate 1(3), like the other pieces has corner motifs which form a completed pattern when four tiles are placed together.[3]

These first three types are quite rare and would be more expensive than most Victorian tiles. The tile in Plate 1(4) is of a much more common type, very stylised and mechanical in execution, but still a pleasant piece of painting. Interestingly, such tiles with 'ox head' corners were copied c.1873 by Robert Minton Taylor, often on small 4-inch tiles.

The two English delftware tiles represent two entirely different facets of production in mid-eighteenth century England. The Bristol example Plate 1(5) is hand painted with great skill and delicacy, the Sadler & Green tile, Plate 1(6), printed at great speed in considerable quantities as noted earlier on p.17. Full details of English delftware tiles are contained

1

2

3

4

5

6

in Anthony Ray's excellent work (see bibliography).

Once transfer printing of this competency could be accomplished, the delftware painter was on the road to redundancy, and the way was open for the mass production of decorative tiles in the Victorian age.

Plate 1.
(1) *Dutch delft. Polychrome painted tile in deep blue, orange and green; simple patterned corners, with the figure of a cow within a five-ring circular frame. 5ins. Attributed to Rotterdam, early 17th century.* **(2)** *Dutch delft. Polychrome painted tile in medium blue, orange, yellow and green; Chinese meander corners, with a fine figure of a hawk within a circular frame. 5ins. Attributed to Makkum, 1650-1660.* **(3)** *Dutch delft. Polychrome painted tile in deep blue, orange, yellow and green; debased Arabesque patterned corners with stylised Renaissance vase of flowers* (bloem potten) *in a square cross-corner frame. 5ins. Attributed to Gouda, 1600-1630.* **(4)** *Dutch delft. Pale blue and white painted tile, having 'ox-head' patterned corners, with a stylised scene of a house with a tower and three sailing ships. 5ins. Probably late 18th century.* **(5)** *English delft. Pale blue tin glaze painted in blue, yellow, orange and green with a basket of flowers within a* bianco sopra bianco *border. 5ins. Probably Bristol, c.1760.* Courtesy Mr. Hartley Asquith. **(6)** *English delft. Sadler & Green printed tile with the 'Blind Man's Buff' scene and a chinoiserie and rococo scroll emblematic border. 5ins. Liverpool, c.1758-1761 (See A. Ray in* EEC Transactions *1973, p.55, Plate 38.)* Courtesy Mr. Hartley Asquith.

2. FLORAL PATTERNS

The use of the flower as a decorative motif on tiles has a very long history, and in the heyday of Victorian tile production, floral motifs were probably the most popular and most frequently produced designs. It is difficult to decide whether this popularity reflected the Englishman's traditional love of the countryside, or whether there was an element of compensation, an attempt to soften the rigours of urban life by placing, sometimes even in the humblest hearths of working class terraced houses, an abundance of painted, printed or colour-glazed flowers, symbols of a fresher, cleaner life beyond the sprawling streets. Be that as it may, the catalogues of Mintons, Maw and the other major firms are crowded with floral designs from which the customer could chose. Colour Plates II and VIII exemplify this.

Moreover, the artistic climate in the 1870s was right for a new approach to floral decoration on pots. The essentially naturalistic — if romantic — rendering of the flower in the first two decades of the century given by Quaker Pegg at Derby and William Billingsley at his many ports of call, had been continued by the Steels at Rockingham and Mintons, and been adapted to the revived rococo forms of these and other factories during the 1840s and 1850s. And though Mintons, Copeland and the other great potteries continued to employ artists whose work, like that of C.F. Hurten for Copeland, was marvellously attractive and wonderfully skilled, yet the type of decoration seen for example on the Copeland pansy tile Plate 6(30) was essentially old-fashioned by 1870. Designs such as Plate 2(9 and 10) had never appeared upon pots. It was the achievement of the designers, men from outside the pottery industry, to make such designs acceptable not merely as tile decorations, but as motifs for the decoration of ceramics of every kind. As far as we know,

7

8

9

10

11

12

John Ruskin never designed a tile in his life, nor did any of the Pre-Raphaelite painters, but their influence operated directly upon those who worked with the tile makers, whether they were powerful and important figures such as William de Morgan, or less well known or even anonymous designers from the smaller factories.

The period of major tile production, c.1870-1910, coincided with a fascinating period in the development of all the arts, the significance and richness of which has only really been recognised in the past twenty years. The result of this recognition has been the production of many fine books of criticism and evaluation on the work of the leading artists and designers. Because of the splendid coverage given to the tile designs of William de Morgan in works by Pinkham, Barnard, and Gaunt and Clayton-Stamm (see bibliography for details) it has been decided to give only a brief treatment of his work in this book. Attention will be focused rather on those designers whose work is less well known or hitherto unrecorded. However, William de Morgan's tiles provide a standard of design which is of outstanding value as a comparative yardstick.

William de Morgan (1838-1917) was very much the artist potter, his concern — even with his pots — was primarily with surface decoration, much more than with form and shape. He had been destined for an academic career — his father was a Professor of Philosophy — but his inclination led him to attend art classes, and in 1859 he entered the Royal Academy Schools which greatly disappointed him and he only stayed for two years. Here his work moved away from the conventional canvas painting towards the applied and decorative arts. He experimented with designs for stained glass, and, almost inevitably in the close-knit world of the arts, he met William Morris, Burne Jones and other members and supporters of Morris's 'firm'. For Morris he did freelance work designing glass and tiles, even painting some furniture panels. Eventually, in 1869 at his parents' home at 40 Fitzroy Square he set up a kiln in order to "dabble in stained glass".

Shortly after his father's death in 1871, de Morgan set the house roof on fire and moved his somewhat dangerous activities to 30 Cheyne Row in Chelsea. Here he began to work with tiles, buying blanks from firms such as the Architectural Pottery Company of Poole, Dorset and Wedgwood, which he decorated in the showy, colourful 'Persian' colours which were to become his hallmark. As demand increased he

Plate 2.
(7) Moulded tile decorated in majolica glazes predominantly of green, ochre and turquoise, with a stylised sunflower motif. 8ins. Mark: 'Minton Hollins & Co Patent Tile Works etc.' c.1875. Courtesy City Museum and Art Gallery, Stoke-on-Trent. *(8) High relief moulded tile depicting sweet corn, leaves and flowers, decorated in greens and white majolica glazes upon a turquoise ground, with a pink ribbon motif. 8ins. Mark: 'MINTON'. c.1860-1870.* Courtesy City Museum and Art Gallery, Stoke-on-Trent. *(9) Stylised fruit and leaf design in 'Persian' colours of blue and green. 6ins. Mark: 'D.M. 98' (William de Morgan). 1898.* Courtesy City Museum and Art Gallery, Stoke-on-Trent. *(10) Flower and leaf design in blues and greens. 6ins. Mark: 'W'm de Morgan Sands End Pottery' in a circle around a stylised rose. c.1888-1897.* Courtesy City Museum and Art Gallery, Stoke-on-Trent. *(11) Simple floral motifs painted on a quartered tile in blue. The frame bears a label 'Tile designed and made by W'm Morris'. c.1865.* Courtesy City Museum and Art Gallery, Stoke-on-Trent. *(12) Relief moulded in quarters with a sunflower and leaves in shades of brown and grey on a white sand ground. 7ins. Mark: 'Southall' (the Martin brothers) c.1879.* Courtesy Sotheby's Belgravia.

moved to larger premises at 36 Cheyne Row, and took on workmen including the brothers Frederick and Charles Passenger who were to remain with the enterprise even after de Morgan had himself retired.

The Chelsea period which lasted until his move to Merton Abbey in 1882 saw the fulfilment of the scientific side of de Morgan's activities. He had already in the 1860s experimented with lustre decoration and the chemistry fascinated him. As his knowledge increased and his control improved over firing cycles and all the difficulties attendant upon lustre decoration, so did his wish to control all stages of the process of making and decorating tiles and pots. He was no longer satisfied with painting patterns on the blanks of other tile makers, or lustreing the earthenware manufactured in Staffordshire to shapes and designs not his own and which were formed of materials whose chemical and physical response to the kiln he could not always predict. These factors and the chance to move to premises adjacent to those of William Morris prompted the move, in 1882, to Merton Abbey, ten miles south of London. Here his instinct for design could be given full rein; he used a thrower to produce pots to shapes he had designed, usually based upon adaptations of Eastern vase and dish forms. Tile production declined somewhat in this period. The great tile *tour de force* of 1877, when he filled the gaps in Lord Leighton's famous Arabian Hall at his Kensington house with copies of the genuine 'Isnik' tiles, and the decoration of the tile panels for the Tsar Alexander III's yacht *Livadia,* were behind him. Major tile schemes were, however, to feature again when after the formation of a partnership with the architect Halsey Ricardo, a new factory for tile and pottery production was built at Sands End, Fulham, and opened in 1889.

The rest of the formal story is easily recounted. By 1892 de Morgan's health had deteriorated and he took to wintering in Italy and running the factory by correspondence. This may sound improbable but, with the experience of the Passenger brothers and Ricardo still on hand, the business remained commercially successful and new ventures such as 'double' and 'triple' lustreing were accomplished, and contracts such as those for tile panels for P. & O. liners were still won and completed.

By the late 1890s, however, business was declining, and despite a new partnership established with the Passengers in 1898 the course was now downhill. Some magnificent pots were still made and decorated, but the loss of the driving impetus of de Morgan, as well as changes in fashion, meant that these later years were not ones of high achievement built upon solid foundations, but of rather tired repetition and enfeebled creativity. In 1907 the factory finally closed, though the Passengers, with permission, still continued to decorate blanks with de Morgan designs for many years.

For the artist potter himself there was a renaissance. From boyhood he had had literary inclinations, and with the pottery defunct he turned his attention to writing novels. At the age of sixty-seven his first novel, *Joseph Vance,* was published, and by the time of his death in 1917 he had written seven in all.

Within the field of tile design and decoration, de Morgan really stands alone and apart. His principal design source, the Persian 'Isnik' tiles of the fifteenth and sixteenth centuries provided the impetus to his own flair for design, especially in flower and leaf motifs, expressed in fluent swirls

Figure 19. Solid clay tile painted underglaze with a large sunflower in brilliant blue, the foliage in shades of green. 6ins. Mark: 'W. de Morgan, Merton Abbey' (small mark). c.1885. Courtesy Manchester Polytechnic Collection.

Figure 20. Solid clay tile painted underglaze with an incomplete design of stylised flowers and fronds in blues and greens. 6ins. Mark: 'W. de Morgan & Co. Sands End Pottery.' c.1890. Courtesy Manchester Polytechnic Collection.

and exotic curves. His outlines were bold and the designs marvellously filled the surface available in rhythmic patterns which still have the power to excite us today. Allied to this design sense was his use of bold and vibrant colours; blues, turquoise, green and yellow impart an intensity which never lapses into the brash and gaudy. His method of tile decoration was unique, but much more 'production line' than one might imagine. His tiles all look individually hand painted, and in a sense they are, but only the basic design and its colour pattern was de Morgan's. The actual decoration was copied by his work people who painted the design on to a sheet of thin paper, tracing the outlines of a master drawing pasted on to a sheet of glass. Beside the painter was a coloured drawing or a completed tile to indicate the colour values. The painted paper was then placed onto a tile covered with a white porcelain slip. This was then brushed over with sodium silicate and powdered glaze was sprinkled on the adhesive surface. The tile was then fired and thus the colour was incorporated with the glaze. The paper was reduced to ash and dispersed by the draught of the kiln.[4]

It was not only in 'Persian' colours that de Morgan excelled. His lustreing was outstanding and his paper on the technique of lustre decoration which he delivered to the Royal Society of Arts, 31st May, 1892, is a classic statement on the history of lustre and of his own experiments in recreating these metallic decorations.[5]

The illustrations Plate 2 (9 and 10), Plate 3 (13-16) and Figures 19 and 20 give a reasonable indication of the range of designs in both Persian colours and lustre (13) of de Morgan's floral patterns on single or matching pairs of tiles. However, his range was very extensive with many multi-tile panels being designed as well as elaborate fireplace schemes (Figure 16). Nor must his animal and ship designs be forgotten, a few examples of which are included in the appropriate sections.

De Morgan was an outstanding designer and his work rightly commands considerable attention. The works by Gaunt and Clayton-Stamm, and Pinkham illustrate hundreds of his designs and his tiles and panels frequently feature, and are illustrated, in Sotheby's Belgravia sale catalogues. But as a glance at these and the price guide at the end of this book will indicate, a long purse is needed if one wishes to specialise in the tiles of William de Morgan. However, armed with knowledge, the occasional bargain may come your way when you recognise a de Morgan tile which has been overlooked by others. Those in our own collection have been acquired in this fashion.

William Morris, the most prominent figure in the Arts and Crafts movement, also designed some tiles. These, however, are very rare. The illustrated example Plate 2(11) shows the simplicity of his stylised treatment of motif, as do the surround tiles to the 'Beauty and the Beast' panels designed by Burne Jones, now at the William Morris Gallery, Walthamstow.[6]

The work of the Martin brothers of Southall is also much sought after. As studio potters, their pieces are individualistic — always an attraction to the collector — but they produced relatively few tiles and, again because their output has been quite fully treated in other books, just one example is illustrated here Plate 2(12).

The placing of floral patterns at the beginning of the illustrations is deliberate, for not only has it been possible to indicate the influence of the designers outside the tile industry upon tile design, but one can also see in this section a wide variety of treatments by different firms of a basic theme — the depiction of the flower.

Plate 2(7 and 8) are of coloured glaze tiles, the Minton Hollins example (7) being quite clearly influenced by de Morgan. The rather earlier Minton high relief group owes more to the fashionable opaque 'majolica' glazes which were such a feature of Minton earthenware production in the period 1850-1890. Both tiles are of very high quality.

Plate 4(18 and 19) are of tiles by Minton Hollins & Co. and both are in the William Morris and de Morgan 'Persian' style. Good examples of this kind were also produced by Maw, and Colour Plate III shows a fine range of what the catalogue calls "tiles richly glazed and decorated with Persian enamels and chiefly of Persian design", from Mintons China Works. A particularly unusual example involving direct imitation of a de Morgan design can be seen in Plate 3(17) a product of the Marsden Tile Co. in the 1890s.

A stylised treatment of one of the popular symbols of the Aesthetic Movement — the sunflower — can be seen in Plate 4(20), an unmarked

Plate 3.
(13) *Pair of tiles decorated in bright red lustre on a white slip ground with the B B B pattern (after the firm of Barnard, Bishop and Barnard who gave de Morgan the first major tile contract). A two tile repeat. 12ins. by 6ins. No mark, dust-pressed tiles, possibly by Wedgwood. c.1880.* **(14)** *Painted underglaze with a quartered design of two flowers in blue and foliage in green, the outline frame in blues. 6ins. Mark: 'Architectural Pottery Co., Poole Dorset'. c.1880.* **(15)** *Solid clay tile painted underglaze in blue, green and yellow with a quartered pattern 'Rose Trellis'. 6ins. Mark: 'W. de M. Merton Abbey' (large mark). 1882-1888.* Courtesy Manchester Polytechnic Collection. **(16)** *Solid clay tile painted in underglaze with two blue sunflowers, the foliage in green. 6ins. Mark: 'W. de Morgan Merton Abbey' (small mark). 1882-1888.* Courtesy Manchester Polytechnic Collection. **(17)** *Solid clay tile, roughly moulded, printed with a floral design in the style of William de Morgan. 6ins. Mark: 'Marsden Tiles, England. 13'. 1895-1900.* Courtesy City Museum and Art Gallery, Stoke-on-Trent.

13

14

15

16

17

18

19

20

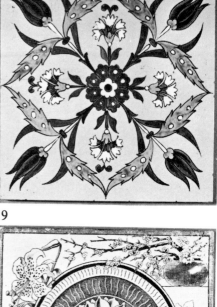

21

22

23

tile which has been traced to its origin, Ambrose Wood, Regent House, Hanley, through the design registration number printed on the back. Even more redolent of the Aesthetic Movement is the unmarked tile (21) which bearing the sunflower, the Japanese prunus, the lily and the daffodil, lacks only a peacock feather to complete the ensemble of aesthetic symbols. Though we may perhaps find the earnestness of the aesthetes amusing, and enjoy the debunking of Gilbert and Sullivan in *Patience (An Aesthetic Opera)*, yet there is much to admire in the skilful adaptations of the familiar motifs by designers influenced by the aesthetes, and in the novelty of many of their ceramic shapes and designs, following what seems to be endless waves of rococo and Gothic revivals in the early Victorian period. The collector who concentrated on tiles of the aesthetic period could assemble a splendid collection of typically attractive patterns, see Plate 53(299 and 300), Plate 59 (335), Plate 61(343), and Figures 21 and 22 for further examples.[7]

Plate 4(22 and 23) illustrates two further somewhat stylised treatments of floral motifs. The latter from the Campbell Brick and Tile Co. being

Figure 21. Sunflower and foliage design set in a circle surrounded by a crazy-paving pattern, printed underglaze in brown and hand painted underglaze in yellow and pink. 6ins. No mark. c.1880.

Figure 22. Printed underglaze in brown on a cream ground with a sunflower pattern. Quarter sunflowers at each corner indicate this is an element in a repeating pattern panel. 6ins. Mark: Moulded 'W' in a circle. c.1880.

Plate 4.
(18) *Leaf patterned 'Persian' style design in dark blue, turquoise, and green coloured glazes on a white slip ground. 8ins. Mark: 'Minton Hollins & Co. etc.' Design registration mark for 1871.* **(19)** *Symmetrical highly stylised floral design in turquoise blue, white, violet and green on a smoky grey ground. 8ins. Mark: 'Minton Hollins & Co. etc.' c.1875.* **(20)** *Stylised sunflower, daffodil and leaf pattern printed in brown and painted underglaze in yellow, black and green on a cream ground. 6ins. Mark: 'No 164' and 'Rd No. 22731', the pattern registered in 1885 by Ambrose Wood, Regent House, Hanley.* **(21)** *Aesthetic pattern of the sunflower, the lily, the daffodil and prunus spray, printed in brown on a cream ground. 6ins. No meaningful mark. c.1875-1880.* **(22)** *Moulded pattern of a star-shaped flower diagonally placed with leaf, stem and bud motifs. Coloured glaze decoration in blue, pink and orange on a grey ground. 6ins. Mark: 'Maw & Co. Benthall Works, Broseley. Salop.' c.1870.* **(23)** *Dado tile with running pattern of flowers and buds within a scroll border motif. Decorated in majolica glazes of white and shades of green upon a red background. 8ins. Mark, within a circle: 'The Campbell Brick and Tile Co. Stoke upon Trent'. c.1880.*

Figure 23. Dado tile with block printed design in greens, black and red with additional enamelling in green of an ivy leaf design. 6ins. Mark: 'Minton Hollins & Co. etc.' c.1885.

part of a border of freize with an identical running pattern repeated on each tile, as is also the case in Figure 23, whereas Plate 4(18) is clearly part of a panel or dado scheme with an incomplete floral motif at each edge. All the tiles Plate 5(24-29) are further examples of floral design of a semi-representational kind; (24), (26) and (29) are fairly conventional but (25) from Mintons China Works and (28) from Wedgwood both give the appearance of being somewhat influenced by the type of design illustrated by Christopher Dresser in his book *Principles of Decorative Design* first published in 1873. This is particularly true of the Wedgwood lotus which closely echoes Figure 2 in Dresser's book. With (27) we are again back with the sunflower and a tentative essay at Japonaiserie.

A different, less consciously 'artistic' treatment can be seen in the tiles Plate 6(30-35). Each design is of a recognisable flower or fruit. A wide range of makers or decorators is represented, Copeland (30), Minton Hollins (31), the Decorative Art Tile Co. (32), T.A. Simpson (33), J.H.B(arrett?) (34) and Mintons China Works (35). Certainly any collector who wishes to collect the tiles from as many factories as possible would find it well worthwhile to do so by concentrating on those tiles decorated with floral motifs — there is plenty of scope.

The illustrations in the text, Figure 24, 25 and 26, continue the same theme. Figure 24 from Mintons is a lovely study of primroses painted in coloured slip ('barbotine'), a process which is noted in connection with Plate 7(39). The Lee of Tunstall tile, Figure 25, and the anonymous example are both printed and painted.

Plate 5.
(24) *Block printed stylised floral pattern in black on a white slip ground. 8ins. Mark: 'Minton Hollins & Co. etc.' c.1875.* **(25)** *Underglaze blue block print on a white ground of a vase of lilies within a hexafoil. Dust pressed. 8ins. Mark: 'Mintons China Works etc.' c.1875.* **(26)** *Block printed underglaze in brown on a white ground with a stylised rose within circular and square frames. 6ins. No mark. c.1885.* **(27)** *Printed underglaze in greeny-grey on a white ground with a stylised pattern of sunflowers and honeysuckle. 6ins. No mark. c.1880.* **(28)** *Printed in shades of underglaze blue on a white ground with stylised lotus blossoms. 6ins. Mark: 'Josiah Wedgwood & Sons etc.' c.1880. Courtesy City Museum and Art Gallery, Stoke-on-Trent.* **(29)** *Printed underglaze in a bluey-grey with a stylised pattern of pine cones. 6ins. Mark: moulded 'I' and 'Registered Design No. 180681.' Late 1891.*

24

25

26

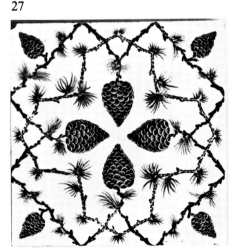

27

28

29

Figure 24. Barbotine painting of primroses and leaves in natural colours on a green background. 12ins. by 6ins. Mark: 'Mintons China Works etc.' c.1870-1875. Courtesy City Museum and Art Gallery, Stoke-on-Trent.

Figure 25. Underglaze brown print on a cream ground of hazel nuts, flowers and foliage set in a rococo scroll frame. Hand painted underglaze in shades of yellow, green and orange. 6ins. Mark: 'L.T. ENGLAND' (for Lee of Tunstall). c.1890-1895.

Figure 26. Underglaze transfer printed in black and hand painted underglaze with a design of violets and leaves within a narrow brown border. No mark. c.1885. Courtesy Rosamond Allwood.

Plate 6.

(30) Plastic clay tile printed in outline on a cream ground with a pansy, which is enamelled in bright and natural colours overglaze. 6ins. Mark: 'COPELAND' and '176 A78' impressed. c.1865. **(31)** Enamel overglaze hand painting in natural colours of a split fruit with seeds, flowers and foliage. 6ins. Mark: 'Minton Hollins & Co. etc.' c.1875. **(32)** Lily flower and foliage printed in outline on a cream ground and painted under the glaze in white, mustard and green. 6ins. Mark: 'Rd No. 67048'. This design was registered on 2nd February, 1887 by the Decorative Art Tile Company, Brian St., Hanley. Probably on a Maw's blank. **(33)** A circlet of daisy-like flowers and leaves, printed underglaze in white, green and yellow on a buff ground. 6ins. Mark: 'T.A.S. Rd No 75842'. This design was registered by T.A. Simpson on 27th June, 1887. **(34)** Tulips and foliage in 'S' scroll central cartouche, printed outline in brown and painted underglaze in red, black, yellow and green. 6ins. Mark: 'J H B (monogram) No C 107/AN'. Probably by J.H. Barrett. c.1895. **(35)** Fine underglaze colour (block) print in shades of green and tan on cream of chestnut leaves and conkers. 6ins. Mark: 'Mintons China Works etc.' This is given as pattern 1694 in the printed catalogue, i.e. introduced c.1879.

30

31

32

33

34

35

36

37

38

39

40

41

It should be noted that these individual studies may be part of sets. For example, the Minton Hollins pomegranate Plate 6(31) is part of a set which included enamelled fruit and flower studies of apples, pears and plums as well as other subjects. Wedgwood issued a set of twelve tiles with different studies of seaweed and sea shells, and the pansy Plate 6(30) is also one of a series of transferred and enamelled single flower studies produced by Copeland.

The group of tiles Plate 7(36-41) are examples of differing techniques of decorative design. (36) and (37) are both from Wedgwood and carry the additional mark 'PATENT IMPRESSED TILE'. The floral design stands quite proud from the surface of the tile, is thick, almost lumpy in appearance and the colours are opaque. In *Victorian Tiles,* Rosamond Allwood draws attention to an article[8] which mentions that "at the famous pottery in Etruria, Messrs. Wedgwood and Sons have been manufacturing ornamental tiles by a system of impressing slips of various colours upon a ground, the design standing up in strong relief". Clearly these tiles were made by this process, a kind of block barbotine painting!

Mention of barbotine painting is a reminder that this method of decoration, the painting of the tile with coloured slip, rather than coloured on-glaze enamels, was very popular for a short period and most factories experimented with it. Plate 7(39) and Figure 24 are examples of the technique. It is, however, time-consuming and much less efficient than colouring-in an already printed design, thus, it was not a process suited to mass production. Plate 7(40) illustrates an example of the mass production method whereby a printed outline could be attractively painted in on-glaze enamel colours by quite unskilled paintresses, but yet which could still be offered as "a hand painted art tile".

Plate 7(38) is an attractive example of a multi-colour block print (see p.50 for details) and Plate 7(41) is a moulded tile decorated with glazes of differing colours which are translucent. This form of decoration was fashionable from the 1880s onwards and all the patterns in the illustrations Plate 8(42 to 47) depict variations upon the basic theme of a tile moulded either in high or low relief which has the pattern highlighted and picked out either in a monochrome glaze (44) and (47) or in a variety of colours as in the other examples on that page. The clear colour glazing came to dominate tile decoration in the art nouveau period of the 1890s and 1900s, as can be seen from the illustrations Plates 11, 12, 13(60-76).

We briefly turn from decorative techniques to explore again the theme of the adaptation of flowers or floral groups to the requirements of a

Plate 7.
(36) *Dust pressed tile moulded in low relief with white daisies and green and brown leaves against a speckled green ground (see above for techniques). 6ins. Mark: 'Josiah Wedgwood & Sons, Etruria, PATENT IMPRESSED TILE', c.1885.* **(37)** *Moulded in low relief with delicate white blossom and green leaves on a pale green ground. 6ins. Mark: as (36). c.1885.* **(38)** *Multi-colour transfer print of daisies and buttercups in shades of green and mustard, on a mottled ground. 6ins. Mark: 'Mintons China Works etc.' c.1885.* **(39)** *Painted in coloured slip (barbotine) in a wide range of colours against a dark brown sponged mottled ground. 6ins. No mark. c.1885-1890.* **(40)** *Underglaze transfer printed in brown, hand coloured on-glaze with green leaves and pink flowers. 6ins. Mark: moulded 'D' within a circle, no attribution. c.1875-1880.* **(41)** *Moulded in high relief with a pattern of liles and foliage in green translucent glaze. Flowers in white on a brown glazed ground. 6ins. Mark: 'ENGLAND'. c.1895.*

42

43

44

45

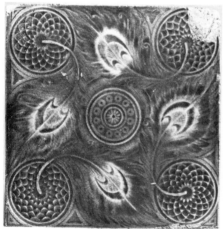

46

47

Figure 27. 'Wild Rose' from the series 'Spirit of the Flowers'. Block printed underglaze in blue. 6ins. Mark: 'Mintons China Works etc.' c.1875 (see text).

pattern designed for a 6-inch square. With the exception of Plate 9(49) and Figure 27, Plates 9 and 10(48 to 59) illustrate this theme. These particular pieces have been selected from potentially hundreds because they come from different factories or have characteristics of design which are very commonly met with. The additional figures in the text (Figures 28-33) were selected on similar criteria.

The Minton tiles Plate 9(49) and Figure 27 'Spirit of the Flowers' are from a series of twelve which seems to be comparatively rare. The subjects listed in the Minton catalogue as pattern No 1347 are:

waterlily
wild rose
poppy
lily of the valley
daisy
foxglove
violet
convolvulus
anemone
snowdrop
lily
primrose

The artist is unknown, but from the style an attribution to Moyr Smith is

Plate 8.
(42) *Moulded in high relief with a sunflower design set in a circular frame. Decorated in green, orange and turquoise translucent glazes. 6ins. No mark. c.1890.* **(43)** *Moulded in relief with a flower and foliage set in a circular double-banded scroll frame. Decorated in translucent glazes in shades of pink, brown, green and white. 6ins. No mark. c.1890.* **(44)** *Moulded in high relief with an open flower design. Glazed overall in a pale cream colour. 6ins. Mark: 'Minton Hollins & Co. etc.' c.1895-1900.* **(45)** *Moulded in high relief with a design of leaves and buds — part of a continuous design. Decorated in a bright blue translucent glaze against a pale green glaze background. 6ins. Mark: moulded 'O'. c.1880.* **(46)** *Moulded with a swirling motif of sunflowers and peacock feathers. Decorated with shades of green glazes. 6ins. No mark. c.1875-1880.* Courtesy City Museum and Art Gallery, Stoke-on-Trent. **(47)** *Lightly moulded with a clover or shamrock motif and decorated with a translucent green glaze. 6ins. No mark. c.1885.*

Figure 28. Underglaze transfer printed and hand painted in colours with a design of various flowers within a narrow floral border. 6ins. No mark. (Barnard, Plate 47, attributes a tile with this border to Wedgwood, see bibliography.) c.1885. Courtesy Rosamond Allwood.

Figure 29. One of a panel of four tiles printed underglaze in brown and hand painted over glaze with a design of pink daisies within an elaborate rococo scroll border. 6ins. Mark: 'L.T. ENGLAND' (for Lee of Tunstall). c.1890. Courtesy Rosamond Allwood.

Figure 30. Printed underglaze in brown and hand coloured with a design of a wild rose in brown, yellow and blue. 6ins. No mark. c.1890.

Figure 31. Printed underglaze in brown with a specimen flower and leaves with ox-eye scrolls in the corners, painted in green and yellow. 6ins. No mark. c.1880.

Figure 32. Stylised underglaze printed design in black of honeysuckle in a quatrefoil frame on a cream ground. Painted in green and red. 6ins. No mark. c.1880.

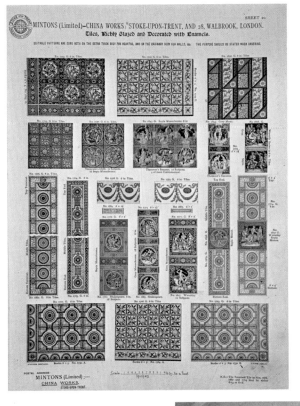

Colour Plate V. Page from the catalogue of Mintons China Works showing a range of tiles "richly glazed and decorated with enamels". Courtesy Royal Doulton Tableware Ltd.

Colour Plate VI. Page from the catalogue of Maw & Co., showing hand painted tiles designed by Walter Crane. Courtesy Royal Doulton Tableware Ltd.

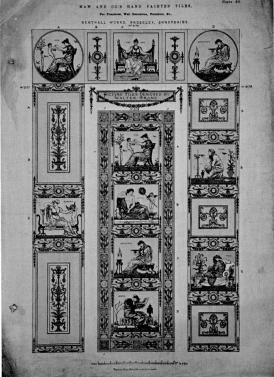

48

49

50

51

52

53

Figure 33. Outline printed underglaze in brown with a bunch of harebells and foxgloves, painted under and overglaze in blue, pink and shades of green. 6ins. Mark: 'Minton Hollins & Co. etc.' c.1880.

a possibility. The name of C.O. Murray (see p.141) could also be considered. Another freelance designer whose work for Mintons is recorded is Robert W. Edis, F.S.A. and an illustration in his book[9] shows eight floral designs for which he was responsible.

Mintons were also responsible for 'Four subjects of Field Flowers', No.1423, "slightly done in the same light blue (turquoise) ground on white". These were to work alternately with six 'Farm and Field' subjects.

Illustrations Plate 11(60-65) return us to the late 1880s and 1890s. All these are examples of relief moulded tiles, usually very low relief, decorated with colour glazes. All are of the early art nouveau period, though none of them could really qualify for designation as an art nouveau tile. It is worth stressing that these are moulded tiles, they are not produced by the tube lining process, they closely resemble it, and indeed are meant to, but mass produced moulding was much more economic than hand decoration by tube lining. Figure 34 is also moulded but Figure 35 is a tube lined example, and interestingly enough, nearly all the piped-on tube lining has flaked off.

The next eight illustrations in this section, Plate 12(66-71) and Plate 13(72-73), are all of tiles from one source, Pilkingtons of Clifton Junction, Manchester. With one exception (66) they represent the work

Plate 9.
(48) *Stylised leaf pattern printed in underglaze blue on white ground. 6ins. Mark: 'Webb's Tileries, Worcester'. c.1880.* **(49)** *Print from the Minton pattern book (Jones, Minton MSS No. 1842). 'Violet', from the series 'Spirit of the Flowers' (see text for details of other tiltles). Mintons China Works. Introduced c.1874.* Courtesy Royal Doulton Tableware Ltd. **(50)** *Spray of blossom, transfer printed outline, painted underglaze in yellows, pale mauve and brown upon a cream ground. 6ins. Mark: 'Rd. No. 158036.' This design was registered on 20th October, 1890 by Timmis and Watkin of Longton.* **(51)** *Spray of large flowers, bud and leaves printed underglaze in brown on a white background set in a border of 'C' scrolls and conventional motifs. 6ins. Mark: 'COV ENGLAND 537'. c.1890 (see p.55).* **(52)** *Small panel of sweet peas set in a border of conventional motifs and buds. Printed underglaze in a dark blue. For a similar border see Plate 43(245). 6ins. Mark: Design registration for 1881. Attributed to T. & R. Boote on the evidence of the border pattern.* **(53)** *Moulded design of a large petalled flower within a framework covered in convolvulus. Painted underglaze in yellow, reds and green. 6ins. Mark: 'Craven Dunnill & Co., Jackfield, Salop.' c.1880.*

Figure 34. Moulded in high relief with a design of apple blossom. Decorated in brown, green, cream and yellow translucent glazes. 6ins. No mark. c.1890.

Figure 35. Tube lined design of a stylised flower and foliage on a cream ground. Decorated in translucent green, and yellow glazes. 6ins. No mark. c.1895.

of two outstanding designers widely known in Victorian England, Lewis F. Day and Walter Crane.

The five designs Plates 12, 13(67, 68, 69, 72, 73) are by Day. They are credited to him in the firm's 1901 Glasgow Exhibition catalogue, or in the 1908 Franco-British Exhibition catalogue (see p.42). Day is also noted as the designer of 'Anthemion Frieze', 'Peony', 'Spring Meadow', 'Feather Leaf', Greek Ivy', and six other unnamed floral motifs described as "cloisonné tiles of conventional floral design, in coloured glazes" of which Plate 12(67) is an example illustrated in the 1901 catalogue. These tiles have not hitherto been recognised as Day's work.

Lewis F. Day (1845-1910) was mainly concerned with the tile side of Pilkington's business, rather than the decorative pottery. He was a Quaker, had been educated in France and Germany, and after setting up in business c.1870, his designs were produced in textiles, wallpapers, stained glass, embroidery, carpets, pottery, glass and books. He was a founder member of the Art Workers Guild (1884) and of the Arts and Crafts Exhibition Society (1888). Examples of his work in various media are illustrated in Gillian Naylor, and Elizabeth Aslin.[10] Day also wrote consistently throughout his career in magazines such as *The Studio Year Book* and *The Art Journal* (see bibliography). His designs were a great

Plate 10.
(54) *Printed underglaze in dark grey with a pattern of daisies surrounded by an inner Greek key border and an outer design of stylised flowers. 6ins. Mark: 'L.T. ENGLAND' (probably Lee of Tunstall). c.1896.* **(55)** *Outline printed in black and painted underglaze in blue, yellow and red with stylised floral branches and sunflowers set in four square frames. 6ins. Mark: 'Minton Hollins & Co. etc.' c.1885.* **(56)** *Outline printed in brown and painted underglaze in shades of green with a stylish pattern of an open flower, buds and leaves. 6ins. Mark: 'ENGLAND' and 'c' moulded in a circle. c.1890.* **(57)** *Outline printed in black with a design of pansies on a cream ground and painted underglaze in yellow, green, blue and pink. 6ins. No mark. c.1885-1890.* **(58)** *Printed underglaze in grey on a white ground with a pattern of daisy-like flowers. 6ins. Mark: 'pattern no. 399' (see p.63). c.1885-1890.* **(59)** *Outline printed in brown with a design of lilies on an ivory ground, crudely painted underglaze with deep yellow and shades of green. 6ins. Mark: 'pattern no. 293' (see p.63). c.1880-1885.*

54

55

56

57

58

59

asset to Pilkingtons, and his style which for many years had inclined to art nouveau flourished in his work for William Burton.

Born in the same year as Day, Walter Crane (1845-1915) was an even more distinguished name to have been associated with Pilkington's venture. He too was a designer with an enormous range of media, and a considerable reputation, though perhaps — as Elizabeth Aslin points out — he was more highly regarded on the Continent as an innovator, than in his own country, though his recognition here was substantial. Crane too was a founder member, and first President, of the Art Workers Guild. In the 1890s he was succesively Director of Design at the Manchester Municipal School of Art, Art Director of Reading University and Principal of the Royal College of Art in South Kensington. Crane was a prolific and delightful illustrator of children's books, and like Day, an author on design theory (see bibliography). His tile designs for Pilkingtons are not particularly novel but are most attractive. The series 'Flora's Train' Plate 12(70 and 71), consisted of six designs, 'Poppy', 'Bluebell', 'Columbine', 'Daffodil', 'Cornflower', 'Anemone'. The pieces according to the 1901 catalogue were "modelled by A.J. Kwiatkowski and painted by John Chambers, Miss Tyldesley and Miss Briggs". The designs resemble his rather sensuous illustrations for the

Figure 36. Moulded with an art nouveau style design of a single flower and stylised leaves in a swirling linear frame. Decorated in translucent green, pink and cream glazes. 6ins. Mark: '10. ENGLAND'. c.1900.

Figure 37. Relief moulded design in art nouveau style of a flower, a bud and foliage. Decorated in translucent shades of green and cream glazes. 6ins. Mark: 'ENGLAND'. c.1905.

Plate 11.
(60) *Moulded quartered pattern with alternate blank and foliage design, the latter decorated in green and yellow coloured glaze, the blank quarters in blue. 6ins. Mark: 'ENGLAND'. c.1895-1900.* **(61)** *Moulded seaweed pattern decorated in cream, blue and brown coloured glazes. 6ins. Mark: 'Mintons China Works etc. Reg'd. No. 278929 (for mid-1896) No. E2777.'* **(62)** *Moulded stylised pattern of flower heads decorated in orange and shades of green coloured glazes. 6ins. Mark: 'ENGLAND. COPYRIGHT', (this relates to the moulding of the back which resembles Sherwin & Cotton's Patent Lock Back.) c.1900.* **(63)** *Moulded stylised ivy leaf pattern decorated with orange, and shades of green coloured glazes. 6ins. Mark: 'ENGLAND'. c.1900.* **(64)** *Moulded chaplet of roses decorated in pink and shades of green coloured glazes. 6ins. Mark: 'L & B No. 1282'. (for Lee & Boulton, Tunstall). c.1900.* **(65)** *Moulded in high relief with a rose and leaves decorated in pink, cream and green glazes. 6ins. Mark: 'ENGLAND. 13 K.' c.1900-1905.*

60

61

62

63

64

65

66

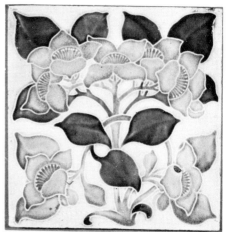

67

68

69

70

71

Plate 12. See page 94 for details.

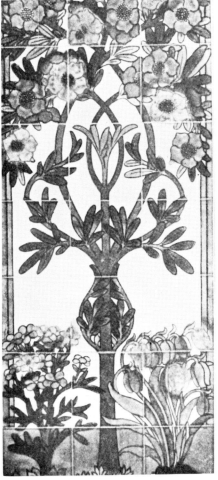

72

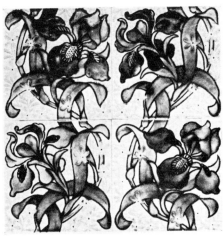

73

74

75

76

Plate 13. See page 94 for details.

book *Flora's Feast,* 1888. Crane also designed the set of five large, 30-inch by 12-inch tile panels of 'The Senses' for Pilkingtons as well as several pieces of art pottery. His designs appear on both pots and tiles made by Maw and are illustrated in Colour Plate VI, and there is evidence that he produced a floral series for Mintons, again based upon 'Flora's Feast', though we have not ourselves seen any examples.

The art nouveau floral motifs evident on Pilkington tiles are echoed in designs of almost every other maker large and small. Some characteristic art nouveau designs are shown in the last three tiles in this section and in Figures 35, 36 and 37. Here also is a possibility for the formation of an exciting and representative collection.

Plate 12. See page 92.
(66) *Moulded design in low relief of a water lily decorated with translucent glazes in shades of green and yellow. The top only of a two-tile design by C.F.A. Voysey. 6ins. Mark: 'P', for Pilkingtons. Reg'd. No. 397655, for early 1902.* **(67)** *Moulded design in a modified art nouveau style of interwoven flowers and leaves decorated with translucent glazes in shades of green and yellow. Designed by Lewis F. Day (see text for details). 6ins. Mark: 'P', for Pilkingtons. c.1898-1900.* **(68)** *Tube lined design of daffodils and leaves, decorated in translucent glazes of yellow and green with a turquoise background. From the earliest group of Lewis F. Day's registered designs for the firm. 6ins. Mark: 'P' for Pilkingtons. Reg'd No. 253079, for 1895. Courtesy Anthony Cross.* **(69)** *Moulded design of stems and leaves very freely drawn, decorated with transparent green glazes on a turquoise glaze background. Designed by Lewis F. Day. 6ins. A second tile completes the design which is continuous to a further pair of tiles. Mark: 'P', for Pilkingtons. Reg'd. No. 257473, for 1895.* **(70 and 71)** *Pair of moulded tiles with designs of 'Poppy' and 'Cornflower' in translucent glazes in shades of green, blue, ochre and red. Part of a set of six designed by Walter Crane for Pilkingtons. 6ins. c.1893 (see text for details). Courtesy Sothebys Belgravia.*

Plate 13. See page 93.
(72) *Illustration of floral tile panel designed by Lewis F. Day for Pilkingtons. Painted by T.F. Evans. Displayed at the Franco-British Exhibition 1908. Size and mark unknown.* **(73)** *Illustration of panel of four tiles designed by Lewis F. Day for Pilkingtons. Painted by W.S. Mycock. Displayed at the Franco-British Exhibition 1908. Size and mark unknown.* **(74)** *Moulded with a floral design in art nouveau style, decorated with green and blue translucent coloured glazes on a cream ground. 6ins. Mark 'C' (moulded), no attribution. c.1905.* **(75)** *Moulded with a stylised floral seed pod and foliage, decorated with ochre and green glaze on a cream ground. 6ins. No mark. c.1890-1895. Courtesy Rosamond Allwood.* **(76)** *Moulded with a poppy and foliage design, decorated in orange and green translucent glazes on a cream ground. 6ins. No mark. c.1890-1895. Courtesy Rosamond Allwood.*

3. LANDSCAPES AND PLACES

The use of topographical scenes as decoration has long been a favourite with English potters. Thus, it is no surprise to find that these self-same potters who, in the 1830s and 1840s, seemed to have drowned the world in a flood of topographical blue printed earthenware, turned again in the 1880s and 1890s to scenes 'of popular resort' at home and abroad to decorate their tiles.

The first ten examples illustrated, Plate 14(77-81) and 15(82-86), are all of Minton manufacture. The factory appears to have produced no fewer than seven different landscape series — and possibly more — which are not always easy to differentiate.

The large view of 'Warwick Castle', Plate 14(77), is a colourful and attractive piece. The Minton catalogue, sheet 34, shows companion studies of 'Kenilworth Castle', also vertical, 'Windsor Castle', horizontal, and three unnamed scenes. These seem to date from c.1890. A slightly later series (c.1896-1900) shown on sheet 53 of the catalogue depicts a set of four panels 12ins. by 6ins., the subjects being 'York Minster', 'Tintern Abbey', 'Fountains Abbey' and 'Canterbury Cathedral'. These are moulded and found with a coloured-glaze finish.

The next three tiles Plate 14(78, 79, 80) show three ways in which a basic transfer print, in this case from an etching, could be treated. 'Edinburgh Castle' (78) has a pale cream-coloured background and the scene printed in brown. 'Boppart on the Rhine' (79) is set within the same border but the ground is whiter and the brown print has been coloured overglaze in enamels. 'Inveraray Castle' (80) has no border and is in fact a teapot stand. Of these three tiles only one (78) is signed by the designer William Wise, one of the leading tile designers at Mintons whose work has hitherto been largely unrecognised (see p.192 for further details of his career). 'Edinburgh Castle' and 'Inveraray Castle' seem to be from the same set, listed in the Minton catalogue as: "Views — Twelve subjects printed on 6in. x 6in. tiles No 2024 and on 8in. x 8in. No 2029.". It is probable that the 'Boppart' (79) is by a different designer and comes from a different series. Other tiles which match it closely are: 'Village of Splugen, the Alps'; 'Dillishun on the Dart'; 'Rodez Cathedral'; 'The West Gate, Warwick'; 'The Old Gateway, Winchelsea'. Yet another series in very much the same style was produced in the 1890s, for entries appear in the pattern books and catalogues with pattern numbers 2175, 2231 and 2251. These latter two are shown as Plate 15(84 and 85) respectively. These views, unlike 'Boppart', are unnamed foreign scenes printed in brown and sometimes coloured, set in a circular and beaded frame with a stylised leaf-type border. Etched copper plates of some of this series are retained by Mintons and the initials L.T.S. are clearly visible, but no recorded name quite fits. Curiously, on finished examples, the L.T.S. initials are not discernible. Clearly more research is required to establish the exact nature and number of these foreign views series, as well as the designers responsible.

A further series of British views is illustrated by the examples Plate 15(82 and 83). These are also unsigned and appear to be of inferior quality in both engraving and printing to Wise's 'Edinburgh Castle'. A view of Swallow Falls, Bettws-y-Coed, has also been noted in this series. A small set, just four subjects entitled 'Landscapes', with a curious out-of-sequence pattern description "No. 58", occurs in the Minton pattern book and the illustration Plate 15(86) shows it to be a design very reminiscent of the type of imaginary scene which so frequently was used by potters of the 1850s, 1860s and 1870s on underglaze blue printed earthenware.

The last Minton tile which merits specific comment is Plate 14(81) of Langton Mill. It is signed in the print 'J.B. Evans', and presents something of a problem. John Bishop Evans was a landscape and marine painter who was associated with Mintons c.1865-1885.[11] He died in 1887. The tile itself is marked 'Made in England', a form of mark not in general use until the present century, and certainly not current before Evans's death. One can only assume that the etching of his view of Langton Mill continued to be used after his death for some considerable

77

78

79

80

81

time. There is no indication in the records that this design was one of a series. Incidentally, a plaque painted by Evans was sold at Sotheby's Belgravia (12th July, 1973) for £75.

Turning briefly to other manufacturers, the Maw company made a series of large topographical plaques, 12ins. by 8ins., and these are recorded in the Order Office pattern book (see p.40) as patterns 2654-61:

'Bridge and river'
'Sailing ships'
'Stone bridge'
'Bridge and brook'
'Absolution'
'Wood, bridge and castle'
'Landscape with cows'
'Fir tree and hills'

The same factory also produced a series of 'Rivers of Great Britain', four titles are illustrated in the catalogue: Shannon, Thames, Clyde and Severn. Each river is represented by a figure in classical attire.

The three simple country scenes, Plate 15(87) and Plate 16(88 and 89), are all very similar in design, though the two latter are coloured and indeed may be by the same maker as technically they are akin. However, they are unmarked and, therefore, must remain anonymous.

The romantic scene, Plate 16(90), is printed on a plastic clay tile and from the indentations — a kind of combed effect — on the back might well be attributable to Copeland. However, it does not appear in any of their tile pattern books, but could well be a transfer from the earthenware department used on a tile. There are indications in the corners of the design that the original print was circular.

The next four designs remind us of the ever-present Oriental or chinoiserie influence. The pattern on the Copeland teapot stand, Plate 16(93), is not the 'Willow' but clearly relates to it, whilst (92) is one of a series of twelve 'Chinese Views' from Mintons — the designer is not known. Plate 17(94) takes us into the twentieth century and judging by the marks on the back, to Pilkingtons of Clifton Junction. No factory of origin can be given to the rather rough clay panel, Plate 17(95), with a good example of on-glaze enamel topographical painting signed by M. Bouquet and dated 1868. I have not been able to identify this artist but clearly he was a man of some technical and artistic skill. It is, of course, possible that the piece is not of English manufacture or decoration.

Plate 17(96, 97, 98) are American scenes printed by Wedgwood. They are of considerable rarity and are much sought after in the United States. To be precise Wedgwood appear to have been responsible for three series

Plate 14.
(77) Engraved picture of Warwick Castle with the river in the foreground. The outline printed in brown underglaze and then finely coloured. 12ins. by 6ins. Mark: 'MINTONS' impressed. c.1890.(78) Etched view of 'Edinburgh Castle from the Grassmarket', printed in brown upon a cream ground. Signed by the designer W. Wise. 8ins. Mark: 'Mintons China Works etc.' c.1885-1890. (79) Etched view of 'Boppart on the Rhine' printed in brown on a cream ground and coloured in enamels. 8ins. Mark: 'Mintons China Works etc.' c.1885-1890. (80) Very fine etched view of 'Inveraray Castle' printed in brown upon an ivory ground. The tile has slightly canted corners and is set upon four circular bun feet to form a teapot stand. 6ins. Mark: 'Mintons China Works etc.' c.1885-1890. (81) Printed and enamelled coloured view of 'Langton Mill'. Signed by the designer J.B. Evans. 6ins. Mark: 'Made in England'. c.1895-1900.

of American views. Plate 49(277) is from a tile series shown in the pattern book, the titles with their pattern numbers are as follows:

T 295, 'Washington Statue, Public Gardens, Boston'
T 297, 'Summer Statue, Public Gardens, Boston'
T 298, 'Trinity Church, Boston'
T 300, 'Public Garden, Boston'
T 417, 'Landing of Pilgrims 1620', Plate 49(277)
T 419, 'The Maplewood White Mountains, New Hampshire U.S.'
T 423, 'Beacon St., Boston'
T 426, 'Maplewood House'
T 486, 'The Boston Common'
T 487, 'Boston Monument (Civil War)'
T 488, 'Museum of Fine Arts, Boston'
T 499, 'St. Mary's Catholic Cathedral'

Dating this series is most difficult as the pattern numbers cover such a wide range. Judging by examples we have seen, these tiles date from the 1880s or later and are to be found printed both in blue and brown underglaze.

The second series is of calendar tiles of rectangular shape which were specifically made by Wedgwood for "Jones McDuffee & Stratton, Pottery Merchants, Boston, U.S.A." Each has a view on one side and an appropriate calendar printed on the reverse. The full list is not known, but the following have been noted:

Bearing dates 1891-1913:
Two views of Trinity Church, Boston
The State House, Boston
The Adjacent Lean-to Houses in Quincey, Mass.
Mount Vernon
Tree in Cambridge, Mass., under which Washington took command of the American army.
Federal Street Theatre
King's Chapel, Boston
Bunker Hill Monument
Harvard Stadium
Pier 46 Mystic Wharves
The Mayflower arriving in Princetown Harbour

Additionally, similarly pierced calendar tiles are recorded for 1923, 'Minute Man, Concorde, Mass.' and for 1926 as illustrated here Plate 17(98) 'Coolidge Homestead.' These two latter items are in the

Plate 15.
(82) *Etched view of 'Conway Castle', printed underglaze in navy upon an ivory ground. 6ins. Mark: 'Mintons China Works etc.' and 'No. 2024'. c.1890.* **(83)** *Etched view of 'Cardinal Beaton's House, Edinburgh', printed underglaze in blue on a white ground. 6ins. Mark: 'Mintons China Works etc.' and 'No. 2024'. c.1890.* **(84)** *Print from the Minton pattern book depicting a landscape set in a circular frame surrounded by geometric and floral motifs. The landscape is printed in black and uncoloured. Pattern number 2231. (Jones, Minton MSS, No. 1842). c.1890. Courtesy Royal Doulton Tableware Ltd.* **(85)** *Print from the Minton pattern book, as (84) but the centre scene is coloured. Pattern number 2251. c.1890. Courtesy Royal Doulton Tableware Ltd.* **(86)** *Print from the Minton pattern book depicting an island house. Pattern "No. 58 — Landscape — 4 subjects". (Jones, Minton MSS, No. 1842). c.1890. Courtesy Royal Doulton Tableware Ltd.* **(87)** *Printed in black upon a cream ground with a view of a small mill with a stream and a waterwheel. 6ins. No mark. c.1885.*

82

83

84

85

86

87

88

89

90

91

92

93

Wedgwood Museum, Barlaston, together with several other American scenes, of which Plate 17(96 and 97) are examples. These are printed in blue on the normal square tiles, but the tile blanks were manufactured by T. & R. Boote and carry their mark as well as the Wedgwood one. Apparently they were made after 1900 when Wedgwood themselves ceased to manufacture tiles, but presumably found it commercially worthwhile to continue the association with America by printing on the products of another firm.

The four tiles at Barlaston are:
'Old South Church, Washington and Mill Street, Tea Party met here 1773', Plate 17(97).
Spirit of '76 Yankee Doodle', Plate 49(278).
'Wadsworth Longfellow House, Portland, Maine.'
'Old State House Boston, East End rebuilt 1712', Plate 17(96).

Although there is no factory of origin marked on the two finely enamelled views, Plate 18(99 and 100), the initials T.H.S. on (99) point to T.H. Simpson, a Minton artist of the mid-century period.[12]

The Doulton picture of 'Otford', Plate 18(101), is one of the most charming tiles in the collection. Although chronologically it falls outside our period, its true quality would appeal to any collector. Desmond Eyles[13] describes how these tiles were produced in the period 1933-1936 from original coloured sketches by Donald Maxwell recording the beauties of the Kentish landscape and architecture. The effect is very striking: "coloured aquatints on clay" is one description. "The outline print was first transferred from an etched copper plate on to a specially made tile with an oatmeal-coloured glaze; the colours were then filled in by hand by Miss A. Lyons and Miss D. Johnson". The first two tiles depicting Yalding and Westerham were presented to George V.

Far less subtle in its effect and finish is the teapot stand with the printed church, Plate 18(102). This type of commemorative design is more commonly found on earthenware.

Plate 18(103) is of a rather nondescript tile. The enamelled scene is of very moderate competency, possibly from an amateur hand, and draws attention to two problems which face the collector. Should he buy this type of enamelled scene which, even when it occurs on a marked tile, seems clearly to fall below the professional standard of factory decoration? Furthermore, in this case, is it worth buying a tile which is only a portion of a design? Such pieces do not afford the satisfaction of

Plate 16.
(88) *Printed and enamel-coloured view of 'The Hermitage, near Dunkeld'. 6ins. No mark but the letter 'D' is moulded in one corner. c.1890-1895.* **(89)** *Printed and enamel-coloured view of a watermill and wheel. 6ins. No mark, but the figure '9' is moulded in one corner. c.1890-1895.* **(90)** *Underglaze blue print of a rustic scene showing a ruined temple or pavilion and two shepherd boys in the foreground, a lake in the background. Plastic clay tile with 'combed' back. 6ins. No mark. Possibly by Copeland. c.1860+.* **(91)** *Printed Oriental scene in fawn with touches of pink and blue enamel colour. 6ins. Mark: the pattern name 'WOODSWORTH'. Unattributed. c.1885.* **(92)** *One of a set of twelve 'Chinese Views', printed underglaze in blue on a white ground. 6ins. A print of this view appears in the Minton pattern book (Jones, Minton MSS, No. 1842). It is given an 'out-of-sequence' pattern number — No.36. c.1885.* **(93)** *A willow type pattern printed in pale blue underglaze on a white ground. The tile is supported on four bun feet to form a teapot stand. 6ins. Mark: 'Copeland 12 98'. This may well denote December 1898.*

94

95

96

97

98

Plate 17.
(94) *Printed underglaze in blue with a 'willow pattern plate.' 6ins. Mark 'P' moulded (Pilkingtons) and 'Made in England'. c.1905.* **(95)** *Rough clay panel enamelled on-glaze with a scene of yachts on a lake with trees in the foreground. Signed. 'M. Bouquet 1868'. 6½ins. by 8½ins.* Courtesy City Museum and Art Gallery, Stoke-on-Trent. **(96)** *Printed underglaze in blue with 'Old State House, Boston, East End rebuilt 1712'. 6ins. Mark: moulded T. & R. Boote mark, printed Wedgwood mark. Post 1900.* Courtesy The Wedgwood Museum, Barlaston. **(97)** *Printed underglaze in blue with 'Old South Church, Washington and Mill Street, Tea Party met here 1773'. 6ins. Mark: moulded T. & R. Boote mark, printed Wedgwood mark. Post 1900.* Courtesy The Wedgwood Museum, Barlaston. **(98)** *Printed underglaze in blue with 'Coolidge Homestead' and on the reverse the calendar for 1926.* Courtesy The Wedgwood Museum, Barlaston.

either a well-decorated object or a whole design, and generally for these reasons alone, irrespective of price, the authors have avoided purchasing such tiles. A couple of pounds or so is better put towards even a fairly routine moulded design such as Plate 18(104) than frittered away on a poor example just because it is hand painted.

Finally, it is worth noting that the *Pottery Gazette,* October 1896, gave details of the work of G.H. Grundy of Derby who produced photo-decorated tiles:

The pictures are printed on the tiles in ceramic colours, and being fired under the glaze they make the most imperishable photographic records known. The tiles are in two colours, white and cream and the subjects are printed from the photograph in black, red, sepia &c as may be desired ... something like fifty different subjects are already printed, and in stock, on 6in. tiles, amongst the subjects:

'Haddon Hall'
'The Albert Memorial'
'St. George's Chapel, Windsor'
'The Aquarium, Brighton'
'The West Pier, Brighton'
'The Castle, Hastings'
'The Forth Bridge'
'The Sands at Ramsgate'
'The High Tor, Matlock' and other places of popular resort.

The only example we have encountered of a photographic tile is one in the Ironbridge Gorge Museum. The subject is identical to one on Grundy's list being of 'The West Pier, Brighton.' However, one cannot say with certainty whether this is a Grundy decorated example on a Maws blank, or one of the factory's own products.

Plate 18. See page 105.
(99) *A fine overglaze enamel painting of a view of 'Chepstow Castle'. No mark. Signed 'T.H.S.' attributed to T.H. Simpson, a Minton artist. 8ins. c.1865-1870. See G.A. Godden, Minton Pottery and Porcelain, p.122 for further details.* **(100)** *A fine overglaze enamel painting of a bridge and a river or lake with mountains in the distance — unnamed. No mark. No signature. This tile was bought as a pair with (99) and is likewise attributed to T.H. Simpson. 8ins. c.1865-1870.* **(101)** *Hand painted with a fine view of 'Otford'. Signed 'D.M.' (Donald Maxwell). One of a series of tiles recording the beauties of the Kentish landscape and architecture. 6½ins. by 5½ins. Mark: Doultons of Lambeth standard mark. c.1933-1936.* **(102)** *On-glaze transfer print in grey with a view of Trinity Congregational Church, Swinton. The tile is mounted on four feet as a teapot stand. Mark: 'Craven Dunnill & Co. etc.' c.1890.* **(103)** *Painted in on-glaze enamels with a coastal scene. This is clearly only one tile from a scenic panel. 6ins. No mark. c.1880.* **(104)** *Moulded in relief with a landscape design of a path passing between trees. Decorated in shades of translucent turquoise and green glazes. 6ins. Mark: 'ENGLAND. Rd. No. 469080', for late 1905.*

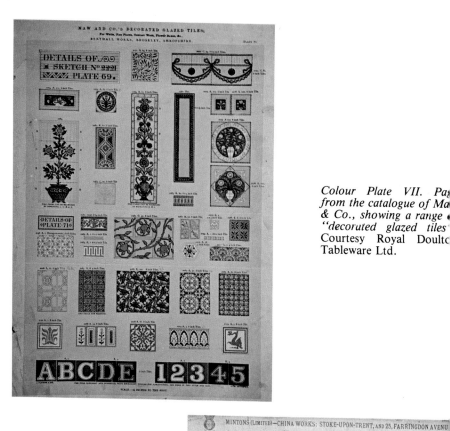

Colour Plate VII. Page from the catalogue of Maw & Co., showing a range of "decorated glazed tiles". Courtesy Royal Doulton Tableware Ltd.

Colour Plate VIII. Page from the catalogue of Mintons China Works showing designs of the 1895-1905 period. Courtesy Royal Doulton Tableware Ltd.

99

100

101

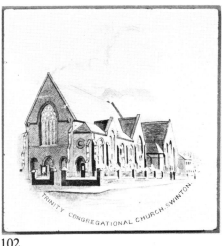

102

103

104

Plate 18. See page 103 for details.

4. ANIMALS, BIRDS AND FISH

Practially every major tile manufacturer produced tiles decorated in one way or another with representations of birds, animals or fish and thus the scope for the collector is again very wide.

Mintons were particularly prolific and the first three illustrations are all examples of their work, Plate 19(105 to 107). They are printed from etchings executed in 1879 by William Wise (see p.192). It was a great delight to find that several of the original copper plates as etched by Wise are still preserved in the engraving shop at the Minton factory.

It is not easy to distinguish between the two main animal series of Wise's. 'Cattle Subjects' consisted of: "four subjects Cows etc., four subjects Horses; four subjects Sheep. No. 2017. On 6 x 6 tiles." 'Animals of the Farm' was "Twelve subjects printed on 6 x 6 tiles No. 1699" which in addition to the three subjects illustrated here had:

'Goats and kids'
'Cow in cowshed'
'Sheep lying down' (Figure 38)
'Two donkeys'
'Shire horses'
'Cattle in the stream'
'Farmyard horses'
'Dairy Cattle'
'Highland Cattle'

Figure 38. Printed underglaze in brown on a white ground with an etched design of sheep lying down. From the series 'Animals of the Farm' by William Wise. 6ins. Mark: 'Mintons China Works etc.' Designed 1879.

This series was also executed in a coloured version, and appears to have been produced later with a subsidiary title of 'Animal Groups'.

In addition to these two series Mintons also produced a set of six 'Farm and Field' subjects: "No 1422 in white, on a light blue, Turquoise, ground to work alternately with four subjects of field flowers". The titles are given as 'cock'; 'hen'; 'turkey'; 'duck'; 'rabbit' and 'kingfisher'. Another fine set from Mintons was entitled 'Natural History': "twelve subjects outlined and painted in monochrome by hand

Plate 19.
(105) *Etched farmyard scene of pigs at a trough and cow. Printed in black on a pale fawn ground. 6ins. Unsigned and unmarked, but see (106).* **(106)** *Etched farmyard scene of sheep printed in black on a pale fawn ground. One of a series of twelve 'Animals of the Farm'. This tile is signed 'W. Wise' and dated '1879'. In the Minton catalogue it is pattern 1699. Mark: 'Mintons China Works etc.' 1879+.* **(107)** *Etched scene of a deer and hind printed in black on a pale fawn ground. 6ins. Unsigned and unmarked but see (106).* **(108)** *Underglaze deep blue printed design of a hind and stag with a geometric patterned border. 8ins. Mark: 'Craven Dunnill & Co., Jackfield, Salop.' c.1885.* **(109)** *Underglaze printed and enamel coloured design of a bird on a branch, within a diced border pattern. 6ins. No mark. Unattributed. c.1890.* **(110)** *Underglaze brown transfer printed design of a bird set amidst blossom. 6ins. Mark: 'No 78' (probably a pattern number). Unattributed. c.1895.*

105

106

107

108

109

110

in blues, No 1899.'' Original watercolour drawings for this series are in the Minton archives in a portfolio labelled: 'Henk's Birds, Animals & Flowers' (Jones, Minton MSS, No.1839, with duplicates in No. 1827). The Henk referred to could either be Christian Henk (fl.1848-1905), or his son (1846-1914), both of whom had long careers at Mintons.[14] The subjects are:

'Thrush and snail'
'Squirrel'
'Two frogs'
'Dragonfly and snail'
'Owl'
'Bird and bee'
'Mouse and acorn'
'Two rabbits'
'Crab and eel'
'Fish, shell and lobster'
'Butterfly and cricket'

Again by virtue of the evidence in the archives, the designer of the series entitled 'Animal Fables' was one of the Henks. This series of twelve is also most attractively painted in monochrome blues. Plate 20(114) gives some impression of the bold clear style of the designer. This set is different from, and rarer than, the 'Aesop's Fables' see Plate 32(181 to 186), with which it could be confused.

A set of birds is advertised in a fairly late, c.1895, version of the Minton catalogue: "sixteen subjects printed on 6 x 6 tiles No 2063. Also done on 8 x 8 tiles No 2079. Twelve of these subjects are coloured by hand in neutral colours No 2133." Also from Mintons is the rather curious, but unmistakable, set of 'The Seven Ages of Bird Life', No. 1653. Various birds, as in Plate 22(127) of two billing and cooing doves labelled 'The Lovers', (in reverse as in the pattern book), depict the Shakespearean stages of man's life. The actual tiles in this series which we have seen have all been printed in black upon a white ground. Lastly in this review of the Mintons series, we may note twelve subjects entitled 'Naturalist' of which an example is shown in the pattern book with a coloured illustration of three wading birds, possibly snipe, see Plate 22(126). The pattern number is given as 1767, but this series does not appear in any of the printed catalogues we have seen, perhaps an indication that it was not a popular series.

Plate 20.
(111) *Fine painting in enamel colours of a heron, set within a circular frame. The outside background is brown, within the circle it is grey. 8ins. Unsigned and unattributed. c.1875.* **(112)** *Set within a narrow gold and white patterned frame, the bird — probably a snipe — and the reeds are painted in raised paste gold and silver, all on a matt black ground. Mark: 'Mintons China Works etc.' 8ins. c.1880.* **(113)** *Watercolour drawing of a bustard from the Copeland archives. Several similar drawings exist. No tiles have been recorded. c.1878. Courtesy The Spode Museum.* **(114)** *Watercolour drawing of 'The Stork and the Frog', one of a series of twelve subjects entitled 'Animal Fables'. Painted in monochrome blue, examples are in the Minton archives (Jones, Minton MSS, Nos. 1816 and 1826). Probably designed by Henk. Pattern 1897 in blue on 6-inch tiles. Introduced c.1882. Courtesy Royal Doulton Tableware Ltd.* **(115)** *A pair of tiles hand-painted in enamel colours. 12ins. by 3ins. The birds and dragonfly are reserved against a dark brown ground. Mark: 'COPELAND' (impressed) and 'L 7'. c.1880.*

111

112

113

114

115

116

117

118

119

120

121

Returning to the earlier illustrations, Plate 19(108, 109 and 110) are examples of pleasant but relatively inexpensive tiles which were purchased a few years ago for sums of £2, 50p and 20p respectively. Though two of them are unmarked their factory of origin might well be discovered by careful research. The finely painted heron, Plate 20(111), is also anonymous, but despite this, one would not expect a hand enamelled tile of this quality to be cheap. The same applies to Plate 20(112), an unusual example from Mintons. A similar tile was sold for £10 at Sotheby's Belgravia as long ago as 20th December, 1973, Lot 80. In one of the Minton Photograph Books[15] these tiles are described as "subjects in raised gold and silver on dry black ground — pattern S1915". The treatment is most effective.

The watercolour drawing of the bustard, Plate 20(113), comes from Copeland. It is possible that tiles were never produced to this design, as it did not appear in the pattern books. Other drawings in the Copeland archives in this series depict the Toucan, Egyptian vulture, Macaw and Penguin. The style is so idiosyncratic — akin to that of the children's toy books of the period — as to be easily recognisable. The herons in Plate 20(115) are much more conventionally delineated. These and the robin, Plate 21(120), in the style of a Christmas card are representative of a fair number of individual animal and bird studies which appear in the Copeland pattern books. The 'Gnomes and Elves' series, Plate 40(227), and the remarkable 'Frog' series, Plate 40(228), should also be remembered as Copeland animal studies.

The remainder of the illustrations of birds are from some of the leading tile makers and designers and include several of considerable rarity. The Minton design signed by Christopher Dresser, Plate 21(116), is naturally unique, but examples of the tile taken from this design do occur from time to time. One was exhibited at the *Minton 1798-1910* exhibition at the Victoria and Albert Museum in the summer of 1976, and this design was exhibited at Wolverhampton in 1978. To the best of our knowledge, however, neither the design in Plate 21(117) nor any related tile have been shown before. This is a 'studio' design from Minton and certainly can be classified as in the style of Dresser, if not actually by him.

Plate 21.
(116) *Pen and wash design in blue on a white ground of three cranes flying over stylised waves. 7½ins. by 11ins. Signed 'Chr. Dresser'. A Minton tile was based on this design. c.1870. Courtesy Royal Doulton Tableware Ltd.* **(117)** *Loose, coloured design of a crane from the Minton archives. 6ins. Mark: 'Mintons Art Pottery Studio Kensington Gore'. Possibly a design by Christopher Dresser. (Jones, Minton MSS No. 1838). c.1872. Courtesy Royal Doulton Tableware Ltd.* **(118)** *Pair of tiles printed underglaze in brown and coloured in green, pink, yellow and blue with a bird on a branch. 6ins. by 3ins. each. No mark. c.1890.* **(119)** *Moulded in medium high relief with a four-part design — two birds and two flowers, decorated overall with a white slip. 6ins. William de Morgan. c.1885. Courtesy City Museum and Art Gallery, Stoke-on-Trent.* **(120)** *Engraved and printed design of a robin on a snow-covered branch with holly, mistletoe, etc. Coloured in red, blue, green and white set in a gold frame with canted corners. 8ins. Mark: 'W.T. Copeland, Stoke-on-Trent'. c.1880.* **(121)** *Decorated with a picture of a kingfisher in gilt on a plain blue ground. 8ins. Mark: 'Wedgwood etc.' and date letters NVK for 1882. Courtesy The Wedgwood Museum, Barlaston.*

Figure 39. Framed solid clay tile decorated in underglaze grey on a white ground with an overall pattern of stylised birds. 6ins. William de Morgan. c.1880. Courtesy Manchester Polytechnic Collection.

Plate 21(119) is good moulded de Morgan design decorated in an effective monochrome white slip, whilst Figure 39, also by de Morgan, depicts similar rather exotic wild fowl, only this time in the more familiar de Morgan underglaze painted technique. Both are quality tiles — and, therefore, likely to be expensive — as is Plate 21(121), the rare Wedgwood example. This is the only example we have seen of this very striking raised gold on blue colour combination. The other examples of outstanding quality in this section on birds are the two parts of the panel in Plate 22(124 and 125) depicting the seven ages of man with the figures those of storks. This set was displayed in the Wolverhampton Exhibition of 1978. In one of the Minton Photograph Books,[16] either this set, or a very similar one, has been photographed and given a reference number of S 1584, which might denote a design emanating from the Kensington Studio. However, a note at the beginning of the first of this set of Photograph Books[17] reads: "This set of designs from 1479 to 1499 were given plain numbers before it was decided to continue the S or London Studio number for Art Tiles and Slabs.

"The first S number given at Mintons is S 1488, the last entry at the London Studio being S 1487".

If this note is accurate — and clearly it was penned well *after* the closure of the London studio in 1875 — then the Stork Seven Ages was a

Plate 22.
(122) *Moulded in high relief with a design of two birds and a dragonfly against a background of leaves and pine cones. Decorated in blue, brown, green and yellow coloured glazes. 6ins. Mark: 'Godwin & Hewitt'. c.1890.* **(123)** *Printed underglaze in black on a white ground with a blue tit feeding in a cage (or trap ?). 6ins. Mark: (moulded) 'Brown-Westhead Moore & Co. Hanley. Ravenscrofts Patent' and printed 'copyright deposé' (see text). c.1885-1890.* **(124)** *'Ye Lovyers' one of a panel of seven tiles painted in yellow and grey with birds (storks depicting 'The Seven Ages'). 6ins. Minton. Probably designed by Stacey Marks. c.1876.* Courtesy Victoria and Albert Museum. **(125)** *"Ye Leane & Slipper'd Pantaloone". (As 124.)* Courtesy Victoria and Albert Museum. **(126)** *Watercolour design from the Minton pattern book of three wading birds (snipe ?) from the series 'Naturalist'. 6ins. Pattern 1767 (Jones, Minton MSS, No. 1842). c.1880.* Courtesy Royal Doulton Tableware Ltd. **(127)** *Printed design in black and white from the Minton pattern book of 'Lovers' from the series 'The Seven Ages of Bird Life'. 6ins. Pattern 1653 (Jones, Minton MSS, No. 1842). c.1878-1879.* Courtesy Doulton Tableware Ltd.

122

123

124

125

126

127

128

129

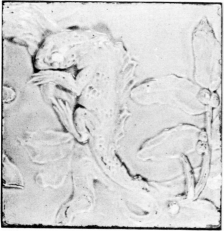

130

131

132

133

factory and not a studio product. Nevertheless, wherever it was produced, it is not unreasonable to attribute the design to that master of quirky medievalism, Henry Stacey Marks. Incidentally, it should be added that the numbers from the Photograph Book just quoted seem to bear no direct relationship to those found in the Minton printed catalogue, and neither to the best of our knowledge, appear on the tiles themselves (at least until the 1890s); thus their importance really lies in establishing a relative chronology whenever possible.

Figure 40. Underglaze printed and enamelled design in shades of green and yellow of a wren on a branch. 6ins. No mark. c.1890.

Figure 41. Moulded in high relief with a rabbit crouched amongst dandelions and other plants decorated in green and brown translucent glazes. 6ins. Mark: 'Godwin & Hewitt.' c.1890.

To return to the more humble and everyday tiles, Plate 21(118) is part of a simple 3-inch wide continuous border pattern, Figure 40 is a companion piece to Plate 19(109), alas, still anonymous, but Plate 22(122 and 123) are both rarities. (122) from Godwin & Hewitt is, like Figure 41, a tile of normal thickness, indeed a not unusual example of a moulded art tile. However, Godwin & Hewitt are much better known for their

Plate 23.
(128) *Plastic clay tile with fawn background incised with a design of horses. The incisions are filled with blue and brown pigments. The tile is somewhat warped and carries the impressed mark 'DOULTON, LAMBETH', between which is the date 1874. 8ins. The monogram of Hannah B. Barlow appears both on the back and the face of the tile. Courtesy Mr. Alan Smith.* **(129)** *Doultons plastic clay tile with an incised design of cows by Hannah Barlow. 8ins. Details as for (128). Courtesy Mr. Alan Smith.* **(130)** *Relief moulded design of a lizard and foliage formed on a plastic clay tile. The whole tile is covered in a rich yellow glaze. 6ins. Mark: the monogram of Burmantofts Faience. c.1890.* **(131)** *Relief moulded design of grotesque birds formed on a plastic clay tile. The whole covered with a dark brown glaze. 6ins. Mark: the monogram of Burmantofts Faience. c.1890.* **(132)** *Intaglio moulded design of a dragon, covered in a thick, pale green glaze which shows darker in the hollows of the design. 6ins. Mark: 'ENGLAND. K.', possibly the work of William England & Sons (see p.56). c.1880.* **(133)** *Relief moulded design of a lion on a form of plinth, with a stippled pattern above and below. Decorated in a pale green translucent glaze. 6ins. Mark: 'P' (moulded) for Pilkingtons. c.1905.*

encaustic tiles (Figure 42 is an earlier example of W. Godwin's encaustic work), and ordinary tiles marked with this firm's name are met with rarely. Of greater rarity still is the bird study, Plate 22(123). Made by one of the major pottery and porcelain manufacturers of the last quarter of the nineteenth century, Brown-Westhead, Moore & Co., it is one of only four tiles we have ever seen from this firm. Perhaps the mark noted in the caption gives a clue that much of their tile production was exported. The mark 'Ravenscrofts Patent' would appear to refer to the moulded form of the back of the tile, but no information is to hand on Ravenscroft.

Minton Hollins produced a set of four bird studies, each subject printed underglaze in blue within a square blue frame. The individual studies carry no titles. The same is true of the twelve-tile Craven Dunnill series of animal studies of which Plate 19(108) is a good marked example.

Figure 42. Encaustic tile decorated with a design of a lion within a shield in orange upon a red body. 6ins. Mark: 'W. Godwin, Lugwardine, Hereford.' c.1865. Courtesy City Museum and Art Gallery, Stoke-on-Trent.

The name of Hannah Barlow is well known to all collectors of English pottery. Her animals incised into the body of Doultons' salt-glazed stoneware are deservedly highly regarded. A product of Mintons' Kensington Studio, she joined Doultons in 1871 and continued to work there until her retirement in 1913.[18] However, her work on tiles is rare, possibly because the Doulton clay body tended to warp in the firing of flat tiles — or so it would seem from these, the two examples seen in Plate 23(128 and 129). Gillian Naylor[19] illustrates another example with

Plate 24.
(134) *An etched and transfer printed design in brown on an ivory ground of a gun dog and a game bird. One of a series of six, pattern T291 (see text). 6ins. Mark: 'Josiah Wedgwood & Sons, Etruria.' c.1880.* (135). *Print from the Wedgwood tile pattern book of a finely etched study of a dog, probably by Thomas Allen, pattern T283 F. One of a series of six (see text). Introduced c.1878.* Courtesy Wedgwood Museum, Barlaston. (136) *Print from the Wedgwood tile pattern book of a camel or dromedary, probably by Thomas Allen, pattern T482. One of a series of four (see text). Introduced c.1886.* Courtesy Wedgwood Museum, Barlaston. (137) *Print from the Wedgwood tile pattern book of 'A Ruski', probably by Thomas Allen, pattern 480. One of a series of four (see text). Introduced c.1886.* Courtesy Wedgwood Museum, Barlaston. (138) *Underglaze dark blue print of a framed design of four fish swimming under water amongst reeds. 6ins. No mark, but pattern number 206, possibly Samuel Fielding & Co. c.1885.* (139) *Finely printed and painted quartered tile with a deep blue background to the fruit and flower study, and a fawn ground for the bird and rabbit. 6ins. Mark: 'Minton Hollins & Co. etc.' 1880-1885.*

134

135

136

137

138

139

tiles set in a cabinet now in the Victoria and Albert Museum, and a six-tile picture of horses is illustrated in Sotheby's Belgravia catalogue 11th November, 1971, Lot 77. The successful bid of £40 seems very cheap nowadays.

The four following tiles, Plate 23(130 to 133), are all moulded and achieve their effect by the use of coloured glazes. The dragon is an intaglio design, the glaze filling the hollows in the surface to produce the effect. The Pilkington lion in (133) is relief moulded. A companion tile was purchased with this latter which had moulded the intertwined initials 'T.L.B.', which were alleged to stand for The Lion Brewery. The illustrations of the Burmantofts pieces Plate 23(130 and 131) perhaps do them less than justice. The rather repulsive lizard would hardly grace the sitting-room, but the grotesque birds are full of character and are reminiscent of Martinware.

As might be expected Maw also produced natural history sets of tiles. The Order Office pattern book at Shrewsbury records two series of birds. The first on 6-inch tiles has a simple three-line square border frame with a small three-line square in the corners. The subjects are:

'Snipe'
'Thrush'
'Partridge'
'Kingfisher'
'Starling'
'Dove'
'Skylark'
'Cuckoo'
'Wagtail'
'Yellow Hammer'
'Blackbird'
'House Swallow' *(sic)*

They are coloured or printed in black and seem based on Bewick engravings. Examples may be seen in the Ironbridge Gorge Museum. A second series of rather inferior draftmanship and inaccurate coloration, again on 6-inch tiles with a simple double-line border, patterns 1577-1584 consists of: 'Cuckoo'; 'Partridge'; 'Swallow'; 'Wren'; 'Moorhen'; 'Goldfinch'; 'Woodpecker'; Woodcock'.

Additionally, two 12ins. by 6ins. panels finely coloured, one of woodcock another of game fish were noted, as were a number of tiles decorated with stylised fish in lustre.

The Minton Hollins firm was also responsible for a series of fine bird studies on 8-inch tiles, these alternating with flower groups. This set is distinguishable by the butterfly which appears in each picture. Another charming series from Minton Hollins is depicted in Plate 24(139), each tile in the series having a different combination of flower, bird, animal and fruit in each quarter. This series is unmistakable even when it occurs on unmarked tiles. The same firm produced an amusing series of canine subjects entitled 'The Road to Ruin'. Stage 2, 'Brawling', shows two dogs fighting with a sub-title 'The True Beginning of our End'. Stage 3 is 'Stealing — a snapper up of unconsidered trifles'. A most attractive series.

In Plate 24(134-137) four examples from the Wedgwood factory are shown. The gun dog and bird (134), an etched example, is one of a series of six studies, pattern T 291. The other subjects are: hare; partridge; gun dog with a 'bag'; woodcock with eggs; cock pheasant. Wedgwood also produced a very attractive series of etched farmyard animals, pattern T 427: goose; turkey cock; pigeons; cock and hen; partridge; quail; cockerel; pheasant; rabbit; guinea fowl; duck; doves. The pattern book also shows six marvellously meticulous and characterful dogs of which Plate 24(135) is one. They are lettered A to F of pattern T 283. Lastly with pattern numbers T 479/480/481 and 482 are four superb animal studies of respectively: a Barbary; a Ruski, Plate 24(137); Arabia; Camel, Plate 24(136).

Figure 43. Solid clay tile moulded with a design of a lion and lioness. Painted underglaze in quarters of cane colour and dark blue; the lions in silver and red lustre. 6ins. Mark: 'William de Morgan'. c.1890. Courtesy Manchester Polytechnic Collection.

Figure 44. Blue painted watercolour of a bull. Design from the Minton archives for a butcher's shop decoration (see also Colour Plate I). (Jones, Minton MSS, No.1856). c.1880. Courtesy Royal Doulton Tableware Ltd.

No examples of these remarkable studies have been seen, but as they appear printed in the pattern book it is more than likely that the tiles do exist. The designer of these outstanding Wedgwood pieces would seem to have been the Art Director, Thomas Allen (see p.140 for fuller details of his work).

The last Plate in this section, Plate 25, shows studies of fish. Both the final example Plate 25(145), a superb tube lined design of swirling movement, and the portion of a de Morgan design Plate 25(144) would not be seen very often. It is perhaps worth remarking of the very colourful de Morgan that even the tail of a fish is better than none at all. If such a tile were to be offered separated from the rest of the design at least the price should be correspondingly reduced. The tropical fish Plate 25(140 and 141) are two of a set of six and, as with most hand painted examples, it is not easy to decide whether they are standard factory products, 'one-offs', or the work of an amateur decorating a set of blanks. No such problems arise with standard tiles either printed, Plate 25(142), or moulded, Plate 25(143) and Figure 43.

Figure 44 is an original drawing from the Minton archives which seems to match very closely the printed version in the factory catalogue shown in Colour Plate I. A hefty addition to the collection whichever way you look at it.

140

141

142

143

144

145

Plate 25.
(140) On-glaze enamel painting in green and pink of a tropical fish. 6ins. Mark: 'Minton Hollins & Co. etc.' c.1880. **(141)** *Painted on-glaze in green and pink enamel with a rather cheeky-looking fish. 6ins. Mark and date as (140).* **(142)** *Printed underglaze in green on a deep cream ground with a Japanese inspired design of a fish, a crane and flowers in circular reserves on a cracked ice and floral ground. 6ins. No mark. c.1880.* **(143)** *Moulded in medium high relief with a fish amongst reeds, decorated with a translucent turquoise glaze. 6ins. Mark: 'Minton Hollins & Co. etc.' c.1885.* Courtesy City Museum and Art Gallery, Stoke-on-Trent. **(144)** *A portion of a panel decorated in blues, yellow, green and cream with fish design. Full size of panel unknown, this tile 6ins. William de Morgan. c.1885.* Courtesy City Museum and Art Gallery, Stoke-on-Trent. **(145)** *Very fine solid clay circular panel, tube-line design of three fish, decorated in green, turquoise and orange translucent glazes. Diameter 10ins. No mark. c.1895-1900.* Courtesy City Museum and Art Gallery, Stoke-on-Trent.

5. LITERARY SUBJECTS

The leading designer of printed pictorial literary scenes was undoubtedly John Moyr Smith. Little has hitherto been published about him or his work, indeed very little seems to be known, but because of his prominence a special study has been made here.

The exact date and place of his birth are unknown, but he was almost certainly born in the 1840s and probably in the north of England (the surname Smith immensely complicates the task of searching through registers and directories, etc.). The first positive evidence occurs in the autobiography of Alfred Darbyshire (see bibliography):

"One of my earliest pupils and assistants was the late J Moyr Smith. Although he stuck manfully to the 'T square,' it was evident that he possessed artistic faculties of a high order. The development of these faculties was encouraged, and, acting on my advice, he went to London. If I remember rightly, he gained admission into the office of the late Sir Gilbert Scott."

Darbyshire set up on his own in 1862, so Smith must have joined him sometime after this date. They parted before Smith had successfully completed his articles of agreement.

The next major source of information is H.M. Spielman (see bibliography), who noted that Moyr Smith worked for *Fun* under Tom Hood's editorship, and was referred to the *Punch* editor Mark Lemon by 'Pater' Evans the printer, this being in 1869. Spielman continues:

"... but he did not work regularly ... until 1872. From this time forward he was one of *Punch's* recognised outside contributors, though he worked for it only when not engaged in making designs for art manufacturers. It was under Shirley Brooks's editorship, and later under Tom Taylor's, that he gave full reign to his passion for classic treatment, and his ornament, which gave a distinct *cachet* to *Punch* up to 1878 was not founded on a mere grotesque treatment of classical subjects, but was the fruit of a close study of and easy familiarity with heathen mythology, classical, Egyptian, and in particular, Norse."

Smith's *Punch* contributions range from the heading for the jottings column 'Punch at Lunch', to an animated drawing of Mr. Punch kicking Lord Lyttleton and Sir Henry Thring out of their office as Endowed

School Commissioners.[20] The style is instantly recognisable to anyone familiar with the tile designs.

It was whilst working in London in 1868 that Moyr Smith's first book, *Studies for Pictures: A Medley,* was published.

His association with Mintons seems to belong principally to the 1870s. There is evidence in the Minton archives which points to Smith having a freelance association with the Kensington Gore Studio, and some of his tile designs were in production in the early 1870s as he used them in his house at Putney, Plate 26(146). The association with Mintons certainly lasted up to 1878 when the Scott series was exhibited at Paris (see p.129) and continued spasmodically for sometime thereafter, see Plate 52(291 and 292).

In the 1870s he illustrated three more books, *Theseus, A Greek Fairy Legend,* London 1872, *An Argive Hero* by Plutarch, London, 1877, and an edition of Charles and Mary Lamb's *Shakespeare for Children, Tales from Shakespeare,* London, 1879. Smith's two major books came in the next decade. Firstly the volume, *Album of Decorative Figures,* London, 1882, is most important as a survey of his work and has been quoted from quite extensively with reference to the illustrations. His scholarly, almost antiquarian, tendencies find full expression in *Ornamental Interiors, ancient and modern,* London, 1887. This is a detailed historical survey which contains little of autobiographical note apart from one passage which is worth quoting in full:

"Here we may claim a small share in the art movement. Besides contributing some of the designs and lithographing all the illustrations in Collinson and Lock's catalogue, the author made some thousands of designs for furniture, decorations, wallpapers, carpets, tapestries, metal work and pottery, which were executed by firms of high standing. Many of these designs, however, were done in the studio of a well-known ornamentalist, and were given to the world as his work.

"About this time the author designed Marcus Ward's new style of Christmas cards and fairy tale books. The illustrations to these books were, we believe, a means of popularising the decorative treatment of figures; the varied sets of figure tiles executed by Messrs Mintons, by Messrs Minton Hollins & Co., and other firms from the author's designs also tended in that direction."

One would dearly love to discover the identity of the "well-known ornamentalist" who issued Smith's designs as his own. Speculation is fruitless, but the present writer would be delighted to hear of any soundly based hypothesis as to whom the ornamentalist might be.

Plate 26.
(146) *'The Green Parlour at Doune Lodge, Putney', the home of J. Moyr Smith, from* The Building News, *15th January, 1875.* **(147)** *Underglaze brown block print on an ivory ground with a scene from 'Una and the Satyrs' and a portrait of the author, Spenser. 8ins. Mark (signed) 'Moyr Smith' and 'Minton Hollins & Co. etc.' c.1875-1880.* **(148)** *Underglaze brown block print on an ivory ground with a scene from 'The Ancient Mariner' and a portrait of the author, Coleridge. 8ins. Mark: as (147).* **(149)** *Underglaze brown block print on an ivory ground of a scene from 'Sardanapalus' and a portrait of the author, Byron. 8ins. Mark: as (147).* **(150)** *Underglaze printed design in blue and grey-green on a white ground of a scene from 'Two Gentlemen of Verona. Act IV', 'WHO IS SYLVIA WHAT IS SHE.' 8ins. Mark (signed) Moyr Smith and 'Minton Hollins & Co. etc.' c.1880.*

146

147

148

149

150

151

152

153

154

155

156

The remainder of Moyr Smith's life and work can be swiftly told. His other recorded publications are, *Ancient Greek Female Costume,* London, 1882, and illustrations for an edition of Shakespeare's *The Tragedie of Macbeth,* London, 1889. His designs appeared in America in conjunction with the work of the Boston architect John Hubbard Sturges. Details of his work on the Sanatorium, Virginia Water, and elsewhere in the United States are given in the *Album of Decorative Figures.* He collaborated with the well-known English architect Bruce Talbert, for his initials appear on some of the illustrations in Talbert's *Gothic Forms* of 1867. Smith may also have had some form of working arrangement with Stacey Marks whom he could well have met through the Minton Kensington Studio. His decorative painting is hardly known at all, though one example was in the Handley Read Collection (D 152). Graves records that he exhibited on three occasions at the Royal Academy:

1888	Cat. 1760	End of a drawing room.
1889	Cat. 1484	"We fly by night midst troops of spirits" *(Macbeth).*
	Cat. 1984	Design for a ceiling at Bloomfield, Queen's Road, Richmond.
1894	Cat. 1453	A phrygian chant.

He is also recorded as exhibiting at three other London exhibitions in the period 1874-1889. Furthermore, in *Works Exhibited at the Royal Society of British Artists 1824-1893* he is noted as having shown in 1874/5 three further examples of his classically inspired works: 'Love's Young Dream'; 'A Greek Tragic Poet'; 'A Greek Rehearsal'.

This then is an outline life of Mintons' most prolific tile designer. His date of death was somewhere between 1894, when he exhibited at the Royal Academy, and 1897 when Alfred Darbyshire described him as "the late Mr. J. Moyr Smith". His self-portrait[21] is too small to give us a clear impression of his features, but he was thin of face with a moustache and pointed beard. Perhaps there are sufficient clues scattered in this brief survey to enable others with a taste for research to follow up this preliminary work and produce a fuller and more rounded picture.

Turning to the illustrations. The entire range from Plate 26-29(146-168) are from Moyr Smith's designs. Of particular interest is the illustration of the room he designed in his own home, Plate 26(146).

Smith describes the room as follows:

"This is a small room in a house recently built for me at Putney by Messrs. Robert Amiss & Co. ... The chimney piece is in unpolished oak with tiles in buff and brown, the subjects being selected from the Industrial and Historical sets designed by me for Messrs.

Plate 27.
(151) *Underglaze blue block print on a white slip ground depicting 'Hagar and Ishmael in the Desert'. 6ins. Signed 'M.S.' No factory mark on this example. Mintons China Works. Introduced c.1872.* **(152)** *As (151) 'Sampson Slaying the Philistines'. Signed 'M.S.' No factory mark.* **(153)** *As (151) 'Elijah and Samuel'. Signed 'M.S.' and the Mintons China Works mark.* **(154)** *Underglaze black block print on a white slip ground depicting 'Going up to Jerusalem', one of twelve 'New Testament' subjects. 6ins. Signed 'M.S.' (for Moyr Smith) and Mintons China Works mark. Introduced c.1872.* **(155)** *Underglaze block print in dark brown and blue on a buff background, depicting 'Vivien', one of a series from Tennyson's 'Idylls of the King'. 6ins. No mark but from Mintons China Works. Introduced c.1873-1874.* **(156)** *As (155) 'Excalibur'. Signed 'Moyr Smith'. Unmarked.*

Mintons. The tiles nearest the grate have floral decoration on a dark blue background; they are of Dutch manufacture. The subjects of the stained glass in this room are Egyptian, Greek and Gothic art. These, as well as the mantelpiece, were done by Messrs. Cox and Son, the actual painting of the glass, however, being done by myself ..."

The present owner kindly informs me that: "the glass mentioned in Smith's article in the *Building News* is still existant — but not the tiles or mantelpiece by Cox — the house having undergone many changes during its various tenancies". The three examples in Plate 26(147, 148 and 149) are from a series of 'Authors and Their Works' done for Minton Hollins & Co. The other titles in the series are:

'Virgil: Aeneas and Dido'
'Shelley: the Witch of Atlas'
'Chaucer: Patient Griselda'
'Goethe: Walpurgis Night'
'Dante: Francesca'
'Scott: The Death of Marmion'
'Burns: The Jolly Beggars'

As these tiles do not appear in either of the Minton & Hollins catalogues we have seen, it is not known whether there were ten or twelve tiles in this series. Similarly, Plate 26(150) is an isolated specimen and no catalogue evidence indicates the full scope of the series.

'The Old Testament' series is by Mintons China Works, pattern 1335, the first of the printed pictorial series Smith designed for them. Three examples are illustrated in Plate 27(151, 152 and 153). The full twelve titles as given in the printed factory catalogue are:

'Adam and Eve driven out of Eden'
'Death of Abel'
'Lot's Wife'
'Hagar and Ishmael'
'Abraham offering Isaac'
'Jacob's Dream'
'Joseph before Pharaoh'
'Death of the firstborn'
'Finding of Moses'
'Samson slaying the Philistines'
'Eli and Samuel'
'David playing before Saul'

The 'New Testament' example, Plate 27(154), is given as pattern 1346 and the series has twelve subjects listed in the Minton catalogue as:

'Adoration of the Wise Men'
'Going up to Jerusalem to the feast'
'Christ disputing with the doctors'

Plate 28.
(157) *As (155) 'Elaine'. Signed 'Moyr Smith'. Unmarked.* **(158)** *As (155) 'Morte D'Arthur'. Signed Moyr Smith. Mark: 'Mintons China Works etc.'* **(159)** *Underglaze block print in dark brown, grey and green on a white slip ground, depicting 'Macbeth. III. iv'. 6ins. One of twenty-four subjects from 'Shakespeare', designed and signed by J. Moyr Smith. Mark: 'Mintons China Works etc.' Introduced c.1873/4.* **(160)** *As (159) 'Much Ado. IV. ii.'* **(161)** *As (159) 'Twelfth Night. III. iv'.* **(162)** *As (159) '1st Part King Henry IV. II . iv.'*

157

158

159

160

161

162

'Christ turning water into wine'
'Christ stilling the tempest'
'Christ blessing little children'
'Christ walking on the sea'
'Jairus' Daughter'
'The Temptation'
'The Crucifixion'
'Christ mocked by the soldiers'
'Christ appearing to Mary Magdalene'
The Tennyson 'Idylls of the King' series, pattern 1465, Plate 27(155 and 156), and Plate 28(157 and 158), was one of the most popular of Minton's series and was done in at least four different colour combinations — as shown in Colour Plate IV — the most striking being the blue, white and dark brown version. The subjects are:

'The coming of Arthur', the lady of the Lake gives the sword to King Arthur.
'Gareth and Lynette', Gareth entering the town.
'Gareth and Lynette', Gareth and Lynette on their journey, Lynette jeers at Gareth.
'Pelleas and Etarre', Pelleas first sees Etarre.
'Pelleas and Etarre', Pelleas finds Gawin and Etarre asleep in the Pavilion.
'Enid', Enid and Limours.
'Enid', Geraint slays Dorm.
'Elaine', Elaine's body in the barge.
'Vivien', Vivien puts forth the charm on Merlin.
'The Last Tournament', Tristram and Isolt.
'Guinevere', King Arthur and Guinevere.
'Morte D'Arthur', King Arthur in the barge with the three Queens.

'Shakespeare', pattern 1408, Plate 28(159, 160, 161, 162) and Colour Plate IV, was also a most popular series, again done in several colour combinations and upon tablewares. It is worth noting that the pattern number given refers to the first entry in the pattern book or printed catalogue, different colour combinations were given different pattern numbers. Also, unlike the Wedgwood examples, the Minton pattern numbers do not appear on the tiles. They are included here for reference, and as a possible help to comparative dating. Twenty-four subjects were designed for the Shakespeare series, as listed below:

'Romeo and Juliet', Act I, scene i and Act III, scene ii.
'Macbeth', Act III, scene iv and Act V, scene vii.
'The Tempest', Act I, scene ii and Act II, scene ii.
'Cymbeline', Act II, scene ii.
'Hamlet', Act I, scene i.
'Antony and Cleopatra', Act IV, scene iv and Act V, scene ii.
'Winter's Tale', Act V, scene iii.
'King Lear', Act I, scene i and Act V, scene iii.
'Twelfth Night', Act II, scene iii and Act III, scene iv.
'Midsummer Night's Dream', Act IV, scene i.
'Troilus and Cressida', Act IV, scene ii.
'Merchant of Venice', Act II, scene ii and Act IV, scene i.
'Othello', Act I, scene iii.
'Taming of the Shrew', Act IV, scene iii.

'Much ado about Nothing', Act IV, scene ii.

'Timon of Athens', Act III, scene vi.

'King Henry the IV', Act II, scene iv.

It is worth noting that the corner motifs to this series were also used for 'Gastronomical', Plate 58(325-328). In all other cases of Minton tiles, the corner motif seems to have been unique to a series. It is thus of assistance in placing doubtful scenes in their correct series.

The most attractive of all the literary designs is the 8-inch series of pictures from 'Waverley', pattern 1607, Plate 29(163-168). Not only is the composition particularly vigorous and harmonious in outline and detail, but the colour combination of black, white, grey and yellowish green also helps to create outstanding and evocative pictures. This set was first brought out at the Paris Exhibition of 1878. Tiles such as these are every bit as desirable in the eyes of most collectors as some of the more consciously 'arty' wares of those who affected to despise the machine-made products of their own age. It is because of work of this quality that the reputation of Moyr Smith is rising, as one of the outstanding designers of the printed pictorial tile.

The other six titles in the series are:

'Ivanhoe', The Death of Bois Gilbert

'The Bride of Lammermoor', Ravenswood and Lucy

'Old Mortality', Morton and Burley

'Kenilworth', Amy Robsart and Leicester

'The Talisman', Sir Kenneth and the Dwarf

'Quentin Durward', Louis, Quentin and Jacqueline

It is worth noting that Moyr Smith either signed or initialled (IMS or MS) many of his designs, but the initials particularly are often difficult to locate as they are partially concealed in the picture, and may even be printed in mirror image.

This brief biography is concluded with a check list of the series designed by J. Moyr Smith for Mintons and the other manufacturers, with a note of the relevant illustrations:

For Mintons China Works:

'Old Testament', Plate 27(151-153)

'New Testament', Plate 27(154)

'Industrial', Plate 52(289 and 290)

'Early English History', Plate 47(265 and 266)

'Fairy Tales', Plate 35(198) and Figures 49, 50 and 51

'Spirit of the Flowers', possibly Plate 9(49) and Figure 27.

'Shakespeare', Plate 28(159-162)

'Idylls of the King, Tennyson', Plate 27(155 and 156) and Plate 28(157 and 158)

'Classical Figures with Musical Instruments', Plate 52(294)

'Husbandry', Plate 52(293)

'Waverley', Plate 29(163-168)

'Thomson's Seasons', Plate 43(241 and 242)

'Anacreon', Plate 57(319 and 320)

'Arts and Sciences', Plate 52(291-292)

For Minton Hollins & Co.:

'Writers and their Works', Plate 26(147-149)

'Shakespeare', Plate 26(150)

'Medieval English History', Plate 47(269 and 270)

Colour Plate IX. A selection of decorative techniques on a variety of pictorial designs.
Top row: Left: 'Autumn', underglaze block printed and decorated with a translucent blue/grey glaze. 6ins. Mark: 'Minton Hollins & Co. etc.' c.1882. Centre: 'Yachting', underglaze printed from an etched design on a cream slip ground. 6ins. Mark: 'Minton Hollins & Co. etc.' c.1890. Right: 'Where are you going to...' painted in enamel colours on-glaze, on a white slip ground, from a design by Walter Crane (p.153), 6ins. Mark: 'Minton China Works etc.' c.1880.
Second row: Left: 'Night, printed underglaze in black on a white slip ground. 6ins. No mark. c.1800-85. Centre: 'Trumpeter', painted underglaze, designed by Edward Hammond (p.191), 6ins. Mark: 'Mintons Art Pottery Studio, Kensington Gore'. c.1872-85. Right: 'Miss Miggs...', underglaze printed from a basic stipple engraving. (Miss Miggs appears in Dickens's Barnaby Rudge). 6ins. No mark. c.1880.
Third row: Left: 'Longbowman', outline printed and enamelled overglaze in colours (p.188), 6ins. Mark: Copeland. c.1878. Centre: 'Reading Stories', underglaze printed on a cream slip ground (p.158), 6ins. Mark: 'Maw & Co. etc.' c.1882-85. Right: 'Music', outline printed and enamelled overglaze in colours (p.188), 6ins. Mark: Copeland. c.1878.
Bottom row: Left: 'Morning', block printed underglaze on a white slip ground. 8ins. Mark: 'Minton Hollins & Co. etc.' c.1875-80. Centre: 'August', outline printed overglaze and enamelled overglaze in colours (p.171), 6ins. Mark: Copeland. c.1879. Right: 'Evening' as 'Morning'.

Colour Plate X. A selection of decorative colour-glaze finishes. All 6ins.
Top row: Left: 'Longfellow', moulded in high relief. Mark: 'M.E. & Co. B' (Malkin Edge & Co. Burslem). c.1890. Centre: Lord Salisbury', moulded in medium high relief. Mark: 'J.C. Edwards, Ruabon B.W.' (Brick Works) c.1896. Right: 'Shakespeare', as 'Longfellow' but unmarked.
Second row: Left: Low relief moulding. Mark: 'Rd.No. 445108' (for 1904) 'England'. Centre: Moulded in high relief. Mark: 'Minton Hollins & Co. etc.' c.1890. Right: Moulded in low relief. Mark: a raised 'C', no attribution, c.1905.
Third row: Left: Moulded in low relief. Mark: 'P' for Pilkingtons and 'Rd.No. 397655' (for 1902) designed by C.F.A. Voysey. Centre: tube-lined. Mark: 'Rd.No. 261518' (for 1895) 'England.' Right: Moulded in low relief. Mark: 'P' for Pilkingtons and 'Rd.No. 380754' (for 1901), designer not known.
Bottom row: Left: Painted underglaze in coloured slips (barbotine, see p.47). No mark. c.1880. Centre: Moulded in low relief. No marks. c.1905. Right: Moulded in high relief. Mark: 'No. M304 M' and monogram 'JHB' for J.H. Barrett & Co. c.1900.

Figure 45. 'The sixth age ... the lean and slippered pantaloon,' painted in enamel colours against a gilt background. One of a set of 'Seven Ages' plaques designed and signed by Stacey Marks. 20½ins. by 10ins. Mark: 'Mintons Kensington Gore Studio'. 1872/1873 date marks. Courtesy Sotheby's Belgravia.

'Nursery Rhymes', Plate 37(208 and 209)
For W.B. Simpson:
'Nursery Rhymes', Plate 37(206 and 207)
'The Months', Plate 44(247 and 248)

Further examples from a number of these series are illustrated in Colour Plates IV and V.

Almost certainly there will be unrecorded designs. The writer would be grateful to hear of these.

It is perhaps inevitable that Shakespearean scenes should figure prominently upon tiles of the 1870s and 1880s. The English stage was enjoying a great period of successful expansion. Henry Irving was astonishing the capital and Charles Calvert had enraptured Manchester with his lavishly authentic Shakespearean 'Revivals'. We have already noted Moyr Smith's lengthy series for Mintons. Clearly Minton Hollins did not wish to be left behind and their series is a sensitively drawn and charming piece of work. In addition to the two subjects illustrated in Plate 30(169 and 170), we also have 'Juliet and Nurse' and 'Othello relating his adventures'. Furthermore 'Hamlet' and 'The Merchant of Venice' are illustrated in the factory catalogue.

Plate 29.
(163) *Underglaze print in grey, black and yellowish green on a white slip ground, depicting a scene from 'The Antiquary'. Ch. XXI. 'Sir Arthur and Dousterswivel'. One of a series of twelve subjects from Sir Walter Scott's 'Waverley' novels; pattern 1607. 8ins. Designed and signed by Moyr Smith. Mark 'Mintons China Works etc.' The series was introduced and exhibited in Paris in 1878.* **(164)** *As (163) 'Fortunes of Nigel. XXVII. Nigel and King James'.* **(165)** *As (163) 'Rob Roy. XXIII. In Glasgow Tolbooth.'* **(166)** *As (163) 'Guy Mannering. LIV. Meg Merrilees and Hatteraick.'* **(167)** *As (163) 'Heart of Midlothian. XXXVII. Jeanie and the Queen'. No mark, but printed on the back with the name of the dealer: 'William England, Mosaic and Tile Works, Bury Place, Oxford Street, London. Established 186? (illegible).* **(168)** *As (163) 'Fair Maid of Perth. XXIII. Bonthron Accuses Rothsay'.*

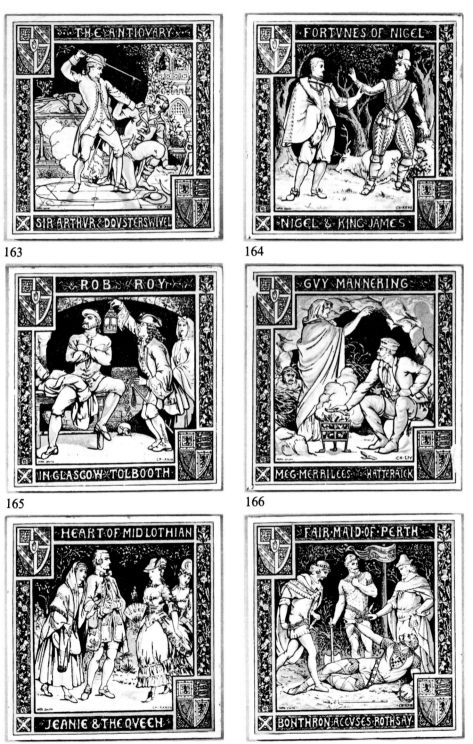

163

164

165

166

167

168

169

170

171

172

173

174

The firm of E. Smith of Coalville was responsible for a Shakespearean series, Plate 30(171 and 172). 'Malvolio' from 'Twelfth Night' has also been noted. Each tile is initialled by the designer 'J.B.', but no positive identification can be given for the artist.

The five examples in Plate 30(173 and 174), Plate 31(175), and Figures 45 and 46, were designed by Henry Stacey Marks, RA (1829-1898). Marks is one of the many Victorian artists whose work is not quite of the highest rank — he is not a Rossetti or an Alma Tadema — but who has perhaps been unduly neglected. His output was varied and included illustrations for the Routledge Shilling *Toy Books,* and simple commissions such as menu cards and memorial programmes. Of more substance is his painting of the proscenium frieze of the redecorated Prince's Theatre Manchester in 1869 with a scene of Shakespeare enthroned between Tragedy and Comedy and supported by figures from the plays, and his design for the frieze of the Royal Albert Hall. Marks worked from a studio in St. John's Wood, and here he designed the business card for Minton's Art Pottery Studio (Figure 6).

Looking at a photograph of a dignified, stoutish figure[22] one is rather surprised to read[23] of a prank which took place in the home of the Agnew family, 'Summer Hill', Pendleton, Salford, in 1870. Apparently, one Sunday morning when the Agnew family was at church, their guests, G.D. Leslie, F. Walker, J.K. Hodgson and Stacey Marks "took possession of the newly-erected billiard room ... a happy thought, with a spirit of mischief in it seized the four distinguished painters. With billiard chalk and soot from the fireplace they proceeded to decorate the walls ... if I remember rightly Marks exercised his humour by drawing cats and dogs as though suspended from the gas brackets." The pictures "were intended as a pleasant surprise for their host and hostess." Seemingly they were successful, for twenty-five years later the pictures still adorned the walls!

Marks had a close connection with Mintons Kensington Studio, and in the Minton archives there are many fine watercolour drawings of Shakespearean subjects, especially of the 'Seven Ages of Man' series, Plate 31(175), for which he devised many alternative designs. As well as the 6-inch tile series he was responsible for a series of plaques, 20ins. by 12ins., examples of which were in the Handley Read Collection (D61, D62). They were dated 1873 and described in the *Art Journal* of that year (p.279) as "distinguished for all the Touchstoneish humour in which his

Plate 30.
(169) *Underglaze print in shades of brown on an ivory ground of the scene of Juliet's death from 'Romeo and Juliet'. Set in a circular frame with a leaf pattern corner motif. 6ins. Mark: 'Minton Hollins & Co.' c.1875-1880.* **(170)** *As (169) printed with a scene depicting Ferdinand and Miranda from 'The Tempest'. Mark: 'Minton Hollins & Co.'* **(171)** *Underglaze blue printed design on a white ground depicting a scene from Act I scene i of 'The Merchant of Venice'. "Lend it not as to thy friend." 8ins. Signed with the initials 'J.B.' (as yet unidentified). Mark: 'E. Smith, Coalville'. c.1885.* **(172)** *As (171) printed in blue with a scene from 'The Tempest', Act I Scene ii. "No I will resist such entertainment till mine enemy has more power."* **(173)** *Block printed in grey on an ivory ground with underglaze painting in tan depicting a scene from 'The Tempest', with Caliban, Stephano and Trinculo. Initialled 'H.S.M.' for Henry Stacey Marks. 8ins. No mark. No attribution. c.1880.* **(174)** *As (173) printed with scenes of 'Falstaff acting the King' from 'Henry IV Part I.' Initialled by Stacey Marks, but otherwise unmarked.*

brush loves to revel, and for all his wonted medieval lore.'' A set of these large plaques was sold at Sotheby's Belgravia, 15th February, 1973, Lot 6, for £290 (see Figure 45). One of the earliest of these sets produced was executed for the Duke of Westminster for Eaton Hall in Cheshire, now unhappily demolished. His quaint bird life, 'Seven Ages' is shown in Plate 22(124 and 125).

Figure 46. Printed in outline und painted in colours with a pseudo-medieval design of a man and woman. 9ins. square. Mark: 'Mintons Art Pottery Studio Kensington Gore' and 'MINTON' impressed. Initialled 'H S M' for Stacey Marks. c.1873.

Marks's delightful neo-medievalism can also be seen on 'The Falconer' panels he designed for Mintons[24] and on the pilgrim bottle also by Mintons now in the Victoria and Albert Museum, which is illustrated both by Elizabeth Aslin and Bevis Hillier.[25] The original watercolour drawings for this latter are preserved by Mintons. A collector who is fortunate enough to obtain even one of Marks's tiles "outlined and painted in colours by hand", such as that in Figure 46, can feel well pleased. As G.D. Leslie wrote of him in the *Furniture Gazette*, 1873: "he has designed for stained-glass, he paints on china plates and wooden cupboards, he designs furniture and costumes and embroidery ... He is my ideal of what a thorough artist should be.''

Plate 31.
(175) *Printed and coloured design from the Minton tile pattern book (Jones, Minton MSS, No. 1842). 'The Soldier' from 'The Seven Ages of Man', designed by Henry Stacey Marks. Pattern 1900. Introduced c.1882.* Courtesy Royal Doulton Tableware Ltd. **(176)** *On-glaze painted design in black and red on a white ground of 'The Schoolboy' from 'The Seven Ages of Man'. Artist unknown. 6ins. Mark: 'Minton Hollins & Co. etc.' c.1880.* **(177)** *Watercolour design from the Copeland pattern book depicting the jester Yorick bearing the child Hamlet on his back (Act V Scene i, Hamlet to Horatio whilst examining the skull: "A fellow of infinite jest, of most excellent fancy; he hath borne me on his back a thousand times"). Pattern book number 1144. Artist unknown. c.1880.* Courtesy The Spode Museum. **(178)** *Mounted watercolour drawing of one of the 'Scenes from Shakespeare' depicting Macbeth and the three witches. For an 8-inch tile. Artist unknown.* Courtesy The Spode Museum. **(179)** *Underglaze print in lilac blue and white of 'Lysander' from the Wedgwood series of 'A Midsummer Night's Dream', pattern T 278. Mark: 'Josiah Wedgwood & Sons Ltd.' Probably designed by Thomas Allen (see text). c.1878.* **(180)** *Print from the Wedgwood tile pattern book depicting 'Moth' from 'A Midsummer Night's Dream series'.* Courtesy The Wedgwood Museum, Barlaston.

175

176

177

178

179

180

181

182

183

184

185

186

Other factories made 'Seven Ages' tiles. A Minton Hollins example, Plate 31(176), has a charming simplicity in contrast to the meticulous medievalism of Marks. Maw too produced a printed 'Seven Ages' series on 6-inch tiles. There is no note of the designer, though each title (pattern numbers 2134-2140) is given on the face (see Figure 14).

From the evidence of their pattern books, Copelands too produced a Sheakespearean series, the first tile of which was brought out early in 1878. As Plate 31(177 and 178) shows, the original, mounted watercolour drawings for the series still exist at the factory, as well as similarly executed entries in the pattern books. The form of lettering on the tile face makes this series quite unmistakable.

In all, the Spode Museum has fourteen mounted 8-inch watercolour Shakespeare designs, and one of 6-inch size — 'Hotspur'. Each is lettered in this very idiosyncratic style with the names of the characters. Of the fifteen designs, which include two different 'Falstaff' scenes, only three also appear in the pattern book. One can only assume that many of the trial drawings were either not made or not entered up — consequently these have not been listed. However, seven designs do appear in pattern books 4 and 5 and are listed below with their pattern numbers. The three marked with an asterisk duplicate with the mounted loose designs:

928 'Touchstone', 'Rosalind and Celia'
1082 'Slender', 'Anne', 'Page'
1087 'Audrey', 'Touchstone'
* 1099 'Pericles', 'Thaisa', 'Simonides'
* 1102 'Kathryn', 'Petruchio'
* 1144 'Hamlet', 'Yorick'
1160 'Ferdinand', 'Ariel'

Additionally, 'Ajax and Thersites' has been reported on a finished tile. Clearly, the full extent of the series is not represented in the pattern books.

Dating from 1878 and entered in the Wedgwood pattern book as pattern T 278 is one of the most sought after of all tile series. This is the set of ten designs depicting scenes from Shakespeare's 'A Midsummer Night's Dream'. Plate 31(179 and 180) shows two of these most desirable pieces which almost certainly were designed by Thomas Allen and which occur in brown, and blue as well as in the lilac of the 'Lysander' example. 8-inch versions have also been noted with a border of leaves surrounding the basic 6-inch square picture. The ten titles listed in the pattern book are:

'Demetrius'
'Lysander'
'Hermia'
'Moth'
'Puck'
'Peasblossom'
'Mustard'

Plate 32.
(181-186) *Six underglaze block printed designs in brown upon a cream body, depicting scenes from 'Aesop's Fables'. Attributed to Thomas Allen of Mintons and Wedgwood (see text). All 6ins. All marked: 'Mintons China Works etc.' c.1872-1875. Many later examples, some printed in blue, are known.*

'Helena'
'Oberon'
'Titania'.

Bruce Tattersall, formerly the Curator of the Wedgwood Museum, Barlaston, in an important article on 'Victorian Wedgwood', *The Antique Collector*, May 1974, illustrates two examples of this series, 'Oberon' and 'Titania', and he firmly attributes the 'Titania' design to Thomas Allen (1831-1915).

Allen is a most interesting figure. He was a native of the Potteries, a student at the Stoke School of Art, and was subsequently employed at Mintons. In 1852 he was awarded the first ever National Scholarship to study at the School of Design in London, where he spent two years. On his return to Mintons he continued to decorate the fashionable Sèvres-revival porcelain with a brilliance which rivalled if not surpassed the work of the famous 'Foreign Legion' of artists which Léon Arnoux, the great Art Director, had gathered round himself. Allen became restless especially as his wages of about £3 per week in 1868 were far below those of the foreign artists. For example, Antonin Boullemeir — also a figure painter — received £400 a year. In 1876 at the age of forty-five Allen left Mintons for Wedgwood, and in 1880 became their Art Director.[26]

Wedgwoods are recorded as having begun tile production c.1870. From the evidence of the factory pattern book, it seems unlikely that any figure patterns were produced before Thomas Allen joined the firm in 1876. A portfolio of Allen's drawings is in the Museum at Barlaston and included therein are original designs and sketches for the 'Ivanhoe' series, two of which Mr. Tattersall illustrates in his article. The scenes shown in Plate 33 (189 and 190) are two of the six subjects printed in the pattern book, though it is there stated that it is a series of ten. The four other known subjects are:

'The black knight exchanges buffets with Friar Tuck'
'Rowena granting safe escort to Rebecca and her father'
'Front de Boeff extorting silver from Isaac the Jew'
'Rebecca repelling the Templar'

Examples of these designs are also known on tableware. Also in the Allen portfolio is the original design for Plate 33(188), pattern T 273 in the pattern book. This too in Mr. Tattersall's opinion is the work of Thomas Allen and has also been noted on porcelain teawares. The date of the introduction of this pattern is c.1878 — pattern T 275 was registered at the Patent Office in March 1878. The 'Aesop's Fables' tiles in Plate 32(181-186) are Minton products. They appear early in the printed catalogue as pattern 1364, and were thus contemporary with some of the earliest of the Moyr Smith patterns of c.1872-1875. What is especially interesting about this series is the stylistic resemblance between them and the Wedgwood 'Where the Carcase is', Plate 33(188), even to the form of the lettering. Certainly these designs have more in common than they have with any of Moyr Smith's work, virtually all of which, even from the first, seems to have been signed by him. The 'Aesop's Fables' were produced when Thomas Allen was at Mintons, 'Where the Carcase is' when he was at Wedgwood where he designed a great many tiles. There does seem sufficient evidence to suggest a tentative attribution of the Minton 'Aesop's Fables' series to Thomas Allen. The six subjects not illustrated are:

'The fox and the goat in the well'
'King Log and King Stork'
'The tortoise and the eagle'
'The wolf and the crane'
'The monkey and the cat'
'The fox and the stork'.

Thomas Allen, a native son of Staffordshire retired in 1900. He has been described by several commentators as "the best Staffordshire porcelain painter of figure subjects of the nineteenth century". Fine examples of his work in this medium can be seen in the Minton Museum at Stoke. His designs on Wedgwood tiles are well worthy of the attention of collectors.

Plate 33(187) and several of the examples in Figure 14 are from a series of 'Aesop's Fables' produced by Maw. Technically the standard of printing is somewhat below that of Mintons and Wedgwood, but the designs have a clear individuality. The initials 'C O M' are clearly visible on the face of the tile and these would seem to fit C.O. Murray (1842-1923) a protégé of Moyr Smith. He possibly worked for a time — probably freelance — for Mintons, though no record of him was noted in the factory archives. As there is no record of Murray in the Maw Order Account Book either, his relationship with them may also have been freelance.[27]

The pattern book/catalogue preserved at Clive House, Shrewsbury gives the pattern numbers of the series as 2225-2236, and the subjects:
'The old man and his ass'
'Small fish better than none'
'The goose which laid the golden eggs'
'Two companions and the bear'
'The boy who cried wolf'
'The swan among the geese'
'Death and the woodman'
'Milkmaid'
'The old man and his sons'
'Pilgrims and the oysters'
'Doctors and the dying man'
'The countryman and the snake'.

Each tile appears to have been titled on the face. The series was decorated in more than one colour combination.

Maws were also the producers of a set of Biblical scenes, Pattern 2141-2151, printed on 8-inch tiles (see Figure 14 for examples). The subjects are:
'Christ entering Jerusalem'
'The Rich Man and Lazarus'
'The Barren Fig Tree'
'A Miracle Healing'
'The Lost Sheep'
'The Wicked Husbandman'
'The Sower'
'The Pharisee and the Publican'
'The Hidden Treasure'
'The Lost Piece of Silver'
'The Foolish Virgins'
'The Prodigal Son'

187

188

189

190

191

192

Each tile has a pattern of foliage or fruit in the corner, and from the examples noted they appear to be finished in a variety of coloured glazes. A similar finish was imparted to another Maw series that was based upon the work of the poet Longfellow — 'The Hanging of the Crane'.[28]

Figure 47. Block printed in brown upon cream with a man cowering from a hooded figure holding a dripping axe, representing 'Death and the Woodman' from 'Aesop's Fables' series. 6ins. Mark: 'Minton Hollins & Co.' c.1880.

Minton Hollins too produced a set of Biblical scenes.[29] Four of the subjects are depicted in their printed catalogue, the pictures are untitled, and no full list of titles is available. Figure 47 illustrates the Minton Hollins 'Death and the Woodman', one of their 'Aesop's Fables' series produced in 6-inch and 8-inch size and easily identified by the border pattern. A set of twenty-four studies from 'Aesop's Fables' all hand painted and framed, was exhibited in 1972 at the Fine Arts Society and illustrated in the catalogue *The Aesthetic Movement and the Cult of Japan.* One of the tiles had the name 'Heaton' pencilled on the reverse, and this whole group, which was clearly by the same hand, was attributed to Clement Heaton of the firm Heaton & Butler & Co. As they do not resemble any known series from the firm Minton & Hollins whose mark they bore, it would be safer to regard these tiles as examples of the work of the outside decorator, not a designer for the factory. Other examples of Heaton's work may well be discovered on the blanks of Minton Hollins or other firms.

Plate 33.
(187) *Underglaze black transfer print of a scene depicting 'The Countryman & the Snake'. One of twelve 'Aesop's Fables'. 6ins. Mark: On the face 'C O M' (probably C.O. Murray, see p.141). Otherwise unmarked, but made by Maw c.1880+.* **(188)** *Print from the Wedgwood tile pattern book 'Where the carcase is, there will the eagles be gathered together', pattern T 273. Attributed to Thomas Allen (see text). c.1878.* Courtesy The Wedgwood Museum, Barlaston. **(189)** *Print from the Wedgwood tile pattern book, 'Ivanhoe and Rowena'. One of ten scenes from 'Ivanhoe', pattern T 335. Attributed to Thomas Allen (see text). c.1880.* Courtesy The Wedgwood Museum, Barlaston. **(190)** *As (189) 'Wamba and Gurtherd the Swineherd' from 'Ivanhoe'.* Courtesy The Wedgwood Museum, Barlaston. **(191)** *Watercolour drawing depicting 'Robin Hood's Last Shoot'. One of a series of twenty-five such designs for Copeland tiles (see text). Pattern 978, for a 6-inch tile introduced c.1878.* Courtesy The Spode Museum. **(192)** *Watercolour design from the Copeland tile pattern book depicting a medieval king with a sword over his shoulder and the legend 'AMOR OMNIA VINCIT', pattern 913. c.1877.* Courtesy The Spode Museum.

The illustrations in Plate 33(191 and 192) are from Copeland. The 'Robin Hood' series with its distinctive thistle corner motif was almost certainly first produced in 1878. Three of the subjects are illustrated in the pattern book, but no fewer than twenty-five designs exist in the form of watercolour drawings. How many were actually produced is a matter for speculation, but the full list is appended exactly as they appear on the face of the tile, with the excruciating mock-medieval spelling. Earthenware plates with the Copeland mark have been noted bearing the 'Robin Hood' scenes in underglaze blue transfer printing:

'Lyttle John Decoys Sheriff'
'Lyttle John and Ye Sheriff's Cook'
'Lyttle John's Prisoner'
'Lyttle John & the IV Beggars'
'Robyn Defeats & Kills Sheriff'
'Ye Poore Knight's Story'
'Robyn Hood & Ye French Pirate' (pattern 1101)
'Lyttle John's Baptism'
'The Poore Knight Asketh for more Time'
'Syr Rich'ds Ladye Askes Robyn Hood to Rescue Hyr Husband'
'Robyn Hood & Ye Abbot'
'Robyn Hood as a Butcher'
'Robyn Hood's Last Shoot' (pattern 978)
'Robyn Hood as a Potter Dines With the Sheriff'
'Robyn and Tinker Hood'
'Robyn Hood and Ye Curtal *(sic)* Friar'
'Robyn Hood Slays Guy of Gisborne'
'Robyn Hood and Ye Tanner'
'Lyttle John Wounded & Saved by Much'
'Ye Bishop Says Mass Unwillingly'
'The King Reveals Hymself' (pattern 1100)
'Robyn's Visit to Squire Gamwel'
'Lyttle John Gives Ye Poore Knight Good Measure'
'Robyn Hood and Lyttle John'
'Robyn Hood & Ye Beggar'

The title of the scene in Plate 33(192) is in Latin. The piece is included as an example of a Copeland pattern which was 'exclusive' as is indicated by the pattern book entry, "the above to be done only for Carr Brothers and Wilson, Sheffield in Great Britain".

6. CHILDREN: NURSERY RHYMES AND FAIRY TALES

Starting in 1865 with the publication of *Cock Robin,* illustrated by Walter Crane, the ensuing two decades saw a flood of excitingly coloured children's story books. Crane's famous *Toy Books* published by Routledge were immensely popular, and were soon followed by Randolph Caldecott's *Picture Books* and the works of Kate Greenaway. The Victorian middle and artisan classes were accustomed to representations of children not only from such books but also from Marcus Ward's Christmas cards, from calendars and from the host of sentimental semi-religious literature which was so fashionable. It is small wonder that the designers of the period should use these popular motifs on tiles for general use, as well as on those intended specifically for the nursery or the children's ward in hospitals.[30]

The first two illustrations of tiles in this section, Plate 34(193 and 194) are photographs from the Copeland pattern book. The children depicted in eighteenth century costume are really small adults engaged upon adult activities. There are three other subjects to accompany (193), 'Music', 'Literature' and 'Science'. A somewhat different convention governs the design of the unattributed etched tile in Plate 34(195). This would appear to be part of a series of country activities of which two other examples are known, a shepherd boy and a mill and waterwheel scene (see Plate 15(87). With Plate 34(196) we have another contrasting style, this time from Mintons. The somewhat Puck-like elf is one of a series of twelve 'Elfins', pattern 1410. Another example, the elfin with the lobster is shown as Figure 48. These tiles are rare and appear to have been introduced c.1875-1876.

The panel tile in Plate 34(197) is part of a set of at least three which together make some kind of frieze. This type of panel was extremely popular in the late 1870s and 1880s, and although the single-tile cherub design is rather rare, the use of *putti* or cherubs for panels and architectural faience was widespread well into the 1890s. In the Minton archives there are scores of watercolour drawings of such schemes by William Wise, H.W. Foster and Antonin Boullemeir. To our eyes, they are amongst the least attractive of the types of design from this period, but this is not a universally accepted judgement.

The twelve tiles designed by Moyr Smith for the Minton series of 'Fairy Tales', Plate 35(198) and Figures 49, 50 and 51 is certainly not Moyr Smith at his best. The lovable looking lion would hardly frighten a pauper much less a Princess. The full series comprises:

'Golden Locks', (Figure 51)
'Snowdrop', (Figure 49)
'Frog Prince'
'The Six Swans', (Figure 50)
'Cinderella'
'The Little Tailor'
'Blue Beard'
'Rumpelstilzchen'
'Puss in Boots'
'Jack and the Beanstalk'
'Beauty and the Beast', Plate 35(198)
'The Sleeping Beauty'

Figure 48. Underglaze block print in blue on a white ground of an elfin taunting a lobster, one of twelve 'Elfins'. 6ins. Mark: 'Minton China Works etc.' c.1875-1880.

Figure 49. Underglaze block print in black on a buff ground with 'Snowdrop' one of twelve 'Fairy Tales'. 6ins. No mark, but Mintons China Works and signed 'J M S' — Moyr Smith. c.1875-1880.

Copelands produced a 'Nursery Rhyme' series, Plate 35(199), which was of good quality and attractive design. The pattern number is 1338 and this places it well into the 1880s, possibly as late as 1887. The designer is unknown. No other subject appears in the pattern book, but watercolour drawings (some of them with the subject in a circular frame and set cross-cornered) exist for the other subjects listed below:

'Old Mother Hubbard'
'Simple Simon'
'Little Red Riding Hood'
'Little Boy Blue'
'Old King Cole'
'Taffy'
'Tom Ye Piper's Son'

Wedgwood made a set of six tiles telling the story of 'Red Riding Hood', Plate 35(200 and 201). The scenes depict her leaving her cottage; meeting the wolf; picking flowers; and the wolf in bed, together with the two final scenes illustrated here.

One of the most attractive fairy tale series we have come across is the anonymous set which in a run of ten tells the story of Cinderella, Plate 35(202 and 203). We first saw these *in situ* forming the window slab in a fishmonger's shop. They looked splendidly bright and fresh, and one

Plate 34.
(193) *Watercolour design from the Copeland tile pattern book, pattern 952, depicting a boy in eighteenth century costume seated at an easel painting. For an 8-inch tile. Introduced c.1878.* Courtesy The Spode Museum. **(194)** *Watercolour design from the Copeland tile pattern book, pattern 888, depicting a boy and girl in eighteenth century costume standing back to back. For a 6-inch tile. Introduced c.1876.* Courtesy The Spode Museum. **(195)** *Underglaze transfer print in black on a cream ground depicting two boys eating fruit. Set in a circular frame with a border pattern of foliage. No mark, no signature. c.1885.* **(196)** *Print from the Minton tile pattern book (Jones, Minton MSS No. 1842) depicting an elf seated upon a toadstool, one of twelve 'Elfins'. For 6-inch tile. Designer unknown. Introduced c.1875-1876.* Courtesy Royal Doulton Tableware Ltd. **(197)** *On-glaze coloured enamel painting on a pale green ground depicting cherubs at play. One of a set of at least three which form a frieze. 12ins by 6ins. Mark: 'Minton Hollins & Co. etc.' c.1875-1880.*

193

194

195

196

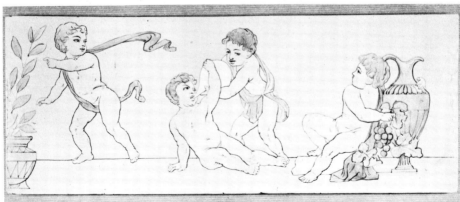

197

page 148

198

199

200

201

202

203

could appreciate why so many of the butchers, fishmongers and dairies in the late Victorian and early Edwardian periods had their shops hygienically tiled throughout in the manner so splendidly illustrated in the coloured catalogues (see Colour Plate I). Needless to say the fishmonger was not inclined to sell his slab there and then. But, in the way these things have of happening, the tiles 'turned up' at a local antiques fair, and we were fortunate to make up a full set. Some of the pieces are damaged, but one in particular has a semi-circular piece cut from the top edge. This serves as a pleasant reminder of its place at the base of a supporting pillar in that now-demolished fishmonger's slab.

Figure 50. As for Figure 49. 'Six Swans' from Mintons 'Fairy Tales'. Mark: 'Mintons China Works etc.'

This series was printed in both blue on white and in brown on cream. No factory of origin can be given and the only mark of any kind is the one of the retailer H. Barralet noted in the caption to Plate 35(203).

The ten subjects are:
'The ugly sisters prepare for the ball'
'The good fairy visits Cinderella'
'Cinderella entering the coach to go to the ball'
'The Prince and Cinderella at the ball'
'The ugly sisters and a jester at the ball'
'Cinderella flies at midnight'

Plate 35.
(198) *Printed underglaze in bright blue on a white slip ground with a scene depicting 'Beauty and the Beast', one of twelve 'Fairy Tales' designed by Moyr Smith. Mark: signed 'J.M.S.' and 'Minton China Works etc.' Introduced c.1874-1875.* **(199)** *Watercolour design from the Copeland pattern book depicting 'Little Bo-Peep'. For either 6-inch or 8-inch tile. Introduced mid-1880s. Courtesy The Spode Museum.* **(200)** *Print from the Wedgwood tile pattern book depicting a scene from the 'Red Riding Hood' series, pattern 276. Designer not known. Introduced 1878. Courtesy The Wedgwood Museum, Barlaston.* **(201)** *As for (200). 'Death of the Wolf' from 'Red Riding Hood' series. Courtesy The Wedgwood Museum, Barlaston.* **(202)** *Underglaze blue transfer print on a white ground depicting 'Cinderella entering the coach to go to the ball' from a series of ten designs for 'Cinderella'. 6ins. Unmarked and unattributed. c.1880.* **(203)** *Underglaze brown transfer print on a cream ground depicting "the ugly sisters and a jester at the Ball". As (202). Mark (of the retailer): 'H. Barralet, 74 Paul Street, London E.C.' c.1880.*

'The courtier and a page show the glass slipper to the ugly sisters'
'The ugly sisters try on the slipper'
'The glass slipper fits Cinderella'
'The Prince invites Cinderella to sit on the throne'.

The full page of illustrations from the Maw factory catalogue, Plate 36(204), includes some of the best known nursery rhyme tiles ever produced, the series designed by Walter Crane. The factory records indicate these as 'hand painted' and they are listed as pattern 2171B. Crane, in describing his ceramic and tile designs, notes:

"About 1874 or 1875, I think, I designed some sets of six and eight-inch fireplace tiles for Messrs. Maw & Co. These, in the first place consisted of figures much in the style of my nursery books, of such characters as 'Mistress Mary', 'Boy Blue', 'Bo-Peep', and 'Tom the Piper's Son'. These were etched on copper in outline, and printed and transferred to the tile, and afterwards coloured by hand. The treatment did not differ much from the treatment of similar subjects in the full pages of "The Baby's Opera" — in fact, I rather think that the square form, size and treatment of the six-inch tiles really suggested the adoption of the same size and treatment for the book, which must have been planned very shortly afterwards. This affords an instance of the suggestive influence one kind of method has upon another."[31]

If Crane's recollection is accurate the "suggestive influence" is quite unusual, as one would normally assume the tile designs were taken from the book, and thus should be given a later date. But here we have the designer's evidence that the tiles pre-date the book from which it is customary to indicate they were copied.

The two other subjects not mentioned by Crane are: 'Jock he was a Person' and 'Little Brown Betty'. As Plate 36 shows each tile is titled on the face.

Crane also comments on the other tiles shown in Plate 36(204), and these are noted in Section 8 — The Calendar.

The pair of tiles in Plate 37(205 and 206) are also from designs by Walter Crane. The quality of printing is rather poor, but the figures have an economy of line and a liveliness rather out of keeping with the mediocre finish of the pieces. The subjects seem to be taken directly from Baby's Own Alphabet. Other titles in this series for which no maker is readily suggested, have kindly been noted for me by Julian Treuhertz of the City Art Gallery, Manchester. They are:

'Great A, little a
Bouncing B
The cats in the cupboard
and can't see me.'

'Boys and girls come out to play'
'Rain, rain, go to Spain'
'Mary had a little lamb'

Plate 36.
(204) *Full page from the Maw & Co. catalogue showing a selection of tiles — nursery rhymes, seasons, sun and moon — designed by Walter Crane. c.1878-1880.* Courtesy Royal Doulton Tableware Ltd.

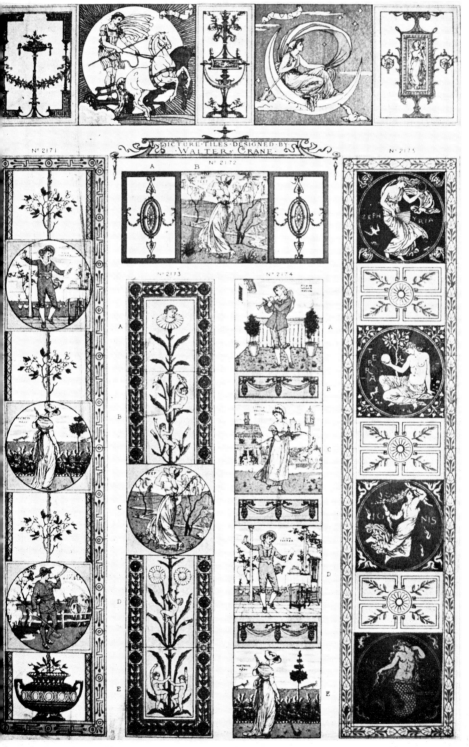

PICTURE·TILES·DESIGNED·BY
WALTER·CRANE·

N° 2171

N° 2172

N° 2173

N° 2174

N° 2175

205

206

207

208

209

210

'Early to bed and early to rise'

'Queen of Hearts she made some tarts'

It seems unlikely that all twenty-six verses of the *Baby's Own Alphabet* were transferred into tile designs, there are probably four further subjects making up a set of a dozen. Curiously Crane does not refer to these tiles in his 1898 article — it is just possible they were made after this date, though more likely the design was pirated. What has happened in the case of Plate 38(213) is more debatable. The tile is entirely hand-painted (no guiding outline print). It is a faithful copy of Crane's well-known 'Buy a Broom', from *Baby's Bouquet* (1877). We have a record of seven subjects all hand-painted on Minton tiles which ordinarily would lead one to believe that Minton had commissioned Crane, or paid him a royalty for the use of these nursery rhyme designs. There does exist, however, some element of doubt. Firstly, no trace of these designs appeared in the Minton archives (though we could well have overlooked them), but furthermore in every instance we have come across Crane's familiar monogram *rebus* is omitted from the painted tile, which is possibly an indication that the tiles were painted by a firm of specialist tile decorators rather than in the Minton factory itself, which would surely have both advertised the sale of these very popular articles by including them in the catalogue, and reproduced the designer's initials on the finished product. An intriguing mystery. Incidentally, the tiles are so well decorated and follow the originals so closely that whoever the decorator was, he or she was not 'an amateur' in the slightly derogatory sense in which the word is usually applied. The seven recorded subjects are:

'The Old Man in Leather' *(Baby's Bouquet)*

'Buy a Broom' *(Baby's Bouquet)*

'Ye Good King Arthur' *(Baby's Opera,* 1877)

'Where are you going to my pretty maid?' *(Baby's Opera* — see Colour Plate IX.)

'Jack and Jill' *(Baby's Opera)*

'How does my Lady's garden grow' *(Baby's Opera)*

'Little Bo-Peep' *(Baby's Opera)*

Just how many other of the illustrations from these two books were used is speculative, but it is likely there would be others. Examples have been recorded in Sussex, North Wales and London, so clearly a number of sets were decorated. A set of seven, framed, was sold at Sotheby's, Belgravia on 1st April, 1976 for £75. Quite a bargain for someone!

With Plate 37(207, 208, 209 and 210) we return to Moyr Smith. 'Little Miss Muffet' and 'Banbury Cross' being taken from illustrations in Smith's *Album of Decorative Figures,* where they are recorded as being from a set of twelve, 8-inch size, "the border is formed by little squares with

Plate 37.

(205) *Underglaze transfer print in brown on a pale cream ground depicting in a central panel 'Sliding on the ice'. From designs by Walter Crane (see text). 6ins. No mark, no attribution. c.1885 + .* **(206)** *As for (205). 'Hark, hark the dogs do bark'. No mark. c.1885 + .* **(207)** *A design taken from J. Moyr Smith's* Album of Decorative Figures *depicting 'Little Miss Muffet' one of twelve 'Nursery Tiles' designed by Smith for W.B. Simpson. Signed: 'M.S.' c.1878.* **(208)** *As for (207), 'Ride a cock horse'.* **(209)** *Underglaze block print in black on a white ground of 'Jack Sprat', one of a series of 'Nursery Rhyme' designs. 8ins. Mark: 'Minton Hollins & Co. etc.' Signed: 'Moyr Smith'. c.1875-1880.* **(210)** *As for (209). 'See-saw Marjery Daw'.*

Figure 51. As for Figure 49. 'Golden Locks' from Mintons 'Fairy Tales'. Unmarked.

alternate ornaments.'' As these designs were executed for W.B. Simpson & Sons who were decorators only, they may be found on the blanks of a number of other firms, with or without a Simpson's mark. Four other titles are illustrated in the *Album,* they are: 'Mistress Mary', 'Old King Cole', 'Humpty Dumpty' and 'Simple Simon'. The remaining six titles are so far unrecorded.

The two Minton Hollins examples, also by Smith, Plate 37(209 and 210) are alleged to have come from a demolished children's hospital "somewhere in Manchester". Be that as it may, they are strikingly attractive in this black and white format, rather less so when printed without a border on a cream ground on a 6-inch tile. The 'Jack Sprat' is particularly evocative of suburban middle class life in the 1870s, and quite alters one's traditional impression of Sprat and his wife as humble cottagers fortunate to eke out their existence because of their mutually complementary tastes in bacon!

Four other subjects have so far been recorded in this series: 'Little Miss Muffet', 'Old King Cole', 'The Queen of Hearts' and 'Little Jack Horner.'

Other nursery rhyme series and fairy tale scenes either printed or freehand painted come to light from time to time. In the Gladstone Pottery Museum collection at Longton a set attributed to Minton tells the story

Plate 38.
(211) *Printed underglaze in black on an ivory ground with 'Ye House' (the one that Jack built). 6ins. Mark: 'Craven Dunnill & Co. Jackfield. Salop.' c.1875.*
(212) *Printed underglaze in blue on a white ground with a composite picture of the nursery rhyme 'Hey diddle-diddle'. 8ins. Mark: 'E. Smith & Co. Coalville'. c.1880-1885. Courtesy Audrey Atterbury.* **(213)** *Painted on-glaze in blue, green and yellow with 'Buy a Broom' (after Walter Crane, see text). 6ins. Mark: 'Mintons China Works'. c.1885.* **(214)** *Printed underglaze in brown on an ivory ground with panel depicting a group of cherubs apple gathering, surrounded by a motif of musical trophies. 6ins. No mark, but pattern T 290. Attributed to Wedgwood. c.1880.* **(215)** *Moulded in low relief with a naked water nymph amongst art nouveau aquatic plants, decorated in green, yellow and white glazes. 8½ins. Mark: Impressed ship mark, painted 'M' or 'M. de C.' (possibly for Carlo Manzoni or Mrs. de Calawe). Della Robbia Co. Ltd., Birkenhead, c.1900. Courtesy Sotheby's Belgravia.* **(216)** *As for (215). One of a frieze of five tiles. Courtesy Sotheby's Belgravia.*

211

212

213

214

215

216

217

218

219

220

221

222

of 'THYS YS YE HOUSE THATTE JACKE BUYLT', the remainder, inscribed in full with mock-medieval spelling depict, 'the priest and the man', 'the farmer and the cock', 'the cat and the dog', 'the malt and the rat', 'the cow and the maid' (shortened titles). The same collection houses an attractively coloured set with the subjects of 'Miss Muffet', 'Jack and Jill', 'A Woman with a Swan', 'Boy Blue', 'Red Riding Hood' and 'Bo-Peep'. A Minton attribution has been given again to these, but neither of the two is recorded in the factory catalogue or archives, which could well imply decoration elsewhere.

The illustration of 'Ye House' in Plate 38(211), is the first of seven subjects from a similar series to that noted above, but in this case emanating from Craven Dunnill, a firm about which very little has ever been published. The catalogue we have seen also pictured an attractive seven-tile series based on the nursery rhyme 'Who killed Cock Robin?' One feels sure that a considerable proportion of their output must have been produced on unmarked tiles, and, hopefully subsequent research will indicate that some of the anonymous pictorial and patterned tiles pictured here were the work of this important Shropshire concern. Much the same remarks could be made in connection with the Leicestershire tile works of E. Smith of Coalville, Plate 38(212). It is doubtful if they matched the output of Craven Dunnill, but with this nursery rhyme tile and the Shakespeare examples, Plate 30(171 and 172) for guidance, it might be possible to add to the known repertoire of this enterprise also.

Problems of attribution occur with the next ten illustrations. Comment has already been made on the question of the painter of Plate 38(213), whereas Plate 38(214) can be correctly attributed to Wedgwood, even though it is unmarked, by the pattern number pre-fixed by 'T' and reference to the factory records. The attributive problem with Plate 38(215 and 216) again concerns the artist responsible. The Della Robbia pottery, perhaps as its name indicates, was one of the most self-consciously 'artistic' of all the art potteries. Founded in 1894 by Harold Rathbone in Birkenhead, its life was short for it closed in 1906. The wares, whether pots, tiles or architectural faience were highly individualistic and it is known that the sculptor R. Anning-Bell, see Plate 51(287), was associated with the firm, as was the Italian sculptor Carlo Manzoni who in 1896 is recorded as having moved from the small Granville Pottery in Hanley to live in Birkenhead and design for Della Robbia. On the evidence of the initials he may have been responsible for the tiles illustrated, although Mrs. de Calawe is also a possibility (see p.185). Apparently, Manzoni was treated very badly by the eccentric Rathbone who was constantly overruling him despite the fact that he was supposed to be in charge of the architectural and sculptural department.

Plate 39.
(217) *Painted freehand underglaze in blue on a white ground, framed with an orange line, depicting a small boy restrained by an adult hand. 6ins. Mark: 'Minton Hollins & Co. etc.' c.1875.* **(218)** *As for (217), depicting two little girls one seated on a lamb.* **(219)** *Painted freehand on-glaze in red enamel on a white ground with two girls with umbrellas. 6ins. No mark, but painted monogram 'GTC' (?). Unattributed. c.1880.* **(220)** *As for (219), with a group of six children. No attribution (see text).* **(221)** *Painted freehand on-glaze in blue with a scene from Through the Looking Glass. 6ins. Mark: 'Mintons China Works etc.' c.1890.* **(222)** *Painted freehand on-glaze in blue with 'Ye King'. 6ins. No mark. c.1890.*

A most interesting article records the reminiscences of two former Della Robbia workers, and adds to our knowledge of this little known enterprise.[32] Their production of 'collectable' tiles cannot have been large and the two pieces shown in Plate 38(215 and 216), from a set of five sold by Sotheby's Belgravia (15th February, 1973, Lot 92) and the plaque illustrated in Plate 51(287), are really very rare items.

The attributive problems of each of the next three pairs of tiles, Plate 39(217 to 222) are the result of all of them being hand-painted. The first pair, Plate 39(217 and 218), are of Minton Hollins manufacture and are two of a set of four, each with different childhood scenes, which together formed a square plant pot stand. As the paintings are underglaze there is no doubt they are factory products. The next pair, Plate 39(219 and 220), are painted overglaze, the tiles are unmarked and the monogram which looks like 'GTC' has not been identified. The designs look very familiar, but we have been unable to place them — they have the appearance of Kate Greenaway or Ellen Houghton rather than Crane or Caldecott. The painting is well-executed and it really is very difficult to decide whether these are factory-decorated or the work of an amateur. On balance the latter seems more likely. There is very little doubt that Plate 39(221 and 222) were the work of an amateur. Four examples were purchased together, the two not shown also had scenes from *Through the Looking Glass* and all look amateurish if competent. All appear to have been painted on Minton blanks.

The final plate in this section begins with a rather unusual early Copeland tile, pattern 420, Plate 40(223), which was "sent to London in 1855". Similar scenes of children's pastimes were produced elsewhere, such as the six-tile series of considerable charm from Maw, patterns 1592-1597. These were etched and framed by a straight-line border with canted corners and a small shell-like motif in each. The subjects: 'Snowball', 'Feeding ducks', 'Skating', 'Playing houses', 'Reading stories' and rather alarmingly 'Teazing *(sic)* cat.' The firm also advertised three panels 12ins. by 6ins., etched with scenes of 'Boys picking apples', 'Girls making daisy chains' and 'Girls picking black-berries'. Like so many of the Maw products, they do not seem to have found their way into any public collection, though perhaps the Ironbridge Gorge Museum Trust's collection might eventually reveal some examples. (See Colour Plate IX for 'Reading Stories'.)

Plate 40.
(223) *Watercolour design from the Copeland pattern book depicting a group of young people dancing, pattern 420, "sent to London November 26th 1855".* *Designer unknown. Courtesy The Spode Museum.* **(224)** *Print from the Wedgwood pattern book depicting a boy and girl 'Fishing' for ducks with a frog! One of six 'Children's pastimes', pattern T 357. Artist unknown. c.1880+.* Courtesy The Wedgwood Museum, Barlaston. **(225)** *Underglaze block print in black on a beige ground depicting a young female water nymph pursuing an amiable looking fish. One of twelve 'Water Nymphs', pattern 1409. 6ins. Mark: 'Minton China Works etc.' c.1875.* **(226)** *Print from the Wedgwood pattern book depicting a young male water baby conducting a choir (or quadrille?) of lobsters. One of six 'Water Babies', pattern T 317. c.1880.* Courtesy The Wedgwood Museum, Barlaston. **(227)** *Watercolour drawing depicting 'Music' one of a series of gnomes and elves prepared for Copeland tiles (see text). 4ins. c.1885.* Courtesy The Spode Museum. **(228)** *Watercolour drawing in shades of blue depicting a frog riding a penny farthing (see text).* Courtesy The Spode Museum.

223

224

225

226

227

228

Wedgwood were the producers also of a charming, printed 'Children's Pastimes' series. The pattern book depicts six scenes under the pattern number T 357. Illustrated in Plate 40(224), is a rather curious and humorous fishing scene, the other subjects are: 'Two children and a calf', 'A boy throwing a frog into the air', 'A boy and girl with a bird's nest', 'A boy and girl with a lamb', 'A boy and girl playing shuttlecock'. Wedgwood also made the very idiosyncratic set of 'Water Babies', Plate 40(226), again with six subjects, pattern T 317. The sense of humour displayed is somewhat foreign to our present tastes, but the full set would be quite an acquisition. They depict:

'A water-baby with three very murderous-looking fish.'
'A water-baby nursing a fish and giving it medicine from bottle labelled 'Physic'.'
'A water-baby blowing a shell at an audience of fish.'
'A water-baby and a lobster.'
'A water-baby riding a fish using a bulrush as a whip.'

No designer can be firmly given for this series, but the style is similar to that of the Wedgwood fishing series, see Plate 41(233 and 234).

By comparison the Minton 'Water Nymphs' series, Plate 40(225), looks rather clumsy and unattractive. The corner motif will act as a hallmark for this series of twelve subjects, pattern 1409. The individual subjects are insufficiently distinctive to make listing them worthwhile.

Lastly, two more drawings from the Copeland archives the 'Gnomes and Elves' series, Plate 40(227), appears both in the pattern book in several places, and in the collection of watercolour drawings. Rather coy in approach, the subjects as listed below would nevertheless appeal to children.

'A message' (a gnome speaks to a blue tit)
'A prize' (a gnome captures a rat)
'Surprise' (a gnome meets a snail)
'Til' and 'Ting', a pair (two elves mounted on mice and jousting)
'Caught' (a gnome in a spider's web)
'Alarm' (a gnome and a frog)
'Harvest' (a gnome plucking ears of wheat)
'Best' (a gnome drinking from a harebell)
'Ambush' (a gnome captures a wasp in a flower cup)

The humour of Plate 40(228) is much more broad. These designs, thirteen in all, in pale blue monochrome are in the Copeland collection, but no trace of them could be found in the pattern books, and it is possible that they were never manufactured, thus the individual subjects have not been noted here. It would, however, be delightful to hear that 'Ye serenade', a frog playing a guitar beneath his lady love's window or 'On ye bat's back', a frog astride a bat, had been produced. These frog tiles would make excellent companions for the splendid frog and mice figures which George Tinworth modelled in saltglaze stoneware for Doulton in the 1880s.

7. SPORTING SCENES

A curious feature of almost all the tile series devoted to sport is that the subject is treated humorously. The Wedgwood series in Plate 41(229) sets the tone, although the scene illustrating 'Tally Ho!' is more straight-forward than the others which are:
  'Master of the hounds'
  'A good shot'
  'Stand back'
  '1st October'
  '1st September'
The Copeland series, Plate 41(231 and 232), is very similar in approach. These scenes are not titled but a number of the drawings are initialled 'W.G.R.B.', but no known Copeland artist seems to fit. The pattern book indicates that this is a twelve-tile series, ''Royal brown printed and painted underglaze''. The pattern number is 969 and a further note records ''sent to London 14 October 1878'' which, as previously explained, gives a clear indication of its date of introduction. Several of the subjects are quite straightforward but a number of the items, such as Plate 41(232), are treated humorously. In the Spode Museum there are sixteen loose watercolour drawings — Plate 41(232) is one, whereas Plate 41(231) was photographed from the actual pattern book — from which presumably a set of twelve was finally chosen for engraving.

The rather curious Copeland bear shooting scene, Plate 41(230), is endorsed '8 subjects', but no further details are given other than the pattern number 949. For this series no loose drawings were located so its true scope is unknown, and its place in this 'sporting' section is really rather tentative.

The Wedgwood fishing series, Plate 41(233 and 234), is very finely printed and really quite amusing. There are six titles altogether, all under pattern T 288 which indicates a date of introduction c.1878. The other four subjects and their titles are:

Figure 52. Coloured print from the Minton pattern book of 'Hunting', one of twelve 'Old English Sports and Games' (Jones, Minton MSS, No. 1842). Courtesy Royal Doulton Tableware Ltd.

Figure 53. As for Figure 52, watercolour drawing of 'Croquet'.

229

230

231

232

233

234

'Fly fishing', the angler 'catches' a hut.
'I think I shall have a rise here', a bull advances on the angler's rear.
'A nibble', the angler eyes a nearby milkmaid.
'In a fix', the line is stuck in a tree.

It is not easy to attribute these designs to a specific artist. Thomas Allen, the Art Director, has to be considered both for this series and for the 'Water Babies' Plate 40(226), but the evidence is scanty and inconclusive. Hopefully more research will reveal who apart from Allen was designing tiles for Wedgwood at this particular period. As the designs are basically circular in form, it is quite likely that they were printed on tableware as a number of other designs from the tile pattern book have been noted decorating plates, soup dishes and even teapots.

Plate 42(235) and Figures 52 and 53 take us to Mintons China Works and the series 'Old English Sports and Games'. In conformity with the medievalism so prominent in the 1870s the subjects are all shown in medieval attire and consist — to quote from the factory catalogue — "of twelve subjects sportively treated, outlined and painted in colours by hand, pattern 1895." The subjects (eleven only are listed) are:

'Hawking'
'Hunting', Figure 52
'Fishing', Plate 42(235)
'Coursing'
'Shooting'
'Cricket'
'Single Combat'
'Skating'
'Croquet', Figure 53
'Chess'
'Football'

The original watercolour drawings are in the Minton archives (Minton MSS, No. 1829), as are a set of pencil sketches (Minton MSS, No. 1838). A fine set of drawings in various stages was illustrated in the catalogue of the Wolverhampton Exhibition of 1978, 'Victorian Tiles', (cat. No. 112). In addition to 'Croquet' and 'Hunting' as shown here, 'Chess' and an amusing 'Cricket' scene were depicted. No designer can firmly be given for this most attractive series, though Edward Hammond the designer of the 'Musicians' series, Plate 53(300), is a possibility. The pattern number evidence suggests a date of introduction c.1882.

Plate 41.
(229) *Print from the Wedgwood tile pattern book of 'Tally Ho!' one of six hunting scenes, pattern T 290, issued c.1878/9. Artist unattributed.* Courtesy The Wedgwood Museum, Barlaston. **(230)** *Watercolour design from the Copeland tile pattern book depicting a uniformed man accompanied by a child, shooting at a bear in a barrel whilst bear cubs play in the background. Pattern 949 for an 8-inch tile. c.1878.* Courtesy The Spode Museum. **(231)** *Watercolour design from the Copeland tile pattern book depicting a huntsman and his horse jumping a fence. One of twelve subjects pattern 969 "sent to London 14th October 1878."* Courtesy The Spode Museum. **(232)** *Watercolour drawing for one of the Copeland 'Hunting' series. (See 231 for details.)* Courtesy The Spode Museum. **(233)** *Print from the Wedgwood tile pattern book depicting 'Jolly', a fisherman sheltering beneath an umbrella in heavy rain. One of six scenes, pattern T288. Designer unattributed. Introduced c.1878.* Courtesy The Wedgwood Museum, Barlaston. **(234)** *As (233), 'Those Horrid Boys'.* Courtesy The Wedgwood Museum, Barlaston.

A second Minton sporting series was produced a little later, c.1886, "twelve subjects printed in brown outline with grey ground, No 2061 and with buff ground 2062." The tiles are titled and appear in hexagonal frames, the dress is contemporary. Six of the series, 'Harehunt', 'Shooting', 'Fishing', 'Deerstalking', 'Hawking' and 'Cricket' may be seen in the Gladstone Pottery Museum collection. Illustrated here, Plate 42(237) is a photograph of the reversed print of 'Racing' from the Minton pattern book (Minton MSS, No.1842).

A third Minton sporting series is not dissimilar in treatment to the Copeland series mentioned earlier. Plate 42(238) is an example from Minton's 'Scenes in the Hunting Field' which is described as "twelve subjects outlined and tinted in colours by hand on 6in. tiles, No 1898, also tinted in monochrome blues or browns No 1902." The following list of subjects has been compiled from watercolour drawings in the Minton archives (Minton MSS, No. 1813):

'Regardless of Expense'
'Master's Luncheon'
''Arry out Hunting'
'Grief over Wire'
'A good Pilot'
'Hills over Head'
'John'
'A Stern Chase'
'If Women will Hunt'
'Keen'
'Faults on both sides'.

Figure 54. Underglaze blue print of Chinese fisherman in a boat. 6ins. Mark: 'Minton Hollins & Co. etc.' c.1885.

The titles appear on the tiles, and the initials 'G.B.' appear on some of the drawings, but no appropriate Minton artist springs to mind. The date of introduction would seem to be c.1882. Examples of these designs on tablewares are to be seen in the Willett Collection in Brighton Museum and Art Gallery.

The fishing scene, Plate 42(236), is an example of a rare group of English tiles dating from the 1870s which were directly imitative of Dutch delft ware. This is clear both from the design and the use of the tin-glaze. Robert Minton Taylor is credited with tiles in this style and Barnard (Plate 90 of his book) illustrates another typical example.

Plate 42.
(235) *Coloured print from the Minton pattern book of 'Fishing' one of twelve 'Old English Sports and Games'. c.1882.* Courtesy Royal Doulton Tableware **(236)** *Tin-glazed tile painted in blue with a scene of a man fishing within a pseudo-Dutch delft frame. Attributed to Robert Minton Taylor. c.1873.* Courtesy City Museum and Art Gallery, Stoke-on-Trent. **(237)** *Reversed print in colours of 'Racing' one of twelve 'Sporting' subjects from the Minton pattern book. c.1886.* Courtesy Royal Doulton Tableware Ltd. **(238)** *Coloured drawing of 'GRIEF OVER WIRE', one of twelve 'Scenes in the Hunting Field'. Initialled 'G.B.' (see text). c.1882.* Courtesy Royal Doulton Tableware Ltd. **(239)** *Printed in brown on a cream ground with 'Blind Man's Buff', one of a series of sports and pastimes. 6ins. No mark. Attributed to Malkin, Edge & Co. c.1895. (See text.)* **(240)** *As (239) 'Shuttlecock'. c.1895.*

235

236

237

238

239

240

Two further series deserve noting. The Minton Hollins catalogue shows six tiles from a sporting series, possibly of twelve. The sportsman is attired in medieval dress and is shown:

'Wielding a whip on a horse'
'Catching an enormous fish'
'Being dragged along by two hounds'
'Training a performing dog'
'Boxing'
'Cockfighting'

These humorous scenes are circular and set in a simple squared frame.

Figure 55. Loose watercolour drawing of an 'aesthetic cyclist' in medieval attire. For a 6-inch tile from Minton's Studio (Jones, Minton MSS, No. 1838). Courtesy Royal Doulton Tableware Ltd.

Lastly, Plate 42(239 and 240), are two tiles from a series of sports and pastimes of which the examples we have seen have all been unmarked, but which Barnard firmly attributes to Malkin Edge & Co., and there is no cause to question this attribution. Both coloured and plain printed versions of this attractive series have been noted, and the subject of each sport is further exemplified by the charmingly appropriate corner motifs.

8. THE CALENDAR

Another popular subject with the tile designers was the calendar. The various facets of time from morning, noon and night through the months of the year, the days of the week, the signs of the Zodiac, the seasons and the elements were all explored.

Although this book is primarily concerned with the single tile and related series, it would be wrong not to draw attention once more to the seasonal tile panels in the Grill Room of the Victoria and Albert Museum, and to note the Longton Baths tile panels now on loan to the Gladstone Pottery Museum, two of which are illustrated in Barnard.[33] These are lively evocations of the seasons' activities made by Minton Hollins.

The first two illustrations, Plate 43(241 and 242), are of Moyr Smith's designs for Mintons' series of Thomson's 'Seasons'. The printed catalogue devotes a whole column to what was clearly a prestige product.

The tiles were done in several different finishes in both 6-inch and 8-inch sizes. The larger size in full colour is most attractive.

Each season has one emblematical tile and two examples. The catalogue reproduces the poems which were the inspiration for the designs. The pieces are themselves briefly titled. Thus Plate 43(241), which is titled 'Come Gentle Spring', has in the catalogue the supplementary line, "ethereal mildness come", whilst the two supporting tiles are labelled 'Ploughing' and 'The Rainbow' (Colour Plate IV), the latter, for example, with the verse:

"He, wondering, views the bright enchantment bend
Delightful o'er the radiant fields, and runs
To catch the falling glory."

It would be tedious to quote each accompanying verse, but to complete the record the other subjects are:

'Summer' — emblematical, Plate 43(242), 'Celedon and Amelia',
    'Musidora and Damon' (Colour Plate IV).

'Autumn' — emblematical, 'Reaping', 'Lavinia and Palemon'.

'Winter' — emblematical, 'The Snowstorm', 'Skating'.

It was a great delight to discover a number — not a full set — of Moyr Smith's original drawings for this series in the Minton archives (*Minton MSS*, No. 1820) in fine clean condition. In watercolour they seemed to sparkle with life, and though the finished results on tiles lack the immediacy of the originals they are, nevertheless, most sensitively rendered. Colour Plate IV reproduces two of these splendid watercolour designs.

The illustrations of the Copeland watercolour drawings, Plate 43(243 and 244), are from a set of five, 'Time' being the additional item. As no trace of them could be found in the pattern books it is possible that they were never produced. There is no doubt that Plate 43(245) was made. This

Figure 56. Watercolour design for tile panel from the Minton archives, depicting two women gathering fruit and grapes, emblematic of 'Autumn'. Signed 'W. Wise' (Jones, Minton MSS, No. 1858). Courtesy Royal Doulton Tableware Ltd.

is one of a comparatively rare T. & R. Boote series, the design of which is credited to Kate Greenaway.[34]

Minton Hollins also produced two series depicting the 'Seasons'. One consisted of four tiles each with a boy and girl engaged in appropriate seasonal and rural activities. The second, of four scenes of seasonal peasant activity, is in grey and black with the titles printed on the tile face.

The charming but anonymous tile showing the points of the compass, Plate 43(246), is reminiscent in its central motif of the designs of Walter Crane for a most attractive series issued by Maws. The hand-painted 8-inch tiles depict women in classical attire, seated (with one exception), in a variety of ancient thrones, chairs and sofas. Colour Plate VI shows a page from the factory catalogue which contains all eight designs. As can be seen the titles appear on the face of each tile. They are: 'AURORA', 'VER', 'AESTAS' (these three have infants with the women). 'MERIDES', 'AUTUMNUS', 'HIEMS', 'NOX' and, not seated, 'VESPER'. Tiles from this series were shown at the Paris International Exhibition in 1878. Crane wrote of them: "a set of eight-inch tile designs (produced in the same way) of the Seasons of the Year and the Times of Day was more ambitious in aim and classical in treatment. The subjects were connected by a slight repeating design by way of open border above and below, which covered the joints when the tiles were placed one above the other in the jambs of a fireplace".[35] He goes on to write of four of the tiles shown in Plate 36(204): "A set of six-inch tiles, representing by single figures in circles the Four Elements, was designed for the same firm a little later". As can be seen from the illustration these are titled on the face 'ZEPHYRIA', 'TERRA', 'IGNIS' and 'ACQUA'. The subjects are again all women, and are set in circular frames with an appropriate corner motif, e.g. a fish supports the mermaid for the element 'ACQUA'. Crane also designed 'LUNA' and 'SOL', a pair of 8-inch tiles, hand painted, pattern 2170, which depict a woman seated in the moon, and a man driving two horses and a chariot in the blaze of the sun. These two subjects are also illustrated as the two top tiles in Plate 36(204). Whatever one's view about the relative merits of neo-classicism or medieval revivalism, there can be little argument that the quality of these tile designs by Walter Crane is quite outstanding. Maws were fortunate to secure his freelance services, though from the scarcity of surviving examples and their correspondingly high price — it seems

Plate 43.
(241) *A design taken from Moyr Smith's* Album of Decorative Figures *depicting 'Come Gentle Spring', one of twelve Thomson's 'Seasons' designed by Smith for Mintons c.1881 (see text).* **(242)** *As (241), 'Refulgent Summer comes', from Thomson's 'Seasons'. Mintons. c.1881.* **(243)** *Mounted watercolour drawing in shades of blue depicting 'SPRING', one of five 'Seasons' prepared for a 6-inch Copeland tile. c.1880. Courtesy The Spode Museum.* **(244)** *As (243), 'TIME' from a set of 'Seasons' designs prepared for Copeland. Courtesy The Spode Museum.* **(245)** *Underglaze transfer print in reddish brown on an off white ground, enamelled overglaze in colours depicting a girl in a garden symbolic of 'SPRING' from a set of 'Seasons'. Unmarked, but attributed to T. & R. Boote on the evidence of the border pattern. The design is attributed to Kate Greenaway and was registered on 19th April, 1881. Courtesy Hilary Evans.* **(246)** *Underglaze transfer print, with supporting underglaze colour painting, depicting the points of the compass represented by seasonal fruits and flowers. Unmarked and unattributed. c.1880. Courtesy Hilary Evans.*

241

242

243

244

245

246

247

248

249

250

251

252

likely that fewer sets were made than might have been anticipated. Returning to the illustrations, Plate 44(247 and 248) are designs by Moyr Smith for a series of months decorated by the London firm of W.B. Simpson & Sons. The style is somewhat different from much of his other work. It betrays a whimsicality well suited to a *Punch* artist. Smith records that the designs were "used for both dessert plates and six-inch tiles." It is also worth noting that the figure on each design wears a costume of a specific period, e.g. 'MAY' is attired as a Cavalier, etc.

William Wise etched a lovely 'Seasons' set for Mintons, of which Winter, a characterful young woman holding a bunch of holly, is reproduced here, Plate 44(249). This tile and a preliminary sketch by the artist were exhibited at the Northern Ceramic Society's exhibition, Collecting English Pottery and Porcelain, held at Temple Newsam, Leeds, in 1974 and were illustrated in the catalogue. In the Minton pattern book the set is given the pattern number 1996 and each tile has a corner design, unlike the plain example here, which came from a surviving member of the Wise family through the generosity and good offices of Reginald Haggar. Wise was also the artist concerned with Figure 56, an example of the many watercolour designs in the Minton archives which were specifically painted in the hope of securing commissions. Many such bore the words: "the amount charged for this original design will be credited if returned in a reasonable time."

The Copeland series of months, Plate 44(250), has both the month name and the appropriate sign of the zodiac, whereas a second Copeland set, hand coloured on 6-inch or 8-inch tiles has merely the name of the month, Plate 44(251) and Plate 45(253). The original drawings done in pen on very thin and brittle paper are in the Spode Museum, (251) is an example, whereas (253) is a finished tile. These very elegant sketches are signed 'L.B.', which may well stand for Lucien Besche a talented French artist and figure painter who worked at Copeland c.1872-1885, having previously been at Mintons. The pattern number is 1088 which gives a date of introduction c.1879. (See also Colour Plate IX.)

Amongst the best known of all the month tiles are the Wedgwood 'Old English', Plate 44(252), or 'Early English' (both titles appear in the

Plate 44.
(247) *A design taken from Moyr Smith's* Album of Decorative Figures. *A bearded fellow in Tudor attire is holding a Valentine card, showing a heart transfixed by an arrow, symbolic of 'FEBRUARY' from 'Months of the year' designed by Smith for W.B. Simpson & Sons. c.1875.* **(248)** *As (247), an angler in early eighteenth century attire removes a hook from the fish he has just caught, symbolic of 'JUNE'.* **(249)** *Underglaze printed in dark brown on a white slip ground with a girl holding a bunch of holly symbolic of Winter, from a set of 'SEASONS'. Mark: Signed by the designer 'W. Wise' and marked: 'Minton China Works Ltd.' Introduced c.1885.* **(250)** *Watercolour design in shades of blue from the Copeland tile pattern book depicting a young girl in a garden holding a bunch of spring flowers symbolic of 'MAY' with the astrological symbol 'GEMINI'. From a series of 'Months of the Year'. Artist unknown. Pattern 946, introduced c.1878. Courtesy The Spode Museum.* **(251)** *Pen and ink drawing on thin brittle paper of a woman holding a sheaf of corn symbolic of 'JULY' from a series of 'Months of the Year' produced by Copeland. Signed 'L.B.' and tentatively attributed to Lucien Besche. c.1879. Courtesy The Spode Museum.* **(252)** *Print from the Wedgwood tile pattern book of a boy and girl on a windy day, symbolic of 'MARCH'. From a series of months, entitled 'Old English' or 'Early English' (see text). Courtesy The Wedgwood Museum, Barlaston.*

Figure 57. Watercolour design for a 6-inch tile from the Minton archives, depicting a classical figure emblematic of 'Spring'. Marked with the Kensington Studio stamp, c.1871-1875 (Jones, Minton MSS, No. 1858. Courtesy Royal Doulton Tableware Ltd.

records). A document in the Wedgwood archives[36] records that this series of designs was registered in March 1878. The tiles are not uncommon, but the Wedgwood name ensures that they are comparatively expensive. They were produced in both 6-inch and 8-inch sizes, and though normally as Plate 45(254) they were printed in blue, brown prints have also been noted.

Examples of a Minton Hollins set of months, printed in red and black with simple early medieval scenes and titled within a circular frame in Gothic script, are illustrated by Barnard.[37] The same firm issued prior to 1878 a four-tile 8-inch series,[38] in which each tile carried the subject title in Gothic lettering, 'Morning', 'Noon', 'Evening' and 'Night'. The characters, a man, his wife and child in medieval dress pursue appropriate occupations (see Colour Plate IX).[39] Additionally, Barnard illustrates[40] a Craven Dunnill piece on which a seated monk wishes us, "A Merry Christmas".

Maws too produced a set of month tiles both in 6-inch and 8-inch size. The border to the 8-inch set is a very distinctive design of a circle, three vertical lines, and then another circle and so on, with altogether six circles and five sets of lines to each side. The only example noted was 'January' which featured a youth with an axe felling a tree. A Craven Dunnill set of months with appropriate designs of figures in costume is shown in their catalogue.

As has been noted, some month tiles have the signs of the Zodiac upon them, but at least two firms made Zodiac tiles which did not name the

Plate 45.
(253) *'June'. Outline printed and painted overglaze in colours with a young woman tending a rose bush. 6ins. Mark: 'Copeland, Stoke-on-Trent.' c.1880. (See also Plate 44(251) and text.)* (254) *'November.' Printed underglaze in blue with a boy on the seashore. 6ins. Mark: 'Josiah Wedgwood & Sons, Etruria.' c.1880. (See also Plate 44(252) and text.)* (255) *'Winter.' Moulded in low relief with the head of an old man, decorated with a brown translucent glaze. 6ins. No mark, no attribution. c.1890.* (256) *Large circular panel modelled in high relief with the head of an old man emblematic of winter, decorated in opaque glazes. 12ins. diam. Mark: 'Maws'. c.1880. Courtesy City Museum and Art Gallery, Stoke-on-Trent.* (257) *As Figure 57, 'Winter.' Courtesy Royal Doulton Tableware Ltd.* (258) *Printed underglaze in black, brown and fawn with 'OLD TIME', a bearded ancient carrying a scythe. 8ins. Mark: 'Steele & Wood, Stoke-on-Trent'. c.1885.*

253

254

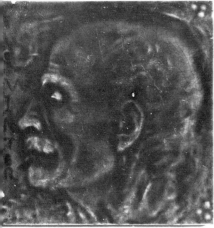

55

256

257

258

259

260

261

262

263

264

months. Maws Zodiac series shows the appropriate animal very simply outlined, e.g. two fish for Pisces. Each is set in a circular frame with a quarter circle at the corners, and normally is done with a coloured glaze, pattern numbers 2158-2169. Four examples can be seen as the corner pieces on Figure 14. The corresponding Minton series is "quaintly represented by Twelve Figure subjects outlined and painted by hand in colours, No 1762." It is yet another essay in quaint mock-medievalism, Plate 46(264) and Figure 58, not without a trace of broad humour as examples in the Minton archives testify *(Minton MSS,* No. 1819).

Three examples have been included in the illustrations of designs featuring old men, symbolic of Winter or the end of the year. Plate 45(255) is a fairly ordinary anonymous tile, but Plate 45(256) is a large architectural example from Maws which could be tempting to the collector despite its considerable weight. The companion seasons similarly modelled can be seen in Figure 8. 'Old Time', Plate 45(258), is an extremely rare example from the firm of Steele & Wood. Very little is known of this concern, and apart from a very highly priced pair of tiles with bird scenes, this is the only example from this firm so far noted. It is this kind of rarity which appeals to those collectors whose aim is to acquire an example from as many manufacturers as possible.

The female 'Winter', Plate 45(257), and the companion 'Spring' (Figure 57) are designs from the Minton Kensington Studio. It is not known whether these were ever made into finished tiles, we have not noted any. Nor is the designer known, though it has been suggested that these were freelance designs by Walter Crane. Stylistically this is a justifiable assumption, but there is, to date, no supporting evidence.

The Minton 'Days of the Week', Plate 46(259-262), "humorously illustrated in seven pictures (with an alternate tile depicting an hour glass) from drawings by Mrs. E.E. Houghton", pattern 1759, are coloured in light reds or in blues. Charming in their simplicity, they are typical of Ellen Houghton's work which also appears in Routledge's toy books and in a delightful souvenir of the 1887 Manchester Royal Jubilee Exhibition — *The Adventures of Little Man-chester.* An entry in the Artists Wages Book (Minton MSS, No. 662) under William Wise (see p.192) is dated 8th July, 1880 and reads: "Engraving, biting in 7 plates for tiles, 'Days of the Week'." This gives a clear indication of the likely date of introduction of this series. Incidentally, copper plates for some of the designs are still retained in the office of the head engraver at Mintons. A complete set of this series in good condition could well fetch over £100.

Finally, calendar tiles seem to have been a late production of several firms. The example in Plate 46(263) is for 1902 from Minton Hollins. The

Plate 46.
(259) *Outline printed and painted in 'bright reds' with a man and woman returning from church, symbolic of 'SUNDAY'. From a set of 'Days of the Week' designed by Mrs. Ellen E. Houghton. 6ins. Mark: 'Mintons China Works etc.' Pattern 1759, introduced c.1880.* **(260)** *As (259), 'MONDAY', fully marked.* **(261)** *As (259), 'FRIDAY', fully marked.* **(262)** *As (259), 'SATURDAY', fully marked.* **(263)** *Underglaze printed calendar tile for 1902 with 'Minton Hollins & Co.'s Compliments.'* Courtesy City Museum and Art Gallery, Stoke-on-Trent. **(264)** *Coloured print from the Minton tile pattern book (Jones, Minton MSS, No. 1842) depicting an archer in medieval costume symbolic of Sagittarius from a series of twelve* Signs of the Zodiac. *Designer unattributed. Pattern 1762, introduced c.1880.* Courtesy Royal Doulton Tableware Ltd.

Figure 58. Printed and coloured design for a 6-inch tile from the Minton archives, depicting a female (Europa?) reclining inelegantly on a bull, emblematic of 'TAURUS'. c.1880. (Jones, Minton MSS, No. 1819). Courtesy Royal Doulton Tableware Ltd.

Wedgwood concern continued with calendar tiles long after normal tile production ceased. Many of these calendar tiles of the 1920s and later were produced for the American market, and had specifically American scenes on them. An example is illustrated in Plate 17(98), and full details given of the scenes and years on pp.98.

9. HISTORICAL, POLITICAL AND PERSONAL

Rather surprisingly tiles which depict historical incidents or personalities are comparatively rare. Only two series have been recorded, one by Mintons, Plate 47(265 and 266) and the other by Minton Hollins, Plate 47(269 and 270). Almost inevitably the designer for both was J. Moyr Smith. The evidence of the development of his style indicates an earlier date c.1872 for the Minton 'Early English History', pattern 1344, than the Minton Hollins. This latter in its coloration and general treatment is closely akin to the Waverley series, see Plate 27(163-168) of c.1878.

The complete list of subjects for 'Early English History' is:
'Landing of the Romans'
'Edy and Elgiva'
'Lilla saving Edwin'

Plate 47.
(265) *Underglaze block print in black upon a beige ground depicting 'Alfred' (and the Cakes), one of twelve 'Early English History' designs. Mark: 'Mintons China Works etc.' Initialled 'J.M.' (S.) for J. Moyr Smith. Pattern 1344, introduced c.1872.* **(266)** *As (265), 'Canute'. Full factory mark. Initialled 'M.S.' for Moyr Smith.* **(267)** *Underglaze blue printed on a white ground depicting 'JOHN BULL extinguishing a Fire-brand'. Mark: 'Copeland & Garrett late Spode.' c.1845 +.* Courtesy City Museum and Art Gallery, Stoke-on-Trent. **(268)** *Fine hand painted portrait in enamel colours of Garibaldi the Italian patriot leader. Unmarked. Solid clay tile with 'combed' back. Attributed to Copeland. c.1865.* Courtesy City Museum and Art Gallery, Stoke-on-Trent. **(269)** *Under glaze block printed in grey, black and yellow, with the scene of the 'MURDER OF A BECKET AD 1171' from a series of 'English History'. Mark: 'Minton Hollins & Co. etc.' Signed: 'Moyr Smith'. c.1880.* **(270)** *As (269), 'MAGNA CARTA A.D. 1215'. Full Minton Hollins mark and signature 'Moyr Smith'. c.1880.*

265

266

267

268

269

270

271

272

273

274

275

276

'Galcactus'
'Canute', Plate 47(266)
'Boadicea'
'Edward the Martyr'
'Death of Harold'
'St. Augustine'
'Alfred', Plate 47(265)
'Harold's Oath'
'Alfred in the Danish camp'.
The Minton Hollins series does not appear in any version of the printed catalogue we have seen, but eight titles have been recorded; they are:
'Murder of à Becket. AD 1171', Plate 47(269)
'Hereward at Ely 1071'
'Richard I — Coeur de Lion and Gourdon 1199'
'Magna Carta. AD1215', Plate 47(270)
'Philippa pleading with Edward III 1347'
'The Armada in Sight 1588'
'The Gunpowder Plot 1605'
'Sir Philip Sidney at Zutphen 1586'
The single Copeland & Garrett tile, Plate 47(267), with the rather vulgar indication of how John Bull should deal with his traditional French adversary, must date from the time of the Copeland & Garrett partnership, i.e. 1833-1847, and thus is the earliest printed tile illustrated here. It is of considerable rarity. So too is the hand-painted portrait of the great Italian patriot leader Garibaldi, Plate 47(268), who, wearing his famous red shirt, led his faithful band of a thousand followers from exile to the eventual triumph of a united Italy. Garibaldi visited England in 1864 and received a rapturous welcome, "never did king or emperor receive such an ovation. From the highest to the lowest, all conspired to do him honour. Never was there such a scene as when he entered London, and all its workmen turned out to meet him. Of course, he was

Plate 48.
(271) *Underglaze printed in black upon a cream ground depicting 'VICTORIA, QUEEN OF ENGLAND, EMPRESS OF INDIA A.D. 1887. THE 50TH OF HER REIGN'. 8ins. Mark: 'Mintons China Works etc.' 1887.* Courtesy City Museum and Art Gallery, Stoke-on-Trent. **(272)** *On-glaze coloured lithographic print entitled 'In Memoriam' depicting Queen Victoria and giving her date of birth and death, and the epitaph 'A thousand claims to reverence, closed In Her as Mother, Wife and Queen'. 6ins. Mark: a moulded 'B'. Unattributed.* Courtesy City Museum and Art Gallery, Stoke-on-Trent. **(273)** *Moulded in relief, decorated with translucent coloured glazes in browns and greens depicting an old man with a beard (Michelangelo? see text). 6ins. Mark: 'FLAXMAN.' c.1890.* **(274)** *Companion tile to (273) with moulded and glazed head and shoulders of an unknown woman. Mark: 'Flaxman' (moulded). c.1890.* **(275)** *Portrait tile moulded* intaglio *(see text for manufacturing method) and covered with a thick green glaze depicting 'Lady Hamilton as Miranda'. The title and mark are incised in the back of the tile: 'Romney Pinxit, Geo. Cartlidge Sculpt. Made by Adams and Cartlidge Ltd. Vine Street, Hanley.' c.1910.* Courtesy Museum and Art Gallery, Stoke-on-Trent. **(276)** *Portrait tile, moulded* intaglio *and covered with a thick brown glaze, depicting W.E. Gladstone. 8¾ins. by 6ins. On the face is inscribed 'From a portrait by H.S. Mendlessohn, G.C. 1898 Sculpt'. On the back: 'Made by Sherwin and Cotton at their works in Hanley in the County of Stafford 1898'.*

presented with the freedom of the city.''[41] This most interesting tile is solid clay and not dust-pressed, and has the 'combed' back often found on Copeland tiles, it too might reasonably be attributed to that factory.

An interesting collection could be formed of individual portraits of distinguished personalities, and high on the list would have to come Queen Victoria, Plate 48(271 and 272). The printed 1887 Jubilee portrait is on a Minton teapot stand. Although in this case it is on an 8-inch tile, the central motif occupies no more than 6ins., and could well appear in that format also. The 'In Memoriam' specimen with its rather lugubrious legend is unattributed as to factory, and appears to be decorated with a lithographic print.

The two colour-glaze tiles, Plate 48(273 and 274), have two especial points of interest. Firstly, an almost identical portrait of the man appears in Barnard[42] on a tile attributed to the Trent Tile Co., New Jersey, USA. It is described as 'head of Michelangelo'. Who then is the companion? As the captions indicate the tiles illustrated are from our own collection and are marked 'Flaxman', a concern not recorded in either Jewitt or Barnard, though one which undoubtedly existed in Longton c.1890-1930. Interestingly, Leonard Brammer the artist whose engravings captured so much of the atmosphere of the Potteries in the 1930s, still retains a copy of one of the fine studies he did of the Flaxman Tile Works.

If there is doubt about the identity of the old man's companion, there should be none about that of Plate 48(275), the celebrated Lady Emma Hamilton. This study and the more sober visage of William Ewart Gladstone, Plate 48(276) are both products of the firm which started out as Sherwin & Cotton (see p.60). They specialised in portraits whose effects were obtained by careful modelling and glazing. It is frequently stated that these tiles were made by a 'photographic process'. This would seem to be incorrect for the modeller responsible, George Cartlidge (b.1868), described his methods of work in two letters to Geoffrey Godden.[43] A model of the subject was first made in clay, from this a plaster cast was taken, and from that a metal die was made. The tile was made, fired, and then dipped in a coloured glaze and placed in the kiln with such care that it lay perfectly flat with the glaze evenly distributed so that the hollows held the deeper pools and the raised portions a thinner layer of colour. Thus a shaded effect was achieved much finer than that on a normal relief tile where the glaze tended to be of even thickness. The effect *looks* like a photograph, but it is not a photographic process. What may have helped to foster this idea is that Cartlidge usually worked from photographs, indeed a number of these are in the City Museum, Stoke-on-Trent, together with a fine collection of Cartlidge's tiles. His first portrait was the Gladstone tile done in 1898, and was followed by many successful portrait tiles which are listed below, they included two Maori chiefs and many First World War personalities. After the war Cartlidge went to America to work for a tile firm, but returned in a few years. His last model was of Thomas Hardy, a limited edition of thirty issued in 1924.

In addition to Gladstone and Hardy, the following portraits are known to have been modelled by Cartlidge, many of them from photographs which he acknowledged in script on the back of the pieces.

Queen Victoria, Diamond Jubilee 1897, 'A Queenly Woman, A

Womanly Queen'

Pope Pius X

Abraham Lincoln, Plate 49(279), on the 100th Anniversary of his birth 12th February 1809 'modelled from the only untouched negative in the United States, taken 1864'

Conrad Dressler (the inventor of the continuous tunnel kiln)

President Woodrow Wilson, 1916

H.C. Sawyer, Esq.

Mr. W.M. Hughes, 'Prime Minister of Australia', sculpt. 1916.

General Smuts, 'Modelled by Geo. Cartlidge after a photograph by Elliott & Fry Ltd.'

J.H. Boycott, Esq.

Sidney K. Dodd

Matene te Nga, a Maori chief

Bella Iles and Sophia Iles, Maori women guides

Admiral Sir David Beatty

General Sir John J. Pershing

'yours faithfully Fred Hodge'

Sidney R. Maw, Esq.

Rt. Hon. David Lloyd George

Rt. Hon. H.H. Asquith

Admiral Sir John Jellicoe

Marshall Foch

General Haig

Whilst he was in America he is known to have modelled General Leonard Wood and General Harding.

Apart from the political and figure subjects noted above, the City Museum, Stoke-on-Trent also possesses examples of 'Gaiety Girls', 'The Village Belle', 'Musicians', 'Compliments of the Season', and several animal studies (cow, bull, dog, stag) and other less easily-defined

Figure 59. Page from the tile catalogue of Sherwin & Cotton showing a number of their standard colour-glazed figure subjects. c.1900-1905. Courtesy City Museum and Art Gallery, Stoke-on-Trent.

277

278

279

280

281

282

subjects produced by the same process. Some are signed by Cartlidge, others are anonymous. From the evidence of the marks it is clear that this type of tile was produced successively by Sherwin & Cotton then Adams & Cartlidge Ltd. and J.H. Barrett & Co. Ltd. A section of a sample catalogue page of Sherwin & Cotton's colour glazed figure tiles is illustrated in Figure 59.

Comment has already been made about the two American scenes, Plate 49(277 and 278), and a list of other topographical and historical scenes is given on pp.97-101.

The next three tiles, Plate 49(280, 281 and 282), are difficult to classify. It is perhaps not inappropriate that 'AMBITION' should follow the political and historical personalities, though perhaps it is stretching the analogy too far to link the politicians with the next two subjects 'IGNORANCE' and 'IDLENESS'! These three tiles are personal studies from a twelve subject Minton series entitled 'Rustic Humours', pattern 1455, introduced c.1875. The other subjects are not listed in the factory catalogue and to date the author has no note of them.

The next three, Plate 50(283-285), examples all depict anonymous women. The Craven Dunnill piece (283) looks very familiar and would seem to be taken from a painting — Alma Tadema or Lord Leighton come to mind — but no correct source can be given. The style of decoration on (284) seems to suggest the work of an amateur. This is not an infrequent occurence, and indeed the work of amateurs does appear on marked tiles as well as unmarked. The standard of accomplishment is very variable and it is not always fair to blame the factory whose name appears on the tile for the poor execution of enamelled decoration — it may be an amateur's first effort!

The next in this personal series, Plate 50(285), 'Rose' is one of a pair with 'Iris'. Though this particular example is in a single glaze colour, there are many examples from Mintons and other factories of panels depicting women, cherubs and other persons in multi-colour glazes or in on-glaze enamels. The Minton archives include many drawings for such panels from various designers, one of the most prolific of whom was Herbert William Foster (1848-1929) who could well have been the designer of 'Rose' and of the two women with the kitten, Plate 51(286), a typical example of a watercolour panel design from the Minton archives.

Plate 49.
(277) *Print from the Wedgwood tile pattern book* — Landing of the Pilgrims 1620, *pattern T 417. Introduced. c.1885-1890 (see text).* Courtesy The Wedgwood Museum, Barlaston. **(278)** *Printed underglaze in blue with an imaginary American War of Independence scene, 'Spirit of '76 Yankee Doodle'. 6ins. Mark: 'T. & R. Boote Ltd.' and the Wedgwood Portland vase mark. Early twentieth century (see text for details).* Courtesy The Wedgwood Museum, Barlaston. **(279)** *Moulded with a portrait of 'Abraham Lincoln, born 12th Feb'y 1809. Copyright 1891 by H. Price. G.C. sculpt.' Decorated with a translucent brown glaze. On the back is incised: 'In commemoration of the One Hundredth Anniversary celebration of the Birth of Abraham Lincoln, February 12th 1809' (see text). 9ins. by 6ins. Mark: 'Made by Sherwin & Cotton, Eastwood Tile Works, Hanley, Staffordshire.'* Courtesy City Museum and Art Gallery, Stoke-on-Trent. **(280)** *Block printed in pale blue on a white ground with a figure of a bearded countryman symbolic of 'AMBITION', one of twelve 'Rustic Humours'. 6ins. Mark: 'Mintons China Works etc.' Introduced c.1875.* **(281)** *As for (280), 'IGNORANCE.'* **(282)** *As for (282), 'IDLENESS'.*

283

284

285

Plate 50.
(283) *Relief moulded tile decorated with a translucent green glaze depicting a reclining figure of a woman watching a parrot feed from a large bowl. 12ins. by 6ins. Mark: 'Craven Dunnill & Co. etc.' c.1890.* **(284)** *Hand painted in overglaze enamel colours with a Dutch-type interior depicting a girl leaning pensively near a window. 12ins. by 6ins. No mark, no signature. c.1885.* **(285)** *Relief moulded tile decorated with a translucent brown glaze depicting a young girl, 'ROSE', surrounded by roses. 12ins. by 6ins. Mark: 'MINTONS' impressed. Pattern number 2609E (the companion 'IRIS' is 2610E). Introduced c.1894.*

Foster was born in Endon and his father and his wife were both artists. Foster himself studied at Hanley Art School and worked for Mintons. Like William Wise he went to the National School of Art in South Kensington, and possibly worked with Wise on the tile panels for the Victoria and Albert Museum. He was also connected with the Mintons Kensington Gore Studio. Foster exhibited at the Royal Academy and after over twenty years as a figure painter at Mintons he left to teach at the life class at Nottingham School of Art.

The large plaque, Plate 51(287), is a further example from the Della Robbia Pottery. It is a finely modelled and sensitive study in a neo-Renaissance style. Rosamond Allwood speculates that the initials 'M de C' might stand for an as yet unidentified member of the family of E. de Calawe whom she records as being Harold Rathbone's partner from c.1900.[44] More than likely it would be Mrs. de Calawe, for Helen Williams records that a Della Robbia employee, Mrs. Threlfall, describes "Mrs. du Calowe" (no Christian name is given) as "a very clever designer".[45] Whoever was responsible for the actual plaque the design is based upon a plaster relief by R. Anning-Bell, the then Director of the Liverpool College of Art who had close connections with the Pottery.

The last of the 'personal' illustrations is the very charming plaque from Mintons, Plate 51(288). It is a most skilful design, fluent and sensitive and represents the best of the more restrained element in art nouveau design. It is well worth the attention of any collector even though the designer, like the young lady, is anonymous.

Plate 51. See page 186.
(286) *Watercolour drawings from the Minton archives depicting two women each nursing a kitten, annotated 'Left' and 'Right', indicative of a pair of tile panels, (Jones, Minton MSS, No. 1858). Attributed to H.W. Foster, c.1880.* Courtesy Royal Doulton Tableware Ltd. **(287)** *Solid clay plaque modelled in relief with a mother and child study, decorated in shades of yellow and green glazes on a mid-blue ground. 17ins. by 8¼ins. Mark: 'D R' (for Della Robbia) 'M de C' and 'No 08'. c.1902 (see text).* Courtesy Birmingham City Museum and Art Galleries. **(288)** *Solid clay plaque moulded in low relief outline with a charming study of a girl holding a flower. Decorated in translucent coloured glazes. 18ins by 12ins. Mark: 'MINTONS', impressed, and year code for 1898.* Courtesy Royal Doulton Tableware Ltd.

286

287

288

Plate 51. See page 185 for details.

10. TRADES, OCCUPATIONS AND COUNTRY LIFE

One of the unintended consequences of the Arts and Crafts movement was the impetus it imparted to a nostalgic romanticism. On tiles more than any other ceramic form this medievalism was prominent. In the depiction of the happy, pre-industrial craftsman, the tile designers gave full expression to the touchingly naïve belief that life was simpler, more dignified, noble and uplifting in the pre-machine days of Merrie England. Moyr Smith was perhaps less affected by this romantic spirit than most designers, though the twelve *Husbandry* subjects he did for Mintons, Plate 52(293), are dressed in the medieval manner. These designs were produced on both 6-inch and 8-inch tiles in a variety of colour treatments including some rare examples with a hand painted finish. The other subjects noted are:

'Scything'
'Fishing'
'A Shepherd'
'A Woodcutter'
'A Gardner'
'Threshing'
'Fruit Gathering'
'Digging'
'Corn Cutting'

The other Minton series Smith designed, 'Industrial', Plate 52(289 and 290), 'Arts and Sciences', Plate 52(291 and 292) and 'Classical Figures with Musical Instruments', Plate 52(294), are more true to his usual classical interpretations. The 'Industrial' series is one of the best known of all Smith's work, and, indeed, has been paid the compliment of being most effectively reproduced in recent years by H. & R. Johnson Richards Tiles Ltd. The twelve titles in the series as given in the printed factory catalogue are:[46]

'Barber'
'Potter'
'Shoemaker'
'Dyer'
'Tanner'
'Painter'
'Smith'
'Weaver', Plate 52(289)
'Tailor'
'Carpenter'
'Plumber', Plate 52(290)
'Mason'.

The series was produced in several different colour finishes.

The 'Arts and Sciences' series appears from the earliest pattern book entry to be a late product. The number given is 2455, which would give a date of introduction c.1892-1894. This is a tentative dating, but certainly the designs are far removed stylistically from Smith's earlier work. Two other subjects are recorded. 'Mechanics' and 'Agriculture'. No note of the series has been observed in the factory catalogue, thus the extent of the series is unknown.

The last of the Moyr Smith designs in this section, Plate 52(294), is from another of the series which were given very rich decorative treatment. Several examples of these 'Classical Figures with Musical Instruments' have been noted with gold backgrounds as well as the multicolour finish of the example illustrated here. The series consists of eight subjects: 'Lute', 'Cymbals', 'Harp', 'Double Flute', 'Sistrum', 'Kithara', 'Tambourine' and 'Pandean pipes'.

Turning to Copelands we see the psuedo-medieval style at its most prominent. Examples are illustrated here of three out of four medieval series emanating from this factory. The lady 'Astronomer', Plate 53(295), is one of a set of probably six subjects, the others being 'Painting', 'Embroidery', 'Literature', 'Music' (Colour Plate IX) and 'Sculpture'. All are enamelled over a printed outline and were produced in both 6-inch and 8-inch sizes. The potter, Plate 53(296) and the serving maid with the horn of wine, Plate 53(298), are from a set for which thirteen designs exist, though probably only twelve were used.

Oddly enough, as the list below indicates, the barmaid *(sic)* is the only female figure in this very attractive series which was produced as an underglaze blue print, and also coloured in enamel overglaze. The subjects are:

'Knight jousting'
'Skittles player'
'Nightwatchman'
'Carpenter'
'Husbandman'
'Armourer'
'Longbowman' (Colour Plate IX)
'Pedlar'
'Crossbowman'
'Maidservant', Plate 53(298)
'Fisherman'
'Musketeer'
'Potter', Plate 53(296).

The designer is not known, though stylistically there is a very close resemblance between these figures, and those of the medieval musicians, Plate 53(299), and to attribute them both to the same person would not be unreasonable. Various names have been suggested for both series,

Plate 52.
(289) *Underglaze block print in blue on a white slip ground depicting 'THE WEAVER' one of a series of twelve designs by Moyr Smith entitled 'Industrial'. Mark: initialled 'J.M.S.', otherwise unmarked but from Mintons China Works, pattern 1342, introduced c.1870-1872.* **(290)** *As for (289), 'THE PLUMBER'. Mark: 'Mintons China Works etc.' and initials 'MS'.* **(291)** *Underglaze print in grey on a pale cream slip ground depicting 'SCULPTURE', one of a series of 'Arts and Sciences'. Mark: 'Mintons China Works etc.' and the signature Moyr Smith. c.1892 (see text).* **(292)** *As for (291), 'ARCHITECTURE', full Minton marks and designer's signature.* **(293)** *Print from the Minton tile pattern book (Jones, Minton MSS, No. 1842) depicting a peasant in medieval attire 'Ploughing'. One of a series of twelve subjects entitled 'Husbandry', designed for Mintons, by Moyr Smith. Pattern 1407, introduced c.1876. Courtesy Royal Doulton Tableware Ltd.* **(294)** *Underglaze block print in blue, pale yellow and brown on a white slip ground depicting a female 'Keltic Harp' player, one of eight subjects in the series 'Classical Figures with Musical Instruments'. 8ins. Mark: 'Mintons China Works etc.' Signed 'Moyr Smith'. Pattern 1466, introduced c.1876-1877.*

289

290

291

292

293

294

295

296

297

298

299

300

including Stacey Marks and Edward Hammond — the designer of Plate 53(300), but until documentary evidence is forthcoming, it is probably wisest to let these most attractive Copeland examples be recorded as "designer — unattributed". It is worth adding that the medieval musician, Plate 53(299), flanked by sunflowers is redolent of the mood of the aesthetic movement.[47] The first pattern book entry is at pattern 920, which indicates a date of introduction of 1878.

The Minton 'Musicians' series, Plate 53(300) and Colour Plate IX, was designed by Edward Hammond assisted by Matthew Elden at the Minton Kensington Studio c.1872-1875, and thus pre-dates the Copeland series by several years.[48] The tiles were originally produced in monochrome blue, sometimes with additional enamelling, and at a rather later date appear to have been re-issued in a moulded low relief version decorated with colour glazes.

A few further occupational designs merit comment. The Wedgwood tile, Plate 53(297), is again medieval in inspiration, and is paired with pattern T 270 which depicts 'YE LAW' and 'YE MEDICINE' with a sun-ray motif in the two remaining quarters.

The Maw factory produced a series of 'Trades'. These designs are set in a circular panel with a simple double-line squared frame. The pattern numbers are listed as 2410-2421 for the following subjects: 'Blacksmith', 'Carpenter', 'Forrester', 'Tailor', 'Painter', 'Cooper', 'Bricklayer', 'Navvy', 'Stone Mason', 'Shoemaker', 'Shipwright', 'Founder'. These are rare, and we cannot recall having seen examples of either this set or of a Maw series of six subjects of Japanese women at work or play.[49] Miss Aslin illustrates two of a set of medieval craftsmen decorated by W.B. Simpson.[50]

Copeland made another series of medieval occupations comprising six male, untitled subjects on 8-inch tiles printed and painted: 'The Blacksmith', 'The Artist', 'The Gardener', 'The Sculptor', 'The Alchemist' and 'The Musician'. The same firm produced a set of six tiles each decorated with a pair of women in classical attire engaged in rural activities: 'fruit picking', 'log gathering', 'corn cutting', 'haymaking', 'seed sowing' and an unidentified subject; the designer was almost certainly Lucien Besche (see p.171). Copeland too was the firm responsible for the 'Chinese Trades' in Plate 56(317 and 318). Seventeen watercolour designs are in the Copeland collection, but there is no sign of

Plate 53.
(295) *Watercolour design from the Copeland tile pattern book depicting a woman in medieval attire studying a terrestrial or celestial globe. Pattern 960, introduced c.1878.* Courtesy The Spode Museum. **(296)** *Watercolour drawing depicting a potter at work, one of a series of 'Medieval crafts' designed for Copelands. The first pattern book entry is for pattern 919 (the carpenter), introduced 1877.* Courtesy The Spode Museum. **(297)** *Print from the Wedgwood tile pattern book of a quartered tile depicting 'YE ARMY' and 'YE CHURCH' (usually printed in underglaze blue), pattern T 269, introduced c.1878.* Courtesy The Wedgwood Museum, Barlaston. **(298)** *Underglaze blue print on a white slip ground, depicting the maidservant from the series noted in (296). 6ins. No mark, but Copelands. c.1880.* **(299)** *Underglaze blue print on a white slip ground depicting a medieval musician seated between two sunflowers. 6ins. No mark, but Copelands. Introduced c.1878 (see text).* **(300)** *Watercolour design from the Minton archives (Jones, Minton MSS, No. 1815) depicting a medieval musician, one of a series designed — and in this instance signed — by Edward Hammond for Mintons China Works. c.1872-1875.* Courtesy Royal Doulton Tableware Ltd.

the series in the pattern books. Nevertheless, the tile (317) would seem to conform to the mounted designs — a curious discrepancy.

Returning from the more general topic of trades and occupations to the specific subject of music, further interesting examples are illustrated in Plate 54(301-305). We are still with Copeland with (301), the top half of a two or three tile design, but from the pre-Raphaelite influence of this hand-painted specimen we return to classical musicians, and one of a set of six such subjects from the Wedgwood factory, Plate 54(302). The two Minton prints, Plate 54(303 and 304), are the only two examples we have seen of either of these two series. The eighteenth century rococo border to the 'Watteau' series of twelve will be helpful in identifying other designs which may well not be based upon a musical theme. The same may be said for the 'Albert Durer' series, again of twelve subjects. This is the only design so far recorded, and though a copper plate for this subject is in the room of the head engraver at Mintons, other examples could not be located. As there is no border pattern to characterise the series, the collector will be on the look out for well etched and engraved scenes from late medieval German life.

The last musical scene is the Minton Hollins example dating from 1875, Plate 54(306), and with it the only other recorded subject from this arts (and sciences?) series, 'Sculpture', Plate 54(305). No designer can be credited with these two pieces which are printed rather faintly. Though they are pleasant, they seem tentative and lacking in conviction, indeed the subject of (305) seems to be a contortionist as well as a sculptress! Two prints in the Minton Hollins catalogue show 'Architecture' and 'Medicine' from a different series.

Examples of the work of William Wise the Minton artist have already been illustrated and commented upon in the sections on Landscapes and Places, Animals, Birds and Fish, and The Calendar.[51]

As Wise figures so prominently in this book it is worth noting the salient facts about him. William Wise was born in 1847 in London and appears to have exhibited artistic talents at an early age. He trained at art school in the period 1867-1871, and during this time was already a married man with children. In the years 1871-1875 he came into contact with the Mintons Kensington Art Pottery Studio, where he may well have met many of the artists and designers such as Dresser, Marks, Moyr Smith and Foster who had connections with this lively if ill-fated venture.

Plate 54.
(301) *Solid clay tile painted freehand underglaze with the head and shoulders of a pre-Raphaelite young man playing a musical instrument (part only of a two or three tile panel). 8ins. Mark: 'Copeland' (impressed) and '4 79' possibly for April 1879.* **(302)** *Print from the Wedgwood tile pattern book of a seated youth playing pipes for a lady. One of a series of six 'Musicians'. Pattern 292, introduced c.1880.* Courtesy The Wedgwood Museum, Barlaston. **(303)** *Print from the Minton pattern book of a boy playing a flute to a seated girl, both in eighteenth century costume. One of a series of twelve subjects entitled 'Watteau'. c.1880-1885 (Jones, Minton MSS, No. 1842).* Courtesy Royal Doulton Tableware Ltd. **(304)** *Print from the Minton Pattern book depicting a man and women in late medieval attire playing musical instruments. One of a series of twelve subjects entitled 'Albert Durer'. c.1885 (Jones, Minton MSS, No. 1842).* Courtesy Royal Doulton Tableware Ltd. **(305)** *Printed underglaze in brown on a cream ground with a female figure symbolic of 'Sculpture'. 6ins. Mark: 'Minton Hollins & Co. etc.' and design registration for 8th November, 1875.* **(306)** *As (305), depicting 'Music.' Introduced 1875.*

301

302

303

304

305

306

307

308

309

310

311

312

He certainly came under the influence there of W.S. Coleman, a fact which can readily be deduced by the style and treatment of many of his subjects especially female figure studies (see Figure 56). A considerable number of such watercolour designs for tile panels and the like are in a portfolio in the Minton archives (Minton MSS, No. 1858) and though not all are signed many are by Wise and date from the 1870s. After the closure of the Studio and the death of his first wife some time previously, Wise moved to Stoke and began his association with Mintons as a freelance designer, etcher and engraver and decorator of pottery and porcelain vases, plates and plaques. His work as a decorator was exhibited in Paris in 1878. His first tile designs were completed a year later — the series 'Animals of the Farm'. At the age of thirty-two he seemed destined for a long and distinguished career, but it was not to be. He was the victim of many pressures not least of which were eight children and, as a freelance, the necessity to work ever harder to support his family at their home in Mayne Street, Hanford, must have taken a considerable toll. Not only was he painting, designing, etching and engraving for Mintons, but he held regular evening classes also. Apparently, his health gave way and he died on 10th September, 1889 aged only forty-two and leaving to his second wife the rather inadequate inheritance of £120 2s. 3d. and eight children.

During his working life with Mintons he was able to command good fees. The Artists Wages Book (Minton MSS, No. 662) contain these entries under Mr. Wyse *(sic)*:

"1877 for engraving the *Anacreon* set. 12 plates by Moir Smith, 25/-per plate. £15:0:0.

Oct. 3rd. Etching a bull plate for Reynolds £1:12:0. (Figure 44).

do of a sheep on 12" tile £1:12:0. (Four days and four hours)

Oct. 31st. one day fireplace (No 1499) painted at home."

Other entries record payments for engraving, sketching, painting, etching, as well as "painting female head on plates", "working at home for biting copper plates" and "16 March 1882. 6 days engraving tiles, butterflies and Kate Greenaway subjects, £4:9:0."

These entries indicate a man of considerable and wide ranging talents employed freelance, in both tile and general pottery business, and often accountable to Alfred Reynolds (the manager of printing processes). Wise's earnings were high for those days. Clearly his work was esteemed.

Of the tiles which he designed we have already noted 'Animals of the Farm', and 'Cattle subjects' (or 'Animal Groups'), the set of 'Seasons' and the 'Landscapes', details of which are given in the appropriate sections. A number of other designs deserve note in this section on

Plate 55.
(307 and 308) *Pulls from the copper plate of scenes from a series of twelve designs by William Wise for Mintons entitled 'Village Life'. Pattern 1801, introduced c.1882.* Courtesy Royal Doulton Tableware Ltd. **(309)** *Print from the Minton pattern book depicting a boy in a stream, one of eight 'Rustic Figures'. c.1885 (see text).* Courtesy Royal Doulton Tableware Ltd. **(310)** *Preliminary pencil drawing by William Wise for a tile in the series 'Village Life'. c.1882.* Courtesy Royal Doulton Tableware Ltd. **(311)** *Printed underglaze in brown on a deep cream ground with an etched design of a girl feeding fowl and pigeons. 6ins. Mark: 'Mintons China Works etc.' Signed: 'W. Wise'. c.1882-1885.* **(312)** *As for (311), a girl feeding ducklings. Mintons. Signed: 'W. Wise'. c.1882-1885.*

'Country Life', though to place all the designs so far recorded in their correct series, is not possible at this stage. The Minton pattern book clearly indicates a series of twelve subjects of 'Village Life', pattern 1801 of which Plate 55(308) is the actual print in the pattern book; Plate 55(307 and 310) are also taken from this series and other subjects which can definitely be assigned to 'Village Life' are:

A woman milking a cow with a boy and a baby nearby

Two women gleaning with a little girl beside them

A shepherd with his dog by a gate

A woman carrying a little girl talking to a boy

A woman standing whilst her companion is on hands and knees — planting potatoes

These subjects may just be discerned in Figure 10. This leaves four subjects not definitely identified. What complicates matters is that though there are plenty of drawings and off-prints in the Minton archives there is no check list of the precise subjects in each set. It might be assumed that Plate 55(309) also belonged to 'Village Life', but this is clearly labelled 'Rustic Figures', eight subjects and an out-of-sequence pattern no. '57'. A further series seems to be indicated by Plate 56(316), again a photograph of the Minton pattern book where the design is untitled, but numbered '2159—12 subjects'. It is into this series that the signed tiles Plate 55(311 and 312) seem to fit; Plate 56(313 and 314) also of women, may well come into this group, whereas Plate 56(315), which is unsigned, can only be given a 'probable' attribution. Other subjects which have been noted and which are definitely by Wise for one or other of these series are:

A woman carrying a basket of apples

A young woman with a deer

A young woman seated under a tree reading

A young woman carrying water over stepping stones

A young woman kneeling and feeding rabbits

Perhaps the correct placing of individual tiles to a series is of academic interest, but Wise's work is so good that it seems worth the effort. It is to be hoped that further research in the Minton archives will reveal additional panels, plaques, individual tiles and complete series which may be credited to this fine designer whose work well repays both study and collection.

William Wise whose mild and kindly face is shown in the self-portrait

Plate 56.
(313) *Underglaze etched transfer print in brown on cream ground depicting a peasant girl with a baby in a basket on her back. Mounted on four bun feet to form a teapot stand. 6ins. Mark: 'Mintons China Works etc.' Designed by William Wise. c.1885.* (314) *As for (313), on a white ground, a girl picking berries. 6ins. Mark: 'Mintons China Works etc.' Signed: 'WISE'. c.1885.* (315) *Underglaze print in black on a white ground depicting a seated young woman and a child, both with bundles of sticks or grasses. 6ins. Mark: 'Mintons China Works etc.' Probably by William Wise. c.1885.* (316) *Print from the Minton pattern book depicting a girl fishing on the seashore. Pattern number 2159, one of twelve subjects. Signed: 'W. Wise'. c.1885-1888.* Courtesy Royal Doulton Tableware Ltd. (317) *On-glaze painted design of a Chinaman. Unmarked, but the plastic clay tile has a 'combed' back. 5ins. Copeland. c.1880.* (318) *Mounted watercolour design depicting a Chinese weaver. One of seventeen coloured drawings of 'Chinese Trades' in the Copeland archives.* Courtesy The Spode Museum.

313

314

315

316

317

318

Figure 60. Self-portrait of the Minton artist William Wise, c.1876. Private collection, by courtesy Royal Doulton Tableware Ltd.

of 1876 (Figure 60), was unusual amongst the generality of Victorian tile designers. He relied upon a meticulous delineation of his etched and engraved subjects for which he himself was responsible at each stage from preliminary sketch, through finished design to engraved copper plate. He was both artist and craftsman displaying both true artistic individuality and creativity, and an awareness of the needs and techniques of industry.

11. FOOD AND DRINK

In this short section attention is drawn to five series which have come to notice, all concerned with food and drink. The five groups of tiles in a rather fascinating manner cover the main lines of approach to Victorian pictorial tiles taken by the designers at two of the main factories. In this small subject area can be seen the very strict classicism of Moyr Smith's 'Anacreon' series, the light and humorous treatment of Solon's 'Cooks', the slightly prim, middle-class stance of the 'Gastronomical' series, the somewhat moralising tone of Thomas Allen's 'Courses of a meal' and finally the fey, whimsical, almost surrealist treatment of the 'Gastronomic Homilies' from Wedgwood. All in all a revealing microcosm of some of the main elements of industrial decorative design of the period.

The first series illustrated, Plate 57(319 and 320), is an unusual set by Moyr Smith known as 'Anacreon'. Very fine coloured and gilt drawings are in the Minton archives of which (319) is an example. Furthermore, one of the factory Photograph Books (Minton MSS, No. 1645) contains pictures of the full series from which the titles which are in Greek and English on the face of the tile have been recorded. This series can be dated to 1877 by an entry in the Artists Wages Book (Minton MSS,

No.662) quoted on p.195, which records that William Wise was paid 25s. each for engraving the twelve copper plates used for printing the designs. The characters in the series are all in classical dress:

'The Host'
'The Hostess'
'The Guest'
'The Grace'
'The Manager'
'The Governor'
'The Cup Bearer'
'The Rose'
'The Master of the Revels'
'The Dessert'
'The Good Listener'
'The Libatior'.

They represent in Smith's words "the chief personages of an Argive Feast". From time to time Minton porcelain dessert plates are noted bearing designs from this series in full enamel colours and at least one such carried an inscription indicating that the series had been exhibited at the 1878 Paris Exhibition.

The next Minton series is, as was indicated earlier, much less earnest and serious. It is a series entitled 'Cooks' or 'Cooking' and its earliest factory pattern book number 2068 indicates a date of introduction in the mid-1880s. The catalogue describes it as "twelve subjects by Solon treated humourously". Four examples are illustrated here, Plate 57(321-324), and they give a rather different impression of "the most celebrated ceramic artist of the era" than one receives from most of his other recorded work.

Marc Louis Solon was born at Montauban in 1835, received his ceramic training at Sèvres and came to England and Mintons in 1870 as a result of the Franco-Prussian war. He remained with Mintons until his retirement in 1904, but continued to work freelance until his death in 1913. His main achievement was his work in the *pâte-sur-pâte* technique, a meticulous and painstaking form of decoration at which he was the acknowledged master. He himself published details of his life and work in *The Studio*, January 1894 and the *Art Journal,* March 1901. He was, of course, a distinguished writer on ceramics, his important books being on *Old English Porcelain, Old French Faience* and *The Art of the Old English Potter*. In front of me as I write is a copy of the illustrated catalogue of the three-day sale of the Solon ceramic collection held in Hanley in November 1912. All the prices are entered and *The Staffordshire Sentinel's* daily reports are stuck in at the end. It is a mouth watering confection of pre-1800 English pottery and porcelain — and the prices!

The great man's lighter touch then is seen in this 'Cooks' series the subjects of which are:

'Sausage machine'
'Smoked haddocks'
'Fried eel'
'Pigeon pie'
'First catch your hare', Plate 57(324)
'Baron of beef'

319

320

321

322

323

324

'Too many cooks', Plate 57(322)

'Executioner'

'Puzzled'

'The last victim'

'Fish supper', Plate 57(321)

'New laid eggs', Plate 57(323).

The third series from Mintons is entitled 'Gastronomical'. Again original drawings are in the Minton archives and Plate 58(326, 327 and 328) are photographs of these drawings. No artist's signature is attached and for the time being they must remain unattributed in this respect. The pattern book example, Plate 58(325), is given the number 1871, and an interesting entry in the Wages Book indicates that on 17th June, 1880 William Wise was paid 2s.3d. for one hour's work for "biting in gastronomical subject replaced". An indication of the date of introduction which fits well with dating derived from the pattern number sequence (see p.35). The series appears on 6-inch and 8-inch tiles, "outlined and painted in colours by hand". The scenes are of a typical middle class Victorian household and depict, for example, the chef preparing the meal, the butler collecting the wine from the cellar, the lady of the house being served with dessert, etc. The series has a corner border pattern identical to that of the Shakespeare series, see Plate 28(159-162), the only occasion so far noted from the Minton factory of the same border motif serving two series.

The last two illustrations are of tiles produced by Wedgwood. Their art director Thomas Allen initialled some of the designs in the five-tile series 'Courses of a Meal'. The pattern books shows:

'Eat thy food with a thankful heart — Mutton'

'Enough means health, more disease — Soup'

'May good digestion wait upon appetite — Fish'

'A little pudding adds to the repast — Pastry', Plate 58(329)

'Eat to live, live to eat — Venison'

Versions of these subjects also appear on dinner wares.[52] It is an open question as to whether Thomas Allen was the designer of the next series, the very remarkable 'Gastronomic Homilies' Plate 58(330). There are certainly resemblances to his style, and the lettering is remarkably akin to that on the previous series, Plate 58(329). If they are Allen's then it is a departure from the norm as remarkable as that of Solon's 'Cooks' series. These designs appear on tableware as well as on tiles and like most

Plate 57.
(319) *Watercolour drawing from the Minton archives depicting 'The Grace' one of twelve subjects entitled 'Anacreon'. Designed by Moyr Smith. 1877 (see text).* Courtesy Royal Doulton Tableware Ltd. **(320)** *Multi-colour block printed tile of 'The Guest' from the 'Anacreon' series. 8ins. Mark: 'Mintons China Works etc.' Signed: 'Moyr Smith'. 1877.* **(321)** *Preliminary design from the Minton archives for 'Fish supper', from a series of twelve designs by M.L. Solon entitled 'Cooks'. c.1885-1888. (Jones, Minton MSS, No. 1810.)* Courtesy Royal Doulton Tableware Ltd. **(322)** *As for (321), 'Too many cooks'.* Courtesy Royal Doulton Tableware Ltd. **(323)** *Print from the Minton pattern book of 'New laid eggs', from the 'Cooks' series. Pattern no. 2072. c.1885-1888. (Jones, Minton MSS, No. 1842.)* Courtesy Royal Doulton Tableware Ltd. **(324)** *As for (323), 'First catch your hare', but pattern number 2068 (see text).* Courtesy Royal Doulton Tableware Ltd.

Wedgwood tiles seem disproportionately expensive (see Price Guide, p.228).

There is a full set of twelve subjects in the Wedgwood pattern book, recorded under pattern T 289 a-l. Each tile depicts these curious child clowns, elves, leprechauns or Chinese clowns — call them what you will, in a variety of ludicrous encounters with everyday household objects. Surrounding the design is an appropriate homily. In every case the joke is predominantly visual with the homily itself also being quietly satirised, for example, the 'little people' are depicted dragging off a roast chicken of comparatively enormous size, the homily is "treason is now owned when 'tis descried, successful crimes alone are justified". Although this series is quite unforgettable once seen, for the sake of a complete record the twelve homilies are recorded below, with the central motif appended in brackets.

'By doing nothing we learn to do ill' (stealing beer)
'He laughs at scars that never felt a wound' (quills)
'The way a man wishes to go, thither his feet will carry him' (balancing on a knife)
'Lowliness is young ambitions ladder', Plate 58(330), (soda siphon)
'Treason is now owned when 'tis descried, successful crimes alone are justified', (chicken stealing)
'He that would eat the kernel, must crack the nut' (nutcracker)
'The circles of our felicities make short arches' (serviette ring)
'Even the ripest fruit does not drop into one's mouth' (melon)
'We lessen our wants, by lessening our desire' (cat in a jar)
'You must be content sometimes with rough roads' (spoon chariot)
'Fly the pleasure that bites tomorrow' (lemon squeezer)
'Let another man's shipwreck be your seamark' (cork popping)

Plate 58.
(325) *Print from the Minton pattern book of a chef at the stove, one of twelve 'Gastronomical' subjects, for 6-inch tiles, pattern number 1871, introduced 1880 (see text). (Jones, Minton MSS, No. 1842.)* Courtesy Royal Doulton Tableware Ltd. **(326)** *Preliminary watercolour sketch of 'The Butler' from the Minton 'Gastronomical' series. 1880. (Jones, Minton MSS, No. 1917.)* Courtesy Royal Doulton Tableware Ltd. **(327)** *As for (326), 'Preparing the meal'.* **(328)** *As for (326), 'Serving the soup'.* **(329)** *Print from the Wedgwood tile pattern book of 'A little pudding adds to the repast — Pastry' from a series of five 'Courses of a Meal' designed by Thomas Allen, pattern number T 277 D. c.1880 (see text).* Courtesy The Wedgwood Museum, Barlaston. **(330)** *Print from the Wedgwood tile pattern book of 'Lowliness is Young Ambitions Ladder' from a series of ten 'Gastronomic Homilies'. Pattern T 289 d. c.1880 (see text).* Courtesy The Wedgwood Museum, Barlaston.

325

326

327

328

329

330

12. MISCELLANEOUS PATTERNS

In this last section the main concern is with abstract patterns and geometric designs of one form of another. These range from designs introduced in the 1840s and continue, though not in strict chronological order, through the century to end with the art nouveau designs of the Edwardian period.

The section starts with several miscellaneous pictorial designs rather loosely linked by the theme of ships and the sea. The first two illustrations, Plate 59(331 and 332), are William de Morgan designs of pseudo-medieval ships. Galleon designs such as these were popular not only with de Morgan who produced similar designs in lustre on pots, but continued in the repertoire of art and studio potters well into the twentieth century as examples from the Poole Pottery and Pilkingtons of the 1910s and 1920s testify.

The anonymous tile, Plate 59(334), the Wedgwood example, is specifically aimed at the American market. It is one of four ship prints which appear next to a lengthy section of American views in the factory pattern book (see p.98). The other three ship prints are 'The Intrepid', pattern T 493, 'The Lillie off Telegraph Hill', pattern T 494, and 'The Rebecca' pattern T 497. These four fine prints are rarely encountered in England. The two Minton 'Japonaiserie' patterns are also rare, but like so many previous examples in other sections reflect the very considerable interest in Japanese design which slowly developed in the years following the Japanese Exhibition in London in 1862.

The next three Plates are roughly in chronological order spanning a period of about fifty years. The first illustration, Plate 60(337), is taken from the Copeland pattern book. It is of a design which appeared on Greek vases, was copied by Josiah Wedgwood from the engravings to Sir William Hamilton's books on his collection, and appears here on Copeland tiles in at least eight different treatments between their pattern numbers 243 and 340.

The Copeland pattern books provide a fascinating perspective of the development of general tile designs. Pattern book one runs from pattern 1-149. A very valuable dating point is provided by an entry against pattern 30, "outline printed in black, Pattern sheet send *(sic)* to London

Plate 59.
(331) *Framed tile painted underglaze in blue with a medieval ship design. 6ins. Mark: Merton Abbey mark of William de Morgan. c.1885.* Courtesy City Museum and Art Gallery, Stoke-on-Trent. **(332)** *Fanciful medieval ship design painted in lustre on a white slip ground. 6ins. Mark: Sands End rose mark of William de Morgan. c.1888-1890.* Courtesy Sotheby's Belgravia. **(333)** *Printed underglaze in blue with a scene of fishermen and their boats, in imitation of Dutch delft. 6ins. Mark: 'ENGLAND 15 K1 pattern 5399'. Early twentieth century.* **(334)** *Print from the Wedgwood pattern book of American sailing ships, 'Running in from the Light Ship'. For 6-inch tile. c.1890.* Courtesy The Wedgwood Museum, Barlaston. **(335)** *Print from a Minton pattern book depicting a Japanese girl waving to ships at sea, set within a fan and surrounded by prunus blossom. Pattern number 1912. For 6-inch tile c.1885. (Jones, Minton MSS, No. 1842.)* Courtesy Royal Doulton Tableware Ltd. **(336)** *Print from a Minton pattern book depicting a Japanese fisherman, as (335). Pattern number 1911 (see text). For 6-inch tile. c.1885. (Jones, Minton MSS, No. 1842.)* Courtesy Royal Doulton Tableware Ltd.

331

332

333

334

336

335

337

338

339

340

341

342

Figure 61. Moulded in low relief with a stylised floral design decorated with a translucent green glaze. 6ins. No mark. c.1895.

November 2/40". Scattered throughout this and the five subsequent pattern books are similar notes which enable a reasonably reliable dating sequence for the introduction of patterns to be established, at least until 1880. From this evidence we can see that many of the patterns in the 1840s, 1850s and 1860s were geometric — often with an affinity to the fashionable neo-Gothic designs. There are many encaustic tile designs and quite a few floral patterns both printed and enamel coloured. One charming 10ins. by 10ins. tile has a border of holly, a sprig of mistletoe in the centre and the legend 'A Happy New Year to You'. As the pattern number is 202, this would seem to date from c.1848 (pattern 313 was "sent to London 8 March 1853").

During the 1850s more pictorial designs appear with scenes of rustic lovers and the like, and landscapes. Sèvres revival designs are also evident, and in the early 1860s the first entry for a private pattern occurs (see p.37). But there is really no fundamental change in the style of design; even the appearance of pattern 817, a circular jug stand printed with the legend 'Allsopp's Pale Ale', is only a temporary departure, though there is a considerable number of patterns of a circular shape for jug stands, not tile centres which might at first glance confuse the unwary. The first figure design of the type we have been discussing throughout this book appears in 1876, pattern 881, several years after

Plate 60.
(337) *Printed and painted design from the Copeland pattern book depicting a classical scene set within an elaborate arrangement of border patterns. For an 8-inch tile, pattern 244. c.1848-1850.* Courtesy The Spode Museum. **(338)** *A printed and hand-coloured elaborate geometric-type pattern set round a plain circular centre. Mark: 'Minton & Co. Stoke-on-Trent. Prosser's Patent'. The tile is pattern 455. c.1855-1860.* **(339)** *An attractive moulded design, glazed in a variety of rich opaque majolica colours. Mark: 'Minton & Co. Stoke-on-Trent'. c.1865-1870.* **(340)** *Moulded repetitive design decorated in opaque majolica glaze colours of pale blue, yellow, red, green and dark blue on a white ground. 8ins. Mark: 'Minton Hollins & Co. etc.' c.1870-1875.* **(341)** *Printed and painted geometric design in shades of orange, brown and turquoise on a white background. 6ins. Mark: 'S.F. & Co.' (Samuel Fielding & Co. Fenton), and registered design number for 1889.* **(342)** *Simple underglaze transfer pattern in shades of grey on a white ground. 6ins. Mark: 'L & B ENGLAND', pattern 486, attributed to Lee & Boulton, Tunstall. c.1900.*

comparable Minton examples. For the next five or six years the number of patterns issued annually rises very considerably, and the style changes too. The geometric and abstract designs continue, but they bear traces of the influence of the Aesthetic Movement rather than the neo-Gothic.

Figure 62. Printed underglaze in black with a stylised swirling design of fruit and foliage on a white ground. 6ins. Mark: pattern number '393' (possibly S. Fielding & Co.). c.1890.

Figure 63. Solid clay tile moulded in medium high relief with a stylised design of foliage and buds decorated in cream and green glazes on a brown ground. 6ins. Mark: 'PATENTED', no attribution. c.1885-1890.

Production continued at Copeland well into the 1890s but the firm seems to have fallen well behind its competitors in the 'art tile' business. In the sixth pattern book the last tile pattern 1357 is entered, and subsequent to this the patterns are all for circular jug stands for such enterprises as 'Bass Pale Ale' and the 'Lancashire and Yorkshire Railway Refreshment Department' (c.1890 in date). A sad declension from the many fine designs both abstract and pictorial produced in the preceding half century.

Returning to the illustrations, Plate 60(338 and 339) both emanate from Mintons. The former with the mark 'Prosser's Patent' is of pattern 455 and would seem to date from the 1850s. Plate 60(339) is somewhat later and is finished in brightly coloured majolica glazes. Despite a date of

Plate 61.
(343) *Printed underglaze in blue on a white ground with a group of aesthetic symbols, a willow pattern plate, a Chinese dragon jar, etc. 6ins. Mark: 'Minton Hollins & Co. etc.' c.1875-1880.* **(344)** *Printed underglaze in turquoise on a white ground with a stylised floral and scale pattern resembling a peacock fantail. 8ins. Mark: 'Minton Hollins & Co. etc.' c.1875.* **(345)** *Part of a continuous repeating pattern of stylised chinoiserie leaves and a passion flower, printed underglaze in blue on a white ground. 8ins. Mark: 'Mintons China Works etc.' c.1875.* **(346)** *Printed underglaze in brown on an off-cream ground with a semi-abstract 'Paisley' type pattern. 6ins. Mark: 'Pattern No. T 358', attributed to Wedgwood. c.1885.* **(347)** *Printed outline underglaze in black, and painted in blue and green underglaze with a stylised classical vase and drapes, set against a foliage background. 6ins. Mark: 'Maw & Co. etc.' c.1880.* **(348)** *Moulded in relief with a neo-classical vase motif surrounded by floral swags. Decorated with a translucent green glaze. 8ins. Mark: 'Minton Hollins & Co. etc.' c.1885.*

343

344

345

346

347

348

349

351

350

352

353

c.1870 it has strong echoes of the earlier Pugin-style encaustic tile designs. Many similar tiles were produced by Maws, T. & R. Boote and other makers. Sometimes patterns originally intended for encaustic tiles reappear as decorative tiles. As has been noted earlier with the pictorial tiles, the tile makers were pleased to advertise their famous designers. The Campbell Tile Company price list claimed "a pattern book and designs by Pugin, Seddon, Gibbs, Dresser and others, sent by post on application to the Manufactory." Many of the abstract and geometric patterns obviously had a distinguished designer, but it is seldom that these can be attributed.

The influence of contemporary trends in the 1870s can be seen in Plate 61(343 and 344). The former recalls the passion for blue and white china of Oscar Wilde and his fellow aesthetes. (344) resembles in stylised fashion one of the symbols of the Aesthetic Movement, the fan-tail of peacock feathers.

Plate 61(345-348) and Plate 62(349-353), are typical examples from the period 1870-1900 from a variety of factories. The captions give full details of each and no further textual comment is called for. However, Plate 63(354), with the Biblical injunction of 'FEED MY LAMBS' is worth further attention. Similar examples from Maws probably were made, but we have not so far encountered them. However, attention has been drawn in the section on Food and Drink to the Wedgwood scenes depicting the diminutive Chinese clowns or possibly leprechauns disporting themselves with various articles of kitchen equipment, with the accompanying homilies such as 'you must be content sometimes with rough roads' which shows one of the little figures being dragged along seated in a teaspoon (see p.202). Furthermore, Barnard illustrates two examples from a series of mottoes, 'Waste Not Want Not' and 'A Place for Everything and Everything in its Place'. These appear in the Minton pattern book as pattern 1644 which would indicate a date of introduction c.1878, though one might have assumed, as Barnard does, an earlier date for their introduction. It is possible that the c.1878 entry represents a re-introduction of an old favourite. A handwritten list at the end of one of the pattern books gives us thirteen other titles in a set of tiles which carry no other pattern than the motto:

'Never trouble others for what you can do yourself'
'Nothing is troublesome that we do willingly'
'Efficiency and promptitude'
'When angry count ten before you speak, when very angry count one hundred'

Plate 62.
(349) *Printed underglaze in black on a white ground with a central oval medallion of musical trophies surrounded by scroll designs. 6ins. No mark. c.1880.* (350) *Underglaze printed design in brown, covering two tiles depicting flowers, fruit and classical ornaments, painted underglaze in yellow, greens and blue on a cream ground. 12ins. by 6ins. No mark. c.1880.* (351) *Printed underglaze with a mosaic pattern in grey, blue, green, orange, black and brown. 6ins. Mark: 'Mintons China Works etc.' c.1880.* (352) *Painted freehand overglaze with a design of a flower pot with lion's head and stylised tulips in green, black and yellow. 6ins. Mark: 'Minton Hollins & Co. etc.' c.1875.* (353) *Moulded design of transverse chevrons, in the centre a shield bearing the white rose. Decorated in translucent colour glazes of turquoise, green, cream and yellow. 6ins. Mark: 'P', moulded, for Pilkingtons, 'Rd. No. 519885', for January 1908.*

354

355

356

357

358

359

Figure 64. Art nouveau and similar designs from a single sheet tile catalogue of Stubbs and Hodgart, Portland Tile Works, Burslem. c.1900-1905. Courtesy City Museum and Art Gallery, Stoke-on-Trent.

'To use the world is nobler than to abuse it'

'To study the world is better than to shun it'

'We never repent having eaten too little'

'Never buy what you do not want because it is cheap'

'To make the world better and happier is the noblest work of man & woman'

'Never put off till tomorrow what you can do today'

'To understand the world is wiser than to condemn it'

'Pride costs us more than hunger thirst & cold'

'The pleasure of doing good is the only one that never ceases'

Plate 63(355) is a curious item and one of a group of tiles in the City Museum, Stoke-on-Trent, which are decorated with what appear to be experimental colour glazes of the type one usually associates with the pottery of Bernard Moore. This example is iridescent and others had glaze effects in a wide variety of colours and lustre. The mark which

Plate 63.
(354) *Decorated overglaze in black enamel with the Biblical injunction 'FEED MY LAMBS' in decorative lettering. 6ins. Mark: 'Maw & Co. etc.' c.1885 (see text).* Courtesy Rosamond Allwood. **(355)** *Solid clay tile moulded in the form of a heraldic shield and decorated in iridescent lustre glaze. 6ins. Mark: 'H & G THYNNE', of Hereford. c.1900.* Courtesy City Museum and Art Gallery, Stoke-on-Trent. **(356)** *Printed underglaze and hand coloured in green, brown and yellow with a 'Japonaiserie' pattern showing a variety of symbols on a cracked ice ground. 6ins. Mark: '723' and an impressed Staffordshire knot (probably Sherwin & Cotton). c.1880.* Courtesy Audrey Atterbury. **(357)** *Moulded with a 'Japonaiserie' pattern of fans and a lotus blossom, decorated with a green translucent glaze. 6ins. Mark: 'Rd. No. 410774', for mid-1903. No attribution.* Courtesy City Museum and Art Gallery, Stoke-on-Trent. **(358)** *Printed underglaze in blue on a white ground with a conventional design of an urn, flowers, scrolls and ribbons. 6ins. Mark: a moulded 'B', no attribution. c.1895.* **(359)** *Moulded in medium high relief with a circlet of flowers and a ribbon. Decorated in translucent pink and green glazes. 6ins. No mark. c.1900.*

Figure 65. Further examples of Stubbs & Hodgart's range of designs. Courtesy City Museum and Art Gallery, Stoke-on-Trent.

appears on only a few of the items is also unusual and may indicate some kind of separation of production in the firm of Godwin and Thynne of Hereford. But to date we have no documentary evidence of this.

Japanese influence already noted in this chapter appears again in the design of Plate 63(356 and 357). The whole of Plate 64(360-365) takes us back in design chronology to the more Gothic phase of tile pattern, and two of the examples are glazed in the opaque majolica colours. The designs, so close to those of encaustic tiles are extremely attractive, probably on account of their relative simplicity. In the next six examples, Plate 65(366-371), we can trace the descent from simplicity and bold outline, especially in (368 and 369), to the elaborate and overfussy as exemplified by Plate 65(370 and 371) and Plate 66(372 and 373). Simpler and perhaps more satisfying designs from a number of manufacturers, Plate 66(374-376) and Plate 67(378-381), conclude this rather miscellaneous group of patterns which cover at least a thirty year span. Their very variety and in many cases, lack of real originality and design sense, is thrown into powerful contrast by the majority of the designs which decorate the art nouveau tiles from the last two tiles in Plate 67 to the end of Plate 70 inclusive, and Figures 64-67, which end the illustrations.

Plate 64.
(360) *Moulded in low relief with a floral/geometric pattern, part of a continuous panel design. Decorated in opaque majolica glazes. 8ins. Mark: 'Robert Minton Taylor, Tile Works, Fenton near Stoke-on-Trent'. c.1872.* Courtesy City Museum and Art Gallery, Stoke-on-Trent. **(361)** *Moulded in low relief with a floral/geometric pattern. Decorated in opaque majolica glazes. 8ins. Mark: 'Campbell Brick and Tile Co. etc.' c.1875-1880.* Courtesy City Museum and Art Gallery, Stoke-on-Trent. **(362)** *Block printed underglaze with a geometric design. 8ins. Mark: as (360). c.1872-1875.* Courtesy City Museum and Art Gallery, Stoke-on-Trent. **(363)** *Block printed in red and blue and orange on a white ground with a geometric pattern. 4ins. Mark: 'Minton Hollins & Co. etc.' c.1885.* **(364)** *Block printed in light and dark brown on a fawn ground with a geometric pattern. 6ins. Mark: 'Mintons China Works etc.' c.1870.* **(365)** *Encaustic tile decorated with a geometric pattern in blue, red and black upon a deep cream ground. 6ins. Mark: W. Godwin, Lugwardine, Hereford'. c.1875.* Courtesy City Museum and Art Gallery, Stoke-on-Trent.

360

361

362

363

364

365

366

367

368

369

370

371

Plate 65. See page 218 for details.

372

373

374

375

376

377

Plate 66. See page 218 for details.

Lewis F. Day had written that "the ordinary run of printed tiles are eminently inartistic in their total effect, obviously cheap, and, to the cultivated eye, proportionately nasty".[53] The tiles representative of the international style known as art nouveau really take us out of the Victorian period, and indeed out of the era of the mass produced printed tile. The art nouveau style seemed to demand other techniques, its swirling rhythmic designs being more suitable to moulded or tube lined surfaces decorated with shining translucent glazes. Thus in the 1890s both the style of design and the techniques of decoration changed. The effects of this have already been noted in an examination earlier of the floral designs. And, indeed, many of the art nouveau tiles depicted in this section, though classed as miscellaneous designs are, in fact, based on floral forms or foliage.

Plate 65. See page 216
(366) *Block printed in black on a white slip ground, coloured in enamel overglaze. Part of a repeating floral/geometric pattern. 6ins. Mark: 'Mintons China Works etc.', and registration mark for 1877.* Courtesy Rosamond Allwood. **(367)** *Moulded in low relief with a 'Moorish' geometrical pattern, decorated in majolica opaque glazes in yellow, navy, turquoise and white. 6ins. Mark: 'Maw & Co. etc.' c.1880.* Courtesy Rosamond Allwood. **(368)** *Block printed underglaze in light and dark brown and yellow on a pale green ground with a repeating floral/geometric design. 8ins. Mark: 'Minton, Hollins & Co. etc.' c.1875.* **(369)** *Block printed underglaze in black and grey on a white ground with a floral/geometric design. 8ins. Mark: 'Minton Hollins & Co. etc.' c.1875-1880.* **(370)** *Printed underglaze in navy on a white ground with a floral/geometric design. 8ins. Mark: 'Minton Hollins & Co.', and design registration for 1883.* **(371)** *Printed underglaze in bluey-grey on a white ground with a geometric design. 6ins. Mark: the Portland vase moulded and 'WEDGWOOD 483' printed. c.1887.*

Plate 66. See page 217
(372) *Printed underglaze in brown and hand-coloured in orange, brown and yellow on a white ground with a central sunflower motif surrounded by a geometric design. 6ins. No mark. c.1880.* **(373)** *Printed underglaze in brown and hand-coloured in orange and brown on an ivory ground with a geometric pattern. 6ins. Mark: Moulded 'P', for Pilkingtons and pattern number 'E 523'. c.1905.* **(374)** *Printed underglaze in green on a white ground with a floral/geometric design. 6ins. Mark: 'ENGLAND'. c.1900.* **(375)** *Printed underglaze in grey on a white ground with a geometric/floral design. 6ins. Mark: 'X' moulded. c.1890.* **(376)** *Printed underglaze in black and coloured in yellow, green, blue and brown on a grey-green ground with a floral/geometric pattern. 6ins. No mark. c.1880.* **(377)** *Printed underglaze in grey on a white ground with a floral/geometric design. 6ins. Mark: 'ENGLAND'. c.1895.*

Plate 67.
(378) *Printed underglaze in tan on a white ground with a stylised floral/geometric motif. 6ins. Mark: 'E. Smith & Co. Coalville'. c.1885.* **(379)** *Printed underglaze in bluey-grey with a floral/geometric pattern on a white ground. 6ins. Mark: 'P', for Pilkingtons. c.1910.* **(380)** *Printed underglaze in black and hand coloured in red and green with a geometric pattern containing flowers and fruit on a white ground. 6ins. No mark. c.1885.* **(381)** *Printed underglaze in green with a swirling pattern on a white ground. 6ins. No mark. c.1885.* **(382)** *Plastic clay tile moulded in high relief with a design of water lily flowers and leaves. Decorated in a translucent green glaze. 8ins. No mark, but said to have been made at Stoke College of Art c.1905-1910.* **(383)** *Moulded in low relief with a design of flowers. Decorated in translucent glazes in brown, shades of green, blue and orange. 6ins. Mark: 'ENGLAND' and registered no. '419660', for 1903.*

378

379

380

381

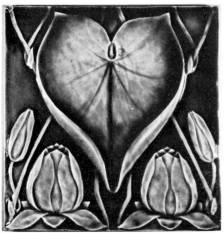

382

383

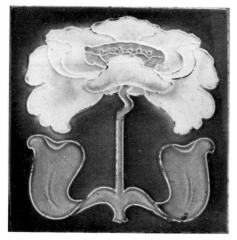

384

385

386

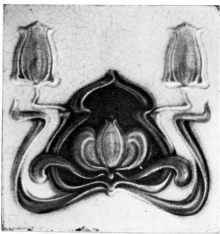

387

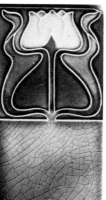

388

389

This is not the place to describe in detail the development of this, the first new and truly international style to emerge since the neo-classicism of the mid-eighteenth century began a seemingly endless series of stylistic revivals. Throughout the nineteenth century as Gothic, revived rococo, Renaissance revival and the other historical styles followed each other, the designers seemed desperately to be looking for a new source of inspiration. To some extent the first stirrings of art nouveau can be found — rather paradoxically — in the pre-Raphaelites. It required the transmutation of some of the complexities of pre-Raphaelite philosophy into the apparent simplicities of the aesthetes before the final step could be taken on the path towards the modern movement. That art nouveau was new is surely apparent from these final illustrations, yet when Walter Crane and Lewis F. Day designed art nouveau tiles for Pilkingtons they were only continuing a progression in their own artistic development, not striking out an entirely new posture for themselves. Thus like all cultural phenomena, the style we call art nouveau was both a product of its own time — and thus unique — and the development of a past tradition — and thus a mere segment in a continuous pattern of change.

Tiles from this period do represent something of a break with the past in technique. As already indicated printed scenes are less popular and indeed printing of any kind is less frequently employed from 1895 onwards. The finish most fashionable was in translucent coloured glazes, and all the examples are so executed. There is a fluidity of line and movement which is very satisfying in the designs. The chosen examples range from the work of art school students on a wet clay tile, Plate 67(382), to the unmarked piece, Plate 70(397), a frequently met-with mass-produced design. In Plate 70(398 and 399) both have a strong Celtic feeling, and this indeed was a major source of influence in art nouveau design. Whilst Plate 70(401), for which watercolour sketches are to be found in the Minton archives (Figure 67) calls to mind a Tiffany lampshade.

The final fling of the art and decorative tile makers was comparatively short. The coloured glaze art nouveau tiles made their appearance in the 1890s and hardly a house in or out of the town, terraced or detached, was complete without a tiled porch, but by 1914, the boom was over. Although strictly speaking the Edwardian period is outside our remit, it is appropriate to end with these stimulating examples of mass-produced design.

Plate 68.
(384) *Moulded with an art nouveau floral design decorated in translucent white, yellow and shades of green glazes. 6ins. No mark. c.1900.* Courtesy City Museum and Art Gallery, Stoke-on-Trent. **(385)** *Moulded with an art nouveau design decorated in translucent pink and green glazes. 6ins. No mark, though same factory as (384). c.1900.* Courtesy City Museum and Art Gallery, Stoke-on-Trent. **(386)** *Moulded in medium high relief with an art nouveau floral design decorated in translucent green glazes. 6ins. Mark: 'Minton Hollins & Co. etc.' c.1900.* Courtesy City Museum and Art Gallery, Stoke-on-Trent. **(387)** *Moulded in relief with a stylised floral design decorated in green and yellow translucent glazes on a cream ground. 6ins. No mark. c.1905.* **(388)** *Moulded in low relief with a quartered pattern of two stylised floral designs decorated in turquoise ground glaze; motifs in green, yellow and orange translucent glazes. 6ins. Mark: 'M.T.W. Co.' — probably Malkin Tile Works & Co. c.1905.* **(389)** *Moulded in low relief with a quartered pattern of two stylised art nouveau floral designs decorated in green ground, with motifs in green and turquoise. 6ins. No mark. c.1905.*

Figure 66. A page of art nouveau tile panel designs from the printed catalogue of Mintons c.1900-1905. (Jones, Minton MSS, No. 1375.) Courtesy Royal Doulton Tableware Ltd.

Throughout the whole of the period from 1840 to 1910 the tile industry had attracted leading designers from other spheres of decorative art. In this way, the production of tiles in the nineteenth century made an important contribution to English ceramic art, and to the applied arts generally. It was an excellent example of that union of art and industry which Sir Henry Cole had first called for in the 1840s, and which though slow to materialise generally, was gradually assisted by the development of schools of art to which firms like Mintons and Doultons sent their young artists to receive formal academic artistic training.

This union of art and industry found vigorous and typical expression not only in the consciously artistic coloured glaze tiles and grand pictorial panels of the latter half of the period, nor merely in the encaustic pavements designed by the great architects in the mid-Victorian years, but also in the printed and painted pictorial tiles of the years 1870-1900. The work of Walter Crane, J. Moyr Smith, William Wise,

Plate 69.
(390) *Moulded highly stylised design decorated with a turquoise translucent glaze ground, and green and orange glazes on the motif. 6ins. Mark: 'ENGLAND'. c.1905.* **(391)** *Watercolour design for a highly decorative tube-lined tile. Mintons. c.1898-1900. (Jones, Minton MSS, No. 1852.)* Courtesy Royal Doulton Tableware Ltd. **(392)** *Moulded in low relief with a highly stylised leaf and flower pattern decorated in orange and green translucent glazes on a cream ground. 6ins. No mark. c.1895-1900.* **(393)** *Moulded with a design of three tulips with interlacing stems and leaves decorated in translucent grey and turquoise glazes. 6ins. No mark. c.1895-1900.* Courtesy Rosamond Allwood. **(394)** *Moulded in low relief with three stylised flowers and foliage decorated overall with a blue glaze. 6ins. Mark: 'C' moulded. No attribution. c.1905.* **(395)** *Moulded in low relief outline of highly stylised leaf motifs decorated with an overall green glaze. 6ins. No mark. c.1900.*

390

391

392

393

394

395

396

397

398

399

400

401

Figure 67. Watercolour drawing showing stages of development of the design of the tile illustrated in Plate 70(401). (Jones, Minton MSS, No. 1852.) Courtesy Royal Doulton Tableware Ltd.

Thomas Allen and other designers of this period which has been illustrated and discussed in detail for the first time in this book, made an important contribution both to art and to industry. These men have left to present-day collectors a rich legacy of fine design which enables us to recreate in our imagination the splendid diversity of life in Victorian times.

Plate 70.
(396) *Moulded in outline with a stylised design decorated with yellow and green translucent glazes on a cream ground. 6ins. No mark. c.1900-1905.* **(397)** *Moulded in low relief with a stylised flower and foliage design decorated in turquoise and green translucent glazes on a pale cream ground. 6ins. No mark. c.1900-1905.* **(398)** *Tube lined with a stylised design reminiscent of a Celtic brooch, decorated in green, blue and red translucent glazes on a white ground. 6ins. Mark: 'P', moulded, for Pilkingtons, and 'Made in England'. c.1900-1905.* **(399)** *Moulded in outline with a highly stylised Celtic design decorated with a deep green glazed background and translucent glazes in orange and shades of green on the motif. 6ins. Mark: 'ENGLAND' and 'Rd. No. 481886', for 1906.* **(400)** *Moulded in outline with a large stylised flower and foliage decorated with a deep maroon glaze background and translucent yellow, green and orange glazes on the motif. 6ins. No mark. c.1905.* **(401)** *Tube lined with a design reminiscent of a Tiffany lampshade (or if turned the other way — stylised leaves and flowers), decorated in orange, blue and green translucent glazes. 6ins. Mark: 'ENGLAND'. c.1895-1900. (See also Figure 67.)*

Chapter Six Footnotes

1. Other examples are illustrated in Berendsen, pp.119, 131, and in de Jonge, Plates 9a, b, c, and 12d.
2. Berendsen, pp.135-136. See also de Jonge, Plate 14c.
3. Berendsen, p.129 and de Jonge, p.21 and Plate 19a.
4. Gaunt and Clayton-Stamm, p.22.
5. Published in the Society's Journal, 24th June, 1892, and reproduced in full in Gaunt and Clayton-Stamm, pp.156-165.
6. Naylor, Plate 16.
7. For details of the movement's many manifestations the books of Elizabeth Aslin and Robin Spencer, both entitled *The Aesthetic Movement,* are recommended.
8. *Art Journal,* 1883, p.222.
9. *Decoration and Furniture of Town Houses,* 1881, Plate 14.
10. E. Aslin, Plates 10, 11, 45, 121, and Naylor, Plates 48, 65.
11. Godden, *Victorian Porcelain,* p.104.
12. op. cit., p.113.
13. Eyles, p.152.
14. Godden, *Victorian Porcelain,* p.92.
15. Minton MSS, No.1645.
16. op. cit., No.1643.
17. op. cit., No.1642.
18. Her work is liberally illustrated both in Eyles, and Dennis.
19. Naylor, Plate 41.
20. *Punch,* 15th August, 1874.
21. Reproduced in Spielman, p.541.
22. Hillier, Plate 173.
23. Darbyshire, pp.71-75.
24. Rhead, p.350.
25. Aslin, Colour Plate 102, and Hillier, Plate 172.
26. Fuller details of Allen's life and work are contained in an article by Reginald G. Haggar in *Proceedings of the Wedgwood Society,* No.6, 1966, pp.61-68.
27. I am indebted to Mr. Roger Pinkham of the Ceramic Department of the Victoria and Albert Museum for these references to Murray's work.
28. This design is moulded on the tiles and is illustrated in Barnard, Plate 27.
29. See Barnard, Plate 90 for an example.
30. See Barnard, Plate 114 for the murals in St. Thomas's Hospital.
31. From *Easter Art Journal,* 1898, to which Gillian Eastwood drew my attention.
32. Helen Williams in the Northern Ceramic Society Newsletter No. 29, March 1978.
33. Plates 105 and 107.
34. Barnard illustrates the remaining three seasons and 'Summer' is reproduced in colour on the cover of Aslin.
35. *Easter Art Annual,* 1898, p.22.
36. *The Pottery and Glass Trades Journal, Registered Designs of the Month.*
37. Plate 85.
38. Jewitt 1878 edition.
39. 'Spring' and 'Winter' are illustrated on Plate 32 of the factory catalogue.
40. Plate 90.
41. J.E. Ritchie, *The Life and Times of Lord Palmerston,* Vol.II, p.283, London n/d.
42. Plate 80.
43. Quoted in Godden's *Antique China and Glass under £5,* pp.69-70.
44. In the catalogue entry for the *Victorian Tiles* exhibition at Wolverhampton.
45. In her article on the reminiscences of two Della Robbia workers, Northern Ceramic Society Newsletter, No.29, March 1978, p.6.
46. The first six subjects are illustrated in Naylor, Plate 39.
47. A set of the twelve tiles in this series, painted in colours, is in the Gladstone Pottery Museum in Longton and is illustrated by Barnard, Plate 29.
48. Interesting comments on Hammond's work are to be found in Rhead, p.357-358.
49. See Barnard, Plate 74 for an example.
50. Aslin, Plate 33.
51. Nothing had been published on this talented artist until the present writer and Paul Atterbury contributed an article to *Collector's Guide,* July 1978.
52. These are illustrated and discussed by Reginald Haggar in his article on Thomas Allen and Silas Rice, *Northern Ceramic Society Journal* Vol.II, 1975-1976.
53. *The Artist,* 1881, p.242.

Price Guide

In compiling this price guide certain important factors have been taken into consideration, some of these were noted in a general sense in Chapter Two, but more specific and detailed influences are recorded here.

The overriding factor which needs to be understood at the outset is that at the time of writing there is no easily-established saleroom price to cover the whole range of tiles shown in this book. I believe it will not be long before Sotheby's Belgravia, Christie's at South Kensington and Phillips start to include groups of tiles in their regular sales much as they currently do with pot-lids, Baxter prints, fairings, Staffordshire figures, commemoratives, etc. When this happens relative prices will be more readily ascertainable. The lack of such obviously handy data has meant that the following list has had to be compiled 'from scratch' as it were. The sources we have used have been varied. We have noted every price fetched by tiles at Sotheby's Belgravia since 1971. The current prices of the major London specialist tile dealers such as those operating in Antiquarius and the Chenil Galleries, Chelsea, and in Kensington Church Street and one or two isolated locations elsewhere have been carefully noted. Additionally, we have visited other antique markets, collectors' fairs, antique shops and junk shops, mainly in the North of England where general antique dealers often include tiles amongst their stocks. From this research it is clear that the market for tiles has not really settled down, as the enormous variety of tiles both in their decorative treatment and subject matter does lead to 'trends' and fluctuations which were not really so noticeable a few years ago. Thus it will be one of the functions of the annual price guide supplements to this book to chart the progress of such fluctuations. To give one simple example. At the moment the well-known Moyr Smith 'Shakespeare', Plate 28(159-162), are fairly common in all colour combinations, and still quite cheap at say £6-£12 per tile; they are not being 'snapped up' the moment they appear. But over the next three years B.B.C. 2 will have produced a major cycle of Shakespeare plays and such a totally extraneous event could well stimulate demand for the Moyr Smith series, or indeed for any Shakespearean scenes. Stranger things have happened in the world of antiques fads and fashions!

Leaving aside that kind of freak influence on prices, certain specific points of wider application are worth stating.

Prices outside the U.K. will be higher than within. Though many tiles were exported at the time of manufacture, the bulk remains in this country, and thus the costs of shipping to collectors and dealers overseas have to be paid for by the eventual purchaser.

Within the U.K., prices in London appear to be higher than elsewhere, but this is only the normal tendency in the antique trade. However, this is somewhat qualified by the question of supply. Vast numbers of tiles were used in the industrial towns of the North in the 1870-1910 period, so these areas are excellent supply grounds as property is demolished, and washstands find their way into local auction houses and dealers' shops. London itself is well-supplied in this way, but the supply of tiles in country areas, the Home Counties and places far from large centres of Victorian and Edwardian housing development is correspondingly smaller and prices tend to be significantly higher than in the North.

A tile which is signed by the artist or designer or which can be reliably attributed to one, will be dearer than an anonymous tile. Many of the hitherto unattributed tiles which are illustrated here for the first time with the designer now recorded and given a brief biography, may well, alas, become more expensive. For example, we bought a perfect tile in the series of 'Musicians', Plate 53(300), which Edward Hammond designed at Mintons Studio c.1872-1875, with both factory and Studio marks in full, for £12 in London at the end of 1978. I would expect this to almost double in price now that the designer can be firmly attributed. The same is true of many of the art nouveau floral designs for which Lewis F. Day was responsible at Pilkingtons, e.g. Plate 12(67, 68 and 69).

Tiles which can be attributed to a specific manufacturer are usually more expensive than anonymous examples. In certain cases this makes an overwhelming difference to the price. Tiles by William de Morgan are really in a class of their own and this is clearly reflected in the prices listed below. Wedgwood too command prices for printed examples throughout their range which are invariably double, and sometimes treble, those of other manufacturers. For example, five of the 'Gastronomic Homilies', Plate 58(330), printed in blue, were recently on offer for £160, had they been marked Maws or Mintons, half that price would have been more than adequate.

Decorative finish is also an important factor conditioning price. Signed on-glaze enamel paintings are more highly esteemed than printed and coloured pieces, unsigned hand painted subjects are still expected to fetch more, probably for the 'wrong' reason that hand painting, however poorly executed and amateurish, seems to be preferred to a print, however well designed it may be.

With printed examples, multi-colour printed tiles will be dearer than monochrome, printed and hand coloured likewise (though the standard of hand painted filling-in in colours is often very untidy and slipshod). Monochrome blue prints are more esteemed than monochrome brown, black, green or grey.

Coloured glaze tiles whether majolica or translucent glazes fetch higher prices than patterned tiles printed with simple outlines and coloured. This is especially true of the many colour glaze designs in the art nouveau style. Currently these latter are much in favour, but they are comparatively so plentiful that prices are held in reasonable check, as the list indicates.

As a general rule 8-inch tiles are dearer than 6-inch, especially so when the same subject appears on both 6-inch and 8-inch tiles — the latter with the addition of a border. In such cases the larger tile is invariably the more expensive.

Condition is an important factor in determining price, but perhaps not of such significance as it is in ordinary ceramic items. The condition of the back of the tile doesn't really matter at all. Slight blemishes to the front in the form of a line of plaster or evidence of stove-blacking should not affect the price as these are easily removed. Snips off the edges do reduce the value a little but proportionately less than, say, on a plate. As yet few people have taken to buying tiles specifically as investment items, but if the buyer does contemplate selling again, then the finer the condition, the more certain will be a good resale. For the dedicated collector, it is better to buy a damaged specimen suitably reduced in price — such as Figure 46 — than to miss such a rarity from the collection.

Tiles bought in sets are normally more expensive per tile than a single specimen would be. This is particularly the case where a complete set is concerned whether it be a four-tile set of 'Seasons', or a five-tile floral pattern vertical run, or the twelve subjects from 'Early English History'. Such sets are sometimes found framed, either reconstructing the vertical 'flower in the pot' type of picture, or bringing together a given number of like tiles. For example, the set of Kate Greenaway 'Seasons' by T. & R. Boote with two matching patterned tiles all six framed, was recently offered for £120. Individually, the 'Seasons' are in the £12-£18 range, the plain patterned tiles far less. However, forming a complete, framed matching set, this price was high, but not extortionate and probably negotiable.

Very often frames have been added to single tiles by enthusiastic collectors or dealers and regrettably, though you may not always want to, you have to pay for the frame in order to secure the desired tile.

Larger tiles and plaques may well have been framed contemporaneously with their manufacture, and in this case it is fitting to retain the original framing provided its condition is sound and appearance attractive. But once again the price for the article will be greater because it is framed.

With these considerations in mind the following list is based upon the assumption that the tile referred to in the illustration is in good condition, and in colour, size and decoration is as described.

The following price guide follows the section sequence in Chapter Six, starting with Section 2, and gives prices, first for the tiles illustrated in the Plates, and then for the Figures, in each section. The prices quoted indicate that you would not normally expect to find the tile at less than the lower figure unless there was significant damage, and again, normally you would not expect to pay more than the upper figure. All prices are in pounds sterling as at summer 1979.

Chapter Six. Section 2. Floral Patterns

	£		
Plate 2(7)	15— 25	(20-21)	3— 7
(8)	20— 35	(22)	5— 10
(9-10)	25— 45	(23)	6— 12
(11)	25— 45	Plate 5(24-25)	8— 15
(12)	25— 45	(26-27)	3— 5
Plate 3(13)	30— 50(the pair)	(28)	7— 12
(14-16)	25— 45	(29)	2— 4
(17)	12— 18	Plate 6(30-31)	7— 14
Plate 4(18)	12— 18	(32-33)	4— 8
(19)	8— 15	(34)	3— 6

(35)	6— 10		Plate 12(66)	8— 14
Plate 7(36-37)	8— 14		(67-69)	10— 15
(38-41)	3— 8		(70-71)	25— 35
Plate 8(42-45)	3— 8		Plate 13(72)	250—350(full panel)
(46)	5— 10		(73)	40— 60(for four)
(47)	2— 4		(74)	4— 7
Plate 9(48)	4— 8		(75-76)	7— 12
(49)	8— 12		Figure 19	25— 45
(50-51)	2— 4		Figure 20	20— 40
(52-53)	6— 10		Figures 21-23	3— 6
Plate 10(54-57)	4— 8		Figure 24	25— 45
(58-59)	3— 6		Figures 25-26	2— 4
Plate 11(60)	3— 6		Figure 27	8— 12
(61)	6— 8		Figures 28-34	2— 4
(62-64)	4— 8		Figures 35-37	4— 6
(65)	2— 4			

Chapter Six. Section 3. Landscapes and Places

Plate 14(77)	15— 25		(91)	4— 8
(78-79)	15— 25		(92)	7— 10
(80)	10— 15		(93)	5— 10
(81)	8— 12		Plate 17(94)	5— 10
Plate 15(82-83)	8— 12		(95)	40— 60
(84-85)	15— 25		(96-97)	30— 50
(86)	6— 10		(98)	25— 45
(87)	8— 10		Plate 18(99-100)	25— 35
Plate 16(88-89)	8— 10		(101)	15— 25
(90)	12— 15		(102-104)	4— 8

Chapter Six. Section 4. Animals, Birds and Fish

Plate 19(105-107)	12— 20		Plate 23(128-129)	75—125
(108)	12— 18		(130-131)	8— 12
(109)	6— 10		(132-133)	5— 8
(110)	3— 6		Plate 24(134)	12— 20
Plate 20(111-112)	15— 25		(135-137)	15— 25
(113-114)	12— 18		(138)	3— 6
(115)	20— 30		(139)	8— 12
Plate 21(116)	25— 35		Plate 25(140-141)	8— 12
(117)	8— 15		(142)	3— 6
(118)	2— 4 (each)		(143)	6— 10
(119)	25— 40		(144)	15— 25
(120)	12— 18		(145)	35— 50
(121)	25— 40		Figure 38	12— 20
Plate 22(122-123)	6— 12		Figure 39	40— 60
(124-125)	25— 35		Figures 40-42	6— 10
(126-127)	8— 12		Figure 43	30— 40
			Figure 44	35— 45

Chapter Six. Section 5. Literary Subjects

Plate 26(147-149)	15— 25		(176)	8— 12	
(150)	15— 25		(177-178)	15— 20	
Plate 27(151-154)	8— 12		(179-180)	18— 25	
(155-156)	10— 15		Plate 32(181-186)	10— 15	
Plate 28(157-158)	10— 15		Plate 33(187)	10— 15	
(159-162)	8— 15		(188)	15— 25	
Plate 29(163-168)	20— 30		(189-190)	20— 30	
Plate 30(169-170)	10— 15		(191-192)	10— 15	
(171-172)	15— 20		Figure 45	500—600 the set	
(173-174)	15— 25		Figure 46	25— 40	
Plate 31(175)	12— 18		Figure 47	7— 12	

Chapter Six. Section 6. Children: Nursery Rhymes and Fairy Tales

Plate 34(193-194)	12— 18		Plate 38(211)	6— 10
(195)	6— 10		(212)	12— 20
(196)	8— 12		(213)	12— 20
(197)	15— 25		(214)	8— 15
Plate 35(198)	8— 12		(215-216)	25— 35 (each)
(199)	15— 20		Plate 39(217-218)	10— 15
(200-201)	20— 30		(219-220)	10— 15
(202-203)	10— 15		(221-222)	6— 12
Plate 36(204)	20— 30		Plate 40(223)	10— 15
	(nursery rhymes)		(224)	15— 25
Plate 37(205-206)	10— 15		(225)	6— 10
(207-208)	12— 18		(226)	15— 25
(209-210)	18— 25		(227-228)	10— 15
			Figures 48-51	8— 12

Chapter Six. Section 7. Sporting Scenes

Plate 41(229)	15— 25		(236)	15— 20
(230)	12— 18		(237-238)	10— 15
(231-232)	12— 18		(239-240)	10— 15
(233-234)	15— 25		Figures 52-53	12— 18
Plate 42(235)	12— 18		Figure 54	4— 8
			Figure 55	15— 20

Chapter Six. Section 8. The Calendar

Plate 43(241-242)	12— 20		(255)	6— 10
(243-244)	10— 15		(256)	30— 40
(245)	12— 18		(257)	12— 18
(246)	8— 14		(258)	18— 25
Plate 44(247-248)	12— 20		Plate 46(259-262)	12— 18 (each)
(249)	20— 25			(£125—£150 the set)
(250)	10— 15		(263)	15— 20
(251)	12— 18		(264)	12— 18
(252)	20— 25		Figure 56	Size unknown, no price
Plate 45(253)	12— 18		Figures 57, 58	12— 18
(254)	20— 25			

Chapter Six. Section 9. Historical, Political and Personal

Plate 47(265-266)	8— 12		(278-279)	25— 35	
(267)	40— 50		(280-282)	10— 15	
(268)	25— 35		Plate 50(283)	15— 25	
(269-270)	15— 20		(284)	12— 18	
Plate 48(271)	25— 35		(285)	15— 25	
(272)	10— 15		Plate 51(286)	Size unknown, no price	
(273-274)	15— 20		(287)	100—150	
(275)	20— 25		(288)	175—250	
(276)	20— 30		Figure 59	18— 25	
Plate 49(277)	30— 50				

Chapter Six. Section 10. Trades, Occupations and Country Life

Plate 52(289-290)	12— 18		(300)	15— 20
(291-292)	12— 18		Plate 54(301)	8— 12
(293)	8— 12			(part design)
(294)	15— 25		(302)	20— 30
Plate 53(295)	18— 25 (8-inch tile)		(303-304)	10— 15
(296)	12— 18		(305-306)	8— 12
(297)	18— 25		Plate 55(307-312)	12— 20
(298)	12— 18		Plate 56(313-316)	12— 20
(299)	12— 18		(317-318)	12— 18
	(£15—£25 coloured)			

Chapter Six. Section 11. Food and Drink

Plate 57(319-320)	15— 25
(321-324)	15— 25
Plate 58(325-328)	12— 18
(329)	20— 30
(330)	25— 30

Chapter Six. Section 12. Miscellaneous Patterns

Plate 59(331-332)	45— 60		Plate 64(360-365)	5— 10
(333)	8— 12		Plate 65(366-370)	7— 12
(334)	25— 30		(371)	2— 5
(335-336)	8— 10		Plate 66(372-377)	2— 5
Plate 60(337)	15— 20		Plate 67(378-381)	2— 5
(338)	5— 8		(382)	10— 15
(339)	7— 10		(383)	6— 12
(340)	10— 15		Plate 68(384-389)	6— 12
(341-342)	3— 5		Plate 69(390-393)	6— 12
Plate 61(343)	7— 10		(394-395)	4— 6
(344-345)	10— 15		Plate 70(396)	4— 6
(346)	8— 12		(397-400)	7— 12
(347-348)	7— 12		(401)	12— 15
Plate 62(349)	4— 7		Figures 61-63	2— 4
(350)	12— 18		Figures 64-65	2— 6 (per tile)
(351-353)	4— 8		Figure 66	45— 60
Plate 63(354-357)	7— 12			(each run of 5)
(358-359)	2— 4		Figure 67	12— 15

Bibliography

General Works
Allwood, Rosamond, Victorian Tiles, catalogue of an exhibition at Wolverhampton Art Gallery, 1978.
Aslin, Elizabeth, *The Aesthetic Movement,* Elek, 1969.
Barnard, Julian, *Victorian Ceramic Tiles,* Studio Vista, 1972.
Berendsen, Anne, *Tiles, A General History,* Faber, 1967.
Furnival, W.J. *Leadless Decorative Tiles, Faience and Mosaic,* 1904.
Gaunt, W. and Clayton-Stamm, M.D.E., *William de Morgan,* Studio Vista, 1971.
Godden, Geoffrey A., *Encyclopaedia of British Pottery & Porcelain Marks,* Barrie & Jenkins, 1964.
Godden, Geoffrey A., *Victorian Porcelain,* Barrie & Jenkins, 1961.
Hamilton, David, *Architectural Ceramics,* Thames & Hudson, 1978.
Haslam, Malcolm, *English Art Pottery 1865-1915,* Antique Collectors' Club, 1975.
Jewitt, Llewellynn, *The Ceramic Art of Great Britain,* 2 Vols., Virtue & Co., 1878, 1 Vol. 2nd edn. 1883.
Jonge, C.H. de, *Dutch Tiles,* Pall Mall, 1971.
Lane, Arthur, *A Guide to the collection of Tiles in the Victoria and Albert Museum,* H.M.S.O., 2nd edn. 1960.
Naylor, Gillian, *The Arts and Crafts Movement,* Studio Vista, 1971.
Pinkham, Roger, *Catalogue of Pottery by William de Morgan,* Victoria and Albert Museum, 1973.
Ray, Anthony, *English Delftware Tiles,* Faber, 1973.
Thomas E. Lloyd, *Victorian Art Pottery,* Guildart, 1974.
Wakefield, Hugh, *Victorian Pottery,* Jenkins, 1962.

Three important exhibition catalogues are worthy of note:
Victorian Church Art, Victoria and Albert Museum, 1971.
Victorian and Edwardian Decorative Art, The Handley-Read Collection, The Royal Academy, 1972.
Minton, 1798-1910 (edited by Paul Atterbury and Elizabeth Aslin), Victoria and Albert Museum, 1976.

Throughout the text detailed references have been made to sections of books, or to articles. For ease of reference these are listed below in alphabetical order of author or title. Documentary sources such as factory pattern books and catalogues are not listed here but are dealt with extensively in Chapter III.
Art Journal, 1839-1912.
The Artist & Journal of Home Culture, 1880-1894.
Atterbury, Paul and Irvine, Louise, *The Doulton Story,* 1979.
Atterbury, Paul and Lockett, Terry, "The Work of William

Wise'',*Collectors Guide,* July 1978.

Coysh, A.W., *Blue and White Transfer Ware 1780-1840,* David & Charles, 1970.

Crane, Walter, *The Baby's Bouquet,* 1877, republished Pan Books, 1974.

Crane, Walter, *The Baby's Opera,* 1877, republished Pan Books, 1974.

Crane, Walter, *The Baby's Own Alphabet.*

Crane, Walter, *Easter Art Journal,* 1898.

Crane, Walter, *An Artist's Reminiscences,* Methuen, 1907.

Darbyshire, Alfred, *An Architect's Experiences,* J.E. Cornish, Manchester, 1897.

Day, Lewis F., *Everyday Art,* London, 1882.

Dennis, Richard, *Doulton Stoneware Pottery (1870-1925),* London, 1971.

Dresser, Christopher, *Principles of Decorative Design,* 1873, reprinted St. Martins Academy, 1973.

Eastlake, Charles, *Hints on Household Taste,* London, 1867.

Edis, R.W., *Decoration and Furniture of Town Houses,* London 1881, reprinted 1972.

Eyles, Desmond, *Royal Doulton 1815-1965,* Hutchinson, 1965.

Fine Art Society, *The Aesthetic Movement and the cult of Japan,* exhibition catalogue, 1972.

Franco-British Exhibition 1908, *Illustrated Review.*

Furniture Gazette 1873-1893.

Godden, Geoffrey A., *Antique China and Glass under £5,* Barker, 1966.

Haggar, Reginald G., "Thomas Allen", *Proceedings of the Wedgwood Society,* No. 6, 1966, and No. 7, 1968.

Haggar, Reginald G., "Thomas Allen and Silas Rice", *Northern Ceramic Society Journal,* Vol.2, 1975-1976.

Haslem, Malcolm, *The Martin Brothers, Potters,* 1978.

Hawkins, Jennifer (ed.), *The Poole Potteries,* Victoria and Albert Museum, 1978.

Hillier, Bevis, *Pottery and Porcelain 1700-1914,* Weidenfeld & Nicholson, 1968.

Ironbridge Gorge Museum Trust (ed. Tony Herbert), *The Jackfield Decorative Tile Industry.*

Kelly's London Directory, various dates.

Kelly's Post Office and Trades Directories, Staffordshire, various dates.

Lawrence, Heather, *Yorkshire Pots and Potteries,* David & Charles, 1974.

McCarthy, James F., *Great Industries of Great Britain,* Vol. III, 1875-1880.

Messenger, M., *Shropshire Pottery & Porcelain,* Shrewsbury Museum, 1974.

Porter, F., *Postal Directory for the Potteries,* 1887.

Pottery Gazette 1877-

Price E. Stanley, *John Sadler, A Liverpool Pottery Printer,* West Kirby, 1948.

Rhead, G.W. and F.A., *Staffordshire Pots and Potters,* 1906, E.P. reprint 1978.

Royal Society of Arts, *Journal,* June 1892.

Smith, J. Moyr, *Album of Decorative Figures,* London, 1882.

Smith, J. Moyr, *Ornamental Interiors, ancient and modern,* London, 1887.

Sotheby's Belgravia, sale catalogues, 1971-1979.

Spencer, Isobel, *Walter Crane,* Studio Vista, 1975.

Spencer, Robin, *The Aesthetic Movement,* Studio Vista/Dutton, 1972.

Spielman, H.M., *History of Punch,* London, 1895.

The Studio and *The Studio Year Book,* 1893-1945.

Tattersall, Bruce, "Victorian Wedgwood", *The Antique Collector,* May, 1974.

Victoria and Albert Museum, *National Art Library Catalogue,* G.K. Hall, 1972.

Williams, Helen, "Della Robbia", *Northern Ceramic Society Newsletter,* No. 29, March 1978.

Wight, Jane, *Medieval Floor Tiles,* Baker, 1975.

Works exhibited at the Royal Society of British Artists 1824-1893, Antique Collector's Club, 1975.

Index

Tile makers whose only appearance in the book is in Chapter Five (an alphabetical listing of the principal tile makers and their marks), are not included in this index.